WINGED
BROTHERS

WINGED BROTHERS

Naval Aviation as Lived by
Ernest and Macon Snowden

Ernest Snowden

Naval Institute Press
Annapolis, Maryland

This book has been brought to publication with the generous
assistance of Marguerite and Gerry Lenfest.

Naval Institute Press
291 Wood Road
Annapolis, MD 21402

Library of Congress Cataloging-in-Publication Data is available.
978-1-68247-296-5 (hardcover)
978-1-68247-295-8 (eBook)

♾ Print editions meet the requirements of ANSI/NISO z39.48-
1992 (Permanence of Paper).
Printed in the United States of America.

26 25 24 23 22 21 20 19 18   9 8 7 6 5 4 3 2 1
First printing

Unless otherwise credited, all photos are courtesy
of the Snowden family.

Contents

Illustrations

Introduction

The business of flying aircraft from ships has lodged itself in the national consciousness since the practice began in the early twentieth century. Naval aviation has tilted the balance in the nation's favor in war and powered its primacy in technological innovation. Throughout its history, naval aviation has been defined by a tight-knit community of high achievers who possessed a certain sangfroid, immense aeronautical skill, and supreme confidence in their own indestructability. As Tom Wolfe so whimsically yet aptly described in *The Right Stuff*, "A young man might go into military flight training believing that he was entering some sort of technical school in which he was simply going to acquire a certain set of skills. Instead, he found himself all at once enclosed in a fraternity. And in this fraternity, even though it was military, men were not rated by their outward rank as ensigns, lieutenants, commanders, or whatever. No, herein the world was divided into those who had it and those who did not."[1]

What follows is an attempt to trace major strides in a long, unbroken stretch of naval aviation history through the overlapping experiences and achievements of two brothers. It is a narrative constructed from deeply researched works of aviation history, personal recollections, officer fitness reports, aviator logbooks, kneeboard cards, and family lore. Where historical facts can be sourced, they are given full credit. Where conversation or motive is reconstructed long after the passing of the protagonists and their contemporaries, the narrative has tried to remain true to the personalities of those involved.

1

Beginnings

*So as we celebrate the centennial of naval aviation and begin to
contemplate the next one hundred years, I encourage all of you to look
back on those who led us through our first century. I urge you to
study their lives and their leadership styles. Then strive to be like them.*

—John McCain

From the four-acre steel flight deck of the aircraft carrier USS *John
C. Stennis* (CVN 74), moored quayside at Naval Air Station North
Island, California, the American public was afforded a most uncommon venue from which to witness the opening celebration of the
centennial of naval aviation. On a cloudless San Diego afternoon in
February 2011, an hours-long procession of meticulously restored and
groomed vintage fighter aircraft paraded in flight, by ones and twos,
up the starboard side of *Stennis*. From the earliest N3N Yellow Peril
biplane trainer to the formation flyover of thirty-five modern carrier-
based tactical aircraft, this spectacle showcased one hundred years of
progress in the evolution of sea-based fighter aircraft.

Left largely to the imagination that afternoon was a sense of the
human scale involved over those one hundred years in bringing the
machines to life—the many committed entrepreneurs, innovators,
designers, aerodynamicists, fabricators, maintainers, and visionary
naval officers—both on the ground and in the air. Through 2010, a
few months before the celebration of the centennial of naval aviation, 170,654 men and women (and a few foreign citizens) have been
trained and designated aviators in the first one hundred years of naval

flight.[1] Entering its second century, the naval aviation profession has spawned—and benefitted mightily—from multigenerational family legacies—fathers and sons, grandsons, and now daughters. The more illustrious family surnames include Flatley, McCampbell, and Lawrence.

Less often have siblings followed the same career path into carrier-based fighters, and rarer still has two brothers' time in uniform spanned so much of the formative years of carrier aviation history. Ernest and Macon Snowden, who graduated fourteen years apart from the U.S. Naval Academy, witnessed firsthand and participated actively in the period during which the profession came of age, proved decisive in the Pacific during World War II, made the difficult transition from propeller planes to jets, carried the war to Vietnam, and affirmed its effectiveness as a preeminent instrument of national policy. The older brother would command a carrier air group in combat from the deck of USS *Lexington* (CV 16) against the Japanese in 1944; the younger brother would command a carrier air wing in combat from the deck of USS *Ticonderoga* (CV 14) against the North Vietnamese in 1965.

The fraternal bond between Ernest, or Ernie, and Macon, whom most knew as Mac, was as much about their mutual regard for naval aviation and their place in advancing their profession as it was their natural fondness as biological brothers. But they viewed their place as brothers in naval aviation as very much a shared endeavor—a common bond. Beginning in their teenage years and continuing throughout adulthood, they called one another "buddy" when together and in their correspondence as a sign of brotherly endearment. A kind of sibling rivalry—and a deep regard for one another—would play out in important ways for the naval service over their combined sixty years in uniform as Ernie's career arced, hit its zenith, and then declined to its nadir to be overtaken by the arc of Mac's career. In making his own way in his naval aviation career, the older brother was the pathfinder and role model for the younger brother. Ernie's encouragement and guidance, an occasional favorable word to his peers or seniors, or just an unprompted assist from a peer to ease the way for the younger brother made a formative difference in Mac's career.

★ ★ ★

Given the gap in their ages, the brothers shared little time under the same roof while growing up; Ernie was already at the Naval Academy before Mac entered grade school. What buttressed their relationship was a shared grief over losing an idolized father to heart disease while in his forties and a shared affection for their doting mother who, as a seamstress, worked a hardscrabble Depression-era existence to hold their home together. The "widow Snowden" was known in their small town of Beaufort, North Carolina, for her work ethic and determination to fashion opportunities for her two boys. She befriended and influenced two successive congressmen to nominate her sons for Naval Academy appointments as the only means to extricate them from a life anchored to the farm or to the local shrimping (and menhaden fishing) industry. Importantly, as the younger brother followed the older to the academy and then into a naval aviation career, a common absorption by and commitment to the business of flying from ships at sea would hold them together.

Mac's esteem for his much older brother deepened with the passing of their father and intensified into unqualified admiration for Ernie's accomplishments in naval aviation. When Mac finally entered naval aviation himself, his competitive nature would drive him to emulate Ernie but to surpass the older brother's career achievements when he could. Through the good fortune of being in the right place at key moments with the skill, experience, and personality to influence events, the two not only would find themselves present for or peripherally involved in many naval aviation milestones, but also would contribute to the maturing of the profession in pivotal ways as testers, developers, tacticians, mentors, and overall leaders of the community.

If viewed through a more modern lens of behavioral science, the development of the brothers' divergent personality traits formed by stressful family circumstances would have been predictable. Ernie, as the only child for his first dozen years, bore the brunt of the hyperinflated expectations of a detached and inaccessible father who demanded tough, dawn-to-dusk physical labor on the farm. In quiet moments at night or with his mother at mealtime, Ernie sought escape by imagining the exploits of adventurers, explorers, and aviators. When those adventures became real in adulthood, he thrived on the adrenaline and risk. By all accounts, he was an affable peer and an encouraging but exacting commander, but the underlying tonic for stressful work and combat flying was compulsive personal behavior, particularly a penchant for excessive partying and drinking that was decried by the institutional Navy as time went by.

Mac, by contrast, endured the loss of his father in his early teenage years and the loss of stature and standing in the community with the onset of the Depression, and he increasingly became the object of his mother's transferred affection from a husband and first-born son who were no longer available. Whether this was the dominant influence in shaping Mac's adult personality cannot be affirmed, but testimonials from naval officer associates suggest a man who, in the military realm, imposed a rigid discipline and exacted complete conformance from subordinates to his views and professional goals. He had a low flash point and was quick to anger when presented with situations or personnel issues that he perceived as inimical to standing orders, squadron instructions, and the strictest interpretation of naval custom. But all who knew him professionally would be quick to note that although "tough," he was "fair," always defaulting to what could produce the best outcome for the naval service.

Whatever their respective personality quirks, the brothers proved able to either subordinate any idiosyncratic or compulsive behaviors or bend them in support of the leadership challenges of their thirty-year professional lives. In the process, they were able to both achieve positive outcomes that propelled their careers forward and to make highly successful and occasionally momentous contributions to naval aviation. On a personal level, however, those same personality quirks would ultimately contribute to the undoing of both careers as they ran their course.

Yet a deeper look at their respective adult lives, from career milestones to personal correspondence to military fitness reports, reveals a close congruity in temperament formed around three readily discernable—and shared—traits. First, they had a love for and transcendent skill in piloting aircraft. Second, they shared an estimable regard for the naval service—not a vainglorious strutting pride in a given airplane, fighter squadron, or even naval aviation, but a more solemn regard for the traditions and ceremonies of the service itself. Third, they had an aptitude for combat leadership that sprang from a genuine care and concern for sailors and junior officers, confident decisionmaking sharpened by a progression of flying achievements, and tough discipline, meted out in ample portions, that bespoke of their particular nurturing and upbringing.

Born in the only bedroom of the family farmhouse in Wildwood, Ernie was the first son of Macon and Helon Snowden, whose attachment to this area of coastal wetland marshes and dense pine forest extended back through Macon's line to the earliest settlements in North Carolina. Isaac Snowden, a great-great-grandfather of Ernie, was recruited from nearby Currituck for service with the 1st Company of the 1st Volunteer Infantry Regiment in the War of 1812.[2] Helon was a direct descendant of Daniel McPherson, a first-generation American born to Scottish immigrant Daniel McPherson in 1690 on their family farm in the tidewater marshes behind Norfolk, Virginia. Ernie's father Macon was a former steam packet captain who piloted ferries bearing horse carriage, early automobile, and pedestrian commuters initially out of Portsmouth, Virginia, and later in the sounds and bays of coastal North Carolina.

By the time of Ernie's birth in 1911, Macon would retire from his early career on the waterways of intercoastal North Carolina and Virginia and take up farming near Beaufort. Before Ernie's ninth birthday, his father moved the family from the more austere farm life of Wildwood into the settled limits of Beaufort for the conveniences that town life could offer. Profits from cabbages, beans, peanuts, potatoes, and the occasional butchered hog on the extensive farm holdings Macon operated just outside town yielded enough down payment to purchase a decade-old Italianate Revival home at 131 Craven Street, only a block from the waterfront. Macon proved adept at farming, and his industriousness made him among the first to successfully raise white potatoes on a large scale in the county—grown both on his farms and through share arrangements with other growers. His enterprising initiative and accumulating profits led him to eventually acquire the Gaskill Brokerage Company to make barrels and containers for farm products and various goods and to corner the local market in the trucking business. This model of paternal industriousness was not lost on sons Ernie and Mac. Their formative experiences in the small southern town of Beaufort were of no particular consequence other than giving both an easy comfort with being on the water and with ocean-going pursuits.

Beaufort, from its earliest days of settlement at the beginning of the eighteenth century, was known as Fish Town. Industrial-scale fishing and fish processing of menhaden—or fatback, as these fertilizer fish were known locally—exploded after the Civil War and sustained Beaufort's economy for one hundred years. Ernie and Mac could later recall the overpowering stench of decomposing fish wafting down Craven Street when the menhaden fleet pulled in and an onshore wind blew into town. Fishing, sailing, and boating of any kind were the vocation of many and avocation of most of Beaufort's population of less than three thousand in the 1920s and 1930s. Fishing and farming supply businesses crowded Front Street. Behind the storefronts on the north side of Front Street, stately homes mostly constructed in the late 1700s extended for several blocks to the northern edge of the town limits. The south side of Front Street, formed mostly from landfill many years earlier, jutted into Taylor Creek, a narrow waterway bounded by Front Street's city docks on its north and by Bird Island on its south side. Opening into Beaufort Channel, Taylor Creek gave open access at its western end to the Atlantic Ocean beyond.

Curiosity was beginning to stir in eastern North Carolina, as in other places, about the means for human flight as early as 1873, well before two brothers from Ohio brought their aerial experiments to the Outer Banks. In Hertford County, about 130 miles due north of Beaufort, farmer James Gatling, older brother of the inventor of the rapid-firing automatic gun, constructed a machine thought to be capable of flight. Gatling is credited with assembling a collection of parts that resembled triangular wings adjoining a sluice box of a fuselage upon which were mounted two rotating drums. The drums, hand-cranked by Gatling the aeronaut, contained fan blades that blew an air stream up onto the underside of wire-controlled wings to theoretically mimic the action of birds' wings. In his one attempt at making his contraption fly, Gatling was injured after a steep, one-hundred-foot descent that resulted in a glide-ending crash in a plowed field. It would be another thirty years before true, sustained flight of a powered, controlled, and manned airplane would be achieved by Orville Wright about one hundred miles northeast of Beaufort in the Kill Devil Hills near Kitty Hawk, North Carolina. The world has since acknowledged that moment in December 1903 as the opening of the age of aviation

and appropriately accorded the Wrights the honor of making it possible. Even so, the Navy in its earliest days gave more deference to
Glenn Curtiss and his early hydroaeroplanes, which had more immediate promise for the Navy's maritime environment.

Beaufort was not without its own aviation pioneer. As North Car-
olinians, many held a certain pride by association with the Wrights'
achievement at Kill Devil Hills in 1903, but it was only four years
later that a native son of Beaufort put the town on the map with an
astonishing achievement for the time and place. William Luther Paul,
anticipating that newspapers and wealthy patrons were lining up to
advance prize money for aviation firsts and spurred on by an inherent restlessness and creative energy, built a monocoque flying machine
with two overhead rotors powered by motorcycle engines and a propeller to impart forward flight. Best described as an early gyrocopter,
it showed great promise by lifting off the ground for a few feet while
still tethered by a rope. Its shape and flight pattern earned it the name
Bumble Bee. Alas, Paul never achieved free flight before his backers
ran out of money and enthusiasm and withdrew their sponsorship. It
would be another thirty years before another native son of Carteret
County, Ernie Snowden, would return to the acclaim of his hometown for his aviation exploits.

In a remarkable juxtaposition of historic beginnings, Ernie was
born in May 1911, the same month and year that historians record
as the birth of naval aviation.[3] On May 8, 1911, Capt. Washington
Chambers placed two requisitions for the Navy's first aircraft—the
A-1 Triad—an amphibious biplane manufactured by aviation inventor and entrepreneur Glenn Curtiss in Hammondsport, New York,
marking that birth. From a twenty-first-century vantage point, the
Triad was a primitive affair, equipped with a metal-tipped propeller
designed to push the craft to achieve speeds of at least forty-five miles
per hour (mph), provisions for carrying a passenger, and dual controls operated by either pilot or passenger. Built from mahogany, canvas, and wire cables, the Triad did not inspire great confidence in any
casual observer about the future of flight in the maritime service. But
it would set in motion a rapid series of revolutionary developments.
Later that same year, building on this confluence of historic events
with Ernie's birth, Lt. Theodore "Spuds" Ellyson would be designated

as the Navy's first naval aviator after taking flying instruction personally from Glenn Curtiss in his "hydro-aero plane."[4]

So began, with Ernie's early life, what would become a story of
two brothers closely linked to the evolution of fighter aircraft and carrier operations at sea. Neither the example of his grandfather's service
in the War of 1812 nor his father's coastal steam packet ferry service
could have presaged young Ernie's interest in and pursuit of a naval aviation career. To understand what may have been a more alluring motivation, one must appreciate the historic and widely recorded events
of the time. In the early twentieth century, aviation was new. Early
aviators were feted as pioneering celebrities who embodied a brash,
devil-may-care mastery of this new technology. They "were dashing
figures in their aviator's caps, goggles, white scarves, and highly pol-
ished boots, and their airplanes, barely more than wooden frames held
together with glue and cotton canvas, were wonders of the modern
world."[5] The American public was spellbound by the news that Navy
flight crews had achieved the very first trans-Atlantic crossing by air
with the touchdown of their NC-4 flying boat near Lisbon, Portu-
gal. The NC-4 was one of three six-man Curtiss-built floatplanes that
attempted the crossing, taking off from Rockaway, New York. NC-1
and NC-3 succumbed en route to a mix of weather and mechanical problems and did not complete the trip. But as Ernie knew at
the time from the newspaper coverage, a junior officer in the NC-1
flight crew would be one of several among the three flight crews that
would be awarded the Navy Cross for their intrepidity in the face
of impossibly hazardous conditions. That officer, Lt. Marc Mitscher,
would have an even more profound effect on Ernie's life and career
nearly a quarter-century later in the carrier combat of the Pacific in
World War II. But in 1919 Ernie was still just eight years old, a boy of
adventurous spirit enthralled by the heroic proportions of this earliest naval aviation achievement. This parade of early aviators and their
incredible accomplishments "were front page news. . . . Pilots featured
especially prominently in boys' magazines and comics, fueling young
imaginations at a time when America and the world had awakened to
the awesome changes happening as automobiles replaced horses, elec-
tricity spread into homes, the new motion pictures vied with vaude-
ville, and the telephone came into widespread use."[6]

By Ernie's teenage years, U.S. military pilots were frequently besting the international competition in a series of high-profile, high-performance airplane races competing for various prizes. The most famous of these was the Schneider Trophy competition, which consisted of a multilap closed course showcase for ever-increasing horsepower and piloting skill. In 1923, the U.S. Navy won first and second place; in 1926, the Navy was the sole representative for the U.S. military and won second and fourth place.[7]

The American entries and the press coverage surrounding their successes were part of a public relations campaign undertaken by both the Navy and the Army to sensationalize U.S. air prowess at a time when funding for the military was in decline. To regain public favor and thereby shape and sway the congressional appropriations process, both services lent their official sponsorship and financial backing to the development of racing aircraft. The Navy took its first serious step in 1922, with lieutenants piloting a Curtiss CR-2 and CR-1 to third and fourth place behind the U.S. Army in the Pulitzer—a closed course for landplanes in Detroit that year. The Curtiss CRs became, in effect, the test beds for technical enhancements that would carry forward to the R2C and R3C racers within two years. A notable upgrade in horsepower from four hundred to more than six hundred, accompanied by a reconfigured engine cooling system with flush-mounted radiators in the upper and lower wing, propelled both Navy and Army Curtiss aircraft to significant performance improvements. In the 1923 Schneider contest at Cowes, Isle of Wight, Marine Corps Lt. David Rittenhouse and Navy Lt. Rutledge Irvine took first and second place, averaging 177 and 173 mph, respectively.[8] The European aviation powers were caught flat-footed by the display of American proficiency and were so agitated that they collectively pulled out of the 1924 race. Faced with an off year, the U.S. Navy team sensed opportunity, setting out to break world speed marks despite the absence of a formally sanctioned contest. Lt. G. T. Cuddihy piloted a CR-3 past the maximum world speed record of 188 mph. Lt. Ralph Ofstie drove a CR-3 past the world record for a one-hundred-, two-hundred-, and five-hundred-kilometer straight course at 178 mph for the first two and 161 mph for the third. Ofstie was poised to repeat a Navy first place when the Schneider competition resumed in 1925, only to be forced out early due to engine problems. That year, the trophy would be claimed by an Army aviator named Jimmy Doolittle. In his early teens, Ernie could not have known that Ofstie would reappear in his life almost thirty years later as a vice admiral and the deputy chief of naval operations for air—in that capacity as Ernie's immediate boss for aircraft carrier matters on the Navy staff.[9]

In the 1926 competition, after a series of unfortunate accidents and fatalities in the run-up to the official race, Navy Lt. William Tomlinson entered with a standard service Curtiss F6C-1 Hawk and still finished fourth in a field of specially configured racing aircraft. The Hawk's respectable finish suggested that aero and propulsion technologies debuted in international racing were beginning to find their way into fleet aircraft designs.[10]

This was the "golden age of air racing," a distant forerunner of today's Reno Air Races. But in the 1920s, air race pilots were the heroes of an adoring American public, which followed their exploits in competitions that also contributed significantly to the advancement of aeronautics. That the Navy's press campaign surrounding their air race achievements succeeded was borne out by the endorsement of Congress through the legislative process. Congress appropriated funding sufficient for the conversion of two battlecruisers to full-fledged aircraft carriers, USS *Lexington* and USS *Saratoga*, both commissioned in 1927.

None of this escaped Ernie's attention as he weighed his chances for appointment to the next class at the Naval Academy. For Ernie, seeking an appointment seemed the surest way to escape the farm and achieve upward mobility. More important, it would satisfy the yearning for adventure that the exploits of those early Navy airmen had nurtured. Representative Charles Abernathy of North Carolina's Third District was delighted to offer Ernie a coveted appointment in 1928. Years later, based on Ernie's example and his personal request, the now-retired Abernathy was pleased to lobby his successor Graham Barden for an appointment for Macon in the spring of 1942. This "pass down" experience would be repeated many times as Ernie, more than a decade ahead of his younger brother, would directly and indirectly pave a path that gave Mac a step up in his own career.

The Naval Academy regimen was wholly unlike the college experience of Ernie's Beaufort High School classmates attending North Carolina State or the University of North Carolina at Chapel Hill. Behind the outward display of uniforms and regimentation, harsh and unrelenting hazing was the norm inside the academy dorm. Those who could push through the emotional and physical torment and emerge with their dignity, wit, and grade point average intact would flourish and develop, by design, a fast and abiding kinship with classmates and fellow alumni who had shared the experience. This was, and in some ways remains, akin to the ancient Spartan way of acculturating young men to a warrior ethos of endurance and persistence through privation, hardship, and loss in battles yet to be fought.

Ernie and Mac hardly resembled each other physically. Ernie was stout and was a varsity wrestler for three years at the academy. Mac was reed-thin and lasted one practice at lightweight football before being knocked senseless and leaving the field. Yet they both possessed traits that became apparent after entering flight training: hyper-keen eyesight, uncanny spatial orientation, and that most necessary trait, facile hand-eye coordination. Both exhibited an abundance of confidence, aggressiveness, and bravura, qualities that would be nurtured in an elite community and that would serve them both well in the years to come as they simultaneously built professional reputations through peace and war. But before they could get to the work of flying—before either could walk the flight line at the air station in Pensacola—they would, in conformance with the policy of the time, go to sea in surface warships to gain experience and an intimate familiarity with the traditional Navy.

2

Foundations

The Navy is the first line of offense and naval aviation, as an advance guard of this first line must deliver the brunt of the attack. Naval aviation cannot take the offensive from shore; it must go to sea on the back of the fleet. . . . The fleet and naval aviation are one and inseparable.

—Rear Adm. William A. Moffett

Naval aviation's second decade opened with a flourish. In a single month—October 1922—two events that were pivotal to the future course of naval aviation unfolded under the watchful gaze of USS *Langley*'s executive officer and early aviation pioneer, Cdr. Ken Whiting. First, as briefed aboard the ship prior to launch, Lt. Virgil Griffin (naval aviator number forty-one) made the first rolling takeoff from the deck of an aircraft carrier, piloting a Chance Vought VE-7 down the length of *Langley*'s flight deck until attaining flying speed off the front end. A week later, Lt. Cdr. Godfrey deC. Chevalier (naval aviator number seven), flying an Aeromarine 39-B biplane, performed a fateful (if unevenly executed) arrested landing at about forty-five knots on the underway *Langley*, steaming at six knots. The press accorded these nearly simultaneous achievements scant attention. Under a spare subhead that failed to plumb the far-reaching consequence of these feats, the major afternoon paper in Washington, D.C., the *Evening Star*, printed a two-hundred-word insert on page thirty-two of the next day's issue: "Land-Type Plane Alights on Deck of U.S. Warship." To a public by then conditioned to speed and distance breakthroughs in the burgeoning domain of aviation, these events amounted to no more than a sideshow or abstract laboratory experiment.

From the vantage point of more than ninety years, these two events, more than any to that point in the embryonic years of experimentation, marked the ascendancy of carrier-based flight as the primary thrust of naval aviation beyond what had been from its inception an emphasis on seaplanes for waterborne operations. Historians Mark L. Evans and Roy A. Grossnick characterize the second decade as one of unprecedented growth, wherein the size, strength, operations, and technological advance of naval aviation accelerated on an increasing scale. The period began with a cumbersome aviation organization built around modest air detachments of mainly seaplanes assigned to each fleet for reconnaissance duties ahead of the battle line of battleships and cruisers. The decade closed with the Navy operating three aircraft carriers with their assigned air groups of fighter, bomber, and scouting squadrons of specialized aircraft and tactics for each mission. Coming to terms with the most effective employment of these newly acquired big decks would play out through the second decade and well into the third inside naval aviation and, more broadly, within the Navy as a whole through a series of Fleet Problems.[1]

Technology moved forward inexorably in the 1920s. Aircraft engines progressed from the standard Dayton–Wright prewar designed water-cooled V-type Liberty to a tripling of available horsepower and improved efficiency obtainable from the Pratt and Whitney Twin Wasp air-cooled radial design. Dissimilar and wholly different types of cockpit instrumentation gave way to a fairly standardized instrument cluster among aircraft types and manufacturers for identical pilot reference going between aircraft. Folding wings and oleo struts for landing gear appeared, easing flight deck handling. Operationally, dive bombing, torpedo attack, and gunfire spotting for the battle line emerged to define warfare specialties and the training and equipment that sustained them.

The exponential growth of the 1920s was predetermined to a great extent by the accumulation of trial results from the first decade. The early pioneers were not content to revel in their newly acquired status as flyers. They set about a vigorous, sometimes precarious path of flight testing intended to push aircraft design limits and challenge the conventional wisdom espoused by staid service traditionalists regarding the limits of the airplane's role in the maritime environment. Each year of that first decade chronicled audacious, often death-defying exhibitions calculated to advance the understanding of what the aircraft could do and how that discovery could be best adapted to the naval service (see Figure 1).

Figure 1. Time Line of Events

1911 Glenn Curtiss taxied his hydroaeroplane alongside USS *Pennsylvania* at anchor in San Diego and sailors manned the cruiser's crane to hoist the aircraft aboard; within the hour, the process was reversed to offload the aircraft for taxi to shore.

1912 Lieutenant John Rogers tested airborne wireless communications, transmitting messages from hydroaeroplane B-1 to Navy torpedo boat *Stringham* over a distance of 1.5 miles.

1913 Lieutenant John Towers established a new world's record for sustained flight in the air—six hours and eleven minutes. Later that year, he reported from his aviation detachment at Naval Station Guantanamo Bay, Cuba, on experiments to gauge bombing, aerial photography, and wireless communications in support of fleet movements: "We have become fairly accurate at dropping missiles, using a fairly simple device gotten up by one of the men. Have obtained some good photographs from the boats at heights up to 1,000 feet and I believe we will get some good results with wireless this winter."

1914 Lieutenant Patrick Bellinger, piloting an observation seaplane from USS *Mississippi*, draws groundfire from Mexican positions off Vera Cruz, marking naval aviation's combat debut.

1915 Lieutenant Commander Henry Mustin made the first catapult launch from a commissioned warship, piloting a Curtiss AB-2 flying boat from the stern of USS *North Carolina* in Pensacola Bay.

1916   Navy Secretary Josephus Daniels, in league with War Secretary Newton Baker, accepted for standard construction of all Navy and Army aircraft a French-derived Deperdussin system for configuring the cockpit with a central control stick for manipulating ailerons and elevators and a rudder pedal for rudder control. The same year, in the Naval Appropriations Act for fiscal year 1917, Congress issued language that authorized establishment of a naval flying corps comprising 150 officers and 350 enlisted.

1917   World War I generated a rapid expansion of naval aviation, producing many firsts:

- The Naval Aircraft Factory at Philadelphia was constructed.
- The Navy was authorized with the Army to take possession of North Island, beginning an unbroken presence for naval aviation in the San Diego area. Concurrently, twenty-seven naval air stations were established on the European continent to prosecute that war.
- A formal progression for flight training, beginning with ground school indoctrination and progressing through preflight and advanced flight training, was established for the naval aviator designation at Pensacola.
- Standard flight clothing was prescribed for summer and winter for aviators, consisting of a tan sheepskin long coat, a short coat and trousers, moleskin hood, goggles, black leather gloves, soft leather boots, waders, brogans, and life belts.
- Secretary Daniels approved as standard uniform wear a winged foul anchor on the left breast signifying a designated naval aviator.

1918 In nineteen months of active involvement in World
War I, naval aviation grew to a fleet of 2,107 aircraft
and 15 airships with manpower of 6,716 officers
and 30,693 enlisted. Flying boats became the visible iconic look of naval aviation, with those aircraft
making 39 recorded attacks on enemy submarines,
sustaining 208 individual casualties by war's end.
Ensign John McNamara made the first recorded
attack on a submarine by a U.S. naval aviator, and
Lt. (jg) David Ingalls scored a fifth aerial victory flying a Sopwith Camel on exchange with Royal Air
Force No. 213 Squadron.

1919 Even as U.S. forces were ramping down following the
armistice, aviation experiments and breakthroughs
continued at a high tempo. Lieutenant Commander
Edward McDonnell became the first to fly an aircraft
from a battleship, launching in a Sopwith Camel from
USS *Texas*. Lieutenant junior grade Harry Sadenwater demonstrated the feasibility of using voice radio
from a flying boat when he carried on a wireless
conversation with Secretary Daniels, who was in his
Navy Department office sixty-five miles away. Finally,
a first for the ages was the record-setting attempt at
a trans-Atlantic crossing by three Curtiss NC flying
boats. Although only one succeeded in making the
complete trip, all of the principal aviators involved in
the three aircraft were presented the Navy Cross.

Source: Evans and Grossnick,
United States Naval Aviation,
1910–2010, 1:4–26, 2:27–58.

The 1910s had firmly cemented naval aviation as a new augmenting
military capability in the minds of Navy flag officers, none of whom
were naval aviators at the beginning of the 1920s. Indeed, there would

not be a first designated naval aviator flag officer until John Towers was promoted to rear admiral near the end of naval aviation's third decade. Yet at this time, there was still nothing approaching unanimity on naval aviation's potential as a primary offensive force at sea. Most recognized that a sufficient concentration in numbers would be needed to obtain a meaningful contribution to the battle line from aircraft at sea. That understanding and the limitations imposed by the Washington Naval Treaty in 1922 provided the necessary impetus to proceed with conversion of two warship hulls, *Lexington* and *Saratoga*, into large deck carriers in the mid-1920s. *Lexington* and *Saratoga* arrived late for Fleet Problem VIII in April 1928, but once on station in proximity to the exercise, they immediately began daily training in the conduct of flight operations. According to author Albert Nofi, "They undertook a series of exercises testing how two carriers could operate together, becoming the first operational carrier division in the fleet. In addition, aviators engaged in a great deal of experimentation, including trials in dive bombing, then a new tactic, while the ships' gunnery officers worked out optimal anti-aircraft tactics."[2] Therefore, *Langley* was the only aircraft carrier to play a dedicated role in Fleet Problems until the arrival of the new big decks. In his consolidated summary conclusions of Fleet Problems II, III, and IV in 1924, commander in chief U.S. Fleet, Adm. Robert Coontz, acknowledged the important, even game-changing, participation by *Langley*'s aircraft; he recommended that the fleet "needed more aircraft, and particularly needed to complete the two aircraft carriers then under construction, *Lexington* and *Saratoga*."[3] Thus, in consideration of the headline-grabbing achievements of the 1910s and the arrival of three aircraft carriers in the 1920s, naval aviation was poised, equipped, and now populated with growing numbers of committed enthusiasts to make the 1920s a decade of matchless growth in technical and tactical prowess and professional reputation of aviation inside the naval establishment.

The formative gestation of naval aviation in the 1920s defined a seagoing aeronautical profession with an allure of derring-do and the camaraderie and stature of an elite guild that the Snowden brothers would be drawn to. Each, in his time and by his own contributions, would add to the luster of the trade. As much as hardware and operational schemes advanced in the 1920s, so too arose a generation of aviation leaders who pioneered the use of aircraft by the fleet, discerning how best to employ the air arm and, crucially, pressing their advocacy in spite of the disdain openly expressed by more hidebound senior battleship officers. Ernie's naval aviation career would intersect with at least three key early trailblazers when they had progressed to positions of senior leadership, and he would draw inspiration from their legendary accomplishments and receive no small amount of encouragement and support from them directly in his career. Younger brother Mac was most animated by the example of a later generation of aviators—those who had made their mark as wartime pilots and leaders of aviation commands in the postwar consolidation and reconfiguration of Navy air—and even by one trailblazer who did not wear a uniform but had an inestimable impact on the hardware that populated the carrier flight decks of the 1950s through the 1970s.

The most prominent voices in the 1920s were those who had midwifed naval aviation's birth the decade prior. This corps of intrepid airmen comprised naval officers who, by their zeal, conviction, and sheer physical bravery, laid the foundations upon which naval aviation would build. Most were Naval Academy graduates from classes in the early 1900s who, after serving the statutory requirement of two years in the fleet before commissioning, deduced from early experiments by the Wrights and Curtiss that aircraft would have an important—if not yet fully defined—role in the fleet. For these young lieutenants, aviation also likely satisfied a personal yearning to distinguish themselves from other naval officers by their display of adventurous spirit and proper wit in harnessing this new technology and priming it for the naval service.

From their ranks would emerge the squadron and air group leaders who would refine tactics and employment concepts through the Fleet Problems of the 1930s and, ultimately, the carrier skippers, division commanders, and task force commanders who would direct a formidable air armada to victory in the global war of the 1940s. Those first aviators formed a small group of pioneering visionaries who, upon mastering the mechanics of yoke, rudder pedal, and throttle, became the early adopters of the new technology and set about pushing the boundaries of aeronautic understanding.

Tragically, Lieutenant Commander Chevalier would perish within a month of his historic landing aboard *Langley*, dying from injuries sustained in a crash of another Vought VE-7. His death underscored one hallmark of the early days of naval aviation: the attendant risk to life and limb assumed by unpracticed aviators placing unstable machines of doped fabric and mahogany into new, unfamiliar flight regimes. Such pluck and fearlessness were common attributes of early (and later) naval aviators. Unsurprising, then, was the steady influx of similarly disposed naval officers intending to enter naval aviation. Of those very first student aviators, Lt. Patrick Bellinger took his flight training with naval aviator number three, John Towers, at Annapolis in 1912. As naval aviator number eight, Bellinger joined Towers with other newly designated aviators in Guantanamo the next year for experimentation and exercise with fleet units, continuing the trials the year after with seaplane launches by catapult from USS *North Carolina*. When hostilities erupted in Mexico, Bellinger accompanied Towers as part of the naval aviation unit attached to fleet warships entering the harbor of Vera Cruz. Operating from USS *Mississippi* to scout enemy movement ashore, he experienced the dubious first of taking ground fire from hostile forces. It was said that next to Chevalier, Bellinger probably had more time in the air than any other officer in the Navy at that time. In 1919, he would command the Curtiss flying boat NC-1 in the trans-Atlantic attempt, and although he would not complete the crossing as planned, he would be lionized along with his colleagues for his intrepidity.[4] Bellinger progressed steadily, reporting to the new Bureau of Aeronautics (BuAer) in 1921 for aviation staff duty, then to aircraft tender USS *Wright* as executive officer. As the 1920s closed, while at the Naval War College, he translated his decade of aeronautical experience into a strikingly prescient forecast:

> The most effective defensive against air attack is the offensive action against the sources, that is enemy vessels carrying aircraft and therefore, enemy aircraft carriers, or their bases and hangars on shore as well as the factories in which they are built. The air force that first strikes its enemy a serious blow will reap a tremendous initial advantage. The opposing force cannot hope to

surely prevent such a blow by the mere placing of aircraft in certain protective screens or by patrolling certain areas. There is no certainty, even with a preponderance in numbers, of making contact with enemy aircraft before they have reached the proper area and delivered their attack, and there is no certainty even if contact is made, of being able to stay them.[5]

Bellinger was at the epicenter of fleet exercises and problem-solving in the 1930s as commanding officer first of aircraft tender USS *Wright* (AV 1), then of USS *Langley* (CV 1), and in Fleet Problem XIX, commanding officer of USS *Ranger* (CV 4). A heart condition kept Bellinger away from the heaviest fighting in World War II, but he would nonetheless ascend to vice admiral in command of Naval Air Forces U.S. Atlantic Fleet for the balance of the war.

Bellinger became an indirect but important link in this narrative: while preparing for the trans-Atlantic attempt in 1919, he was instrumental in drafting as his navigator in NC-1 Lt. Cdr. Marc Mitscher, whose "combined record as a pilot and an executive singled him out for a place in the trans-Atlantic crew."[6] He would occupy a central role in the career, professional growth, and recognition of Ernie Snowden and scores of other aviators a generation later, but as a principal in the historic NC flight, he was already building an enviable reputation for singular competence in the air and on the ground. Beginning with his winging in 1916 as naval aviator number thirty-three, he was a significant participant in aviation experiments from USS *North Carolina* that year and by 1918 was in command of the naval air station at Rockaway, New York, the jumping-off point for the Curtiss flying boat trans-Atlantic attempt. As the pace of training for entry into World War I quickened, he was ordered to take command of the naval air station at Miami, guiding its growth into one of the largest primary training stations during the war build-up. Mitscher began the 1920s in command of the naval air station at Anacostia, adjacent to the District of Columbia. Within six months, he was ordered to staff duty in the new Bureau of Aeronautics as an assistant—and sometime muse—to BuAer chief Rear Adm. William Moffett, drafting the admiral's retorts to radically new notions advanced by Army general Billy Mitchell for establishing a separate and equal service branch for aviation. Mitscher testified before the president's aviation board on the Navy position, which ultimately prevailed for retaining aviation as a fleet component.[7] Mitscher progressed to command of the *Saratoga* air wing during important trials in Fleet Problems of the mid-1930s and to command of *Hornet* delivering the Doolittle raiders to the launch point. Mitscher would command Task Force 58 in USS *Lexington* in 1944, where Ernie, as air wing commander in *Lexington*, would have frequent face-to-face opportunities to gauge the man and to profit by his mentorship.

Barely two months after Chevalier made the historic landing on *Langley*, another naval officer entered aviation service with the winging of Lt. Forrest Sherman in December 1922. Sherman was a gifted aviator and would benefit by exposure to frontline service in carrier squadrons throughout the 1920s and early 1930s. His immediate assignment after flight training was in Fighter Squadron (VF) Two (VF-2), transitioning from seaplanes attached to tender USS *Aroostook* to what were then termed land-planes preparing to embark in *Langley* for participation in Fleet Problem III—which overlapped the annual Grand Joint Army–Navy Exercise Number 2 in 1924. VF-2 would become the first squadron trained to operate from *Langley*. Its performance as part of *Langley*'s first appearance in a Fleet Problem prompted a laudatory commendation from Vice Adm. Newton A. McCully, commander of the scouting fleet: "Great credit is due her aviators for their effective work against so much superior air forces, and it indicates the power of the air attack even when the forces may appear insignificant, and the enemy greatly superior."[8] With that experience, Sherman was reassigned to shore duty as a faculty member in the department of seamanship and flight tactics at the Naval Academy. He would return to the fleet to assume command of VF-1 in *Saratoga*, leading that squadron to capture the fleet aircraft gunnery trophy for 1932–33 and garnering a commendation from the Secretary of the Navy for the squadron's exemplary combat efficiency. He would personally take the Navy battle efficiency "E" for dive bombing and fixed gun scores.[9]

Felix Stump was another early aviator whose career would later intersect with those of both Ernie and Mac. Stump earned his wings in 1921, the year after Mitscher attempted his trans-Atlantic crossing in NC-1. Stump initially was assigned to Torpedo Squadron Two in *Langley*, overlapping Forrest Sherman's time in VF-2 in the same air group. He briefly commanded the naval air station at Hampton Roads, doing early test and evaluation of airborne torpedoes. After three years in cruiser scouting squadrons, he returned to sea in *Saratoga* in 1936 in command of Scouting Squadron Two, in the air group then commanded by Marc Mitscher. He later assumed command of USS *Langley* prior to the start of World War II. Stump would command *Lexington* in late 1943 and early 1944, relinquishing command just as Mitscher came aboard as commander, Task Force 58 to use *Lexington* as his flagship. Felix Stump rose to full admiral and command of the U.S. Pacific Command by 1953. It was in those later years that Ernie would engage with Stump again on behalf of younger brother Mac.

Countless individuals invested their time and energy on behalf of naval aviation in its second decade, but the person who exerted the greatest influence in nurturing the Navy's nascent air arm was Rear Adm. William Moffett. In July 1921, Moffett was named chief of the newly formed BuAer, which replaced the position of director of aeronautics. Absolute discretion and authority for all that related to the designing, building, fitting out, and repairing of aircraft were vested in the BuAer position. Three successive terms as the chief of the bureau gave Moffett the platform he needed to consolidate naval aviation and lead it into its third decade.

Moffett seemed, at first inspection, ill suited as the senior principal advocate for naval aviation. He was not a designated naval aviator. His career bona fides as a "gun club" battleship officer were well established, having served as a junior officer under no less an exemplar of the type than Alfred T. Mahan in USS *Chicago*, and he also had skippered USS *Mississippi*. But upon taking his new position, it became clear that he "comprehended the tactical, strategic and political implications of naval aviation, and he was willing to dedicate his career as a flag officer to bringing aviation into the fleet and then to guaranteeing its role as a powerful arm of the modern Navy."[10] Taking the reins of authority as chief of the new bureau, a position and organization that he personally lobbied for, Moffett set about accreting ownership to BuAer of all the principal aviation functions that previously had been balkanized among competing bureaus. From the bureaus of construction and repair, steam engineering, and ordnance, he absorbed the production of airframes and their structural appurtenances, aircraft engines and radios, and all manner of airborne weapons. From the Bureau of Navigation, he sought concessions or at least shared accountability for training and career assignments of aviators. In addition, BuAer benefitted from the transfer of administrators, technicians, and fiscal resources from each bureau.

The 1920s were a period of retrenchment as the assets of all the services were scaled back from their wartime expansion. In the labyrinth of competing administrative and congressional agendas that was Washington, D.C., Moffett proved equally adept at public relations and at maneuvering in the political realm. He encouraged and enabled Navy participation in the air races of the day, not only as a means to appraise relevant new technologies but also as a way to gain publicity for the Navy's record-setting performances (and consequent favorable consideration of legislative requests). He effectively neutralized the Army Air Corps' irascible zealot, Gen. Billy Mitchell, and his proposal for a separate consolidated air service by means of a finely crafted shaping campaign, presenting airtight logic in congressional questioning and testimonies for the record and in well-placed media inserts. He effected a compromise between aircraft industrialists and the naval aircraft factory in Philadelphia that redirected the government facility to design and manufacture only one-off prototypes while opening the field for private industry to compete for longer full-rate production runs. He was largely responsible for stabilizing those production runs by pursuing and obtaining 1926 legislation authorizing a one-thousand-airplane buy over five years.[11]

The technical and organizational trajectory of naval aviation advancement in the 1920s continued unabated, due in large measure to Moffett's stewardship of BuAer. Nearing the end of his third term as chief of the bureau, the effects of the stock market crash and a general downturn in the economy dampened much of the steady growth of the previous period. However, the proliferation of public works spending fostered by the Depression had a spillover effect on naval aviation. Work begun in the 1920s continued, yielding more accurate bombsights, force induction engines, retractable landing gear, hydraulic arresting gear, and catapults. Significantly, squadron proficiencies showed rising scores across a number of measures, whereas previously those same gains were indicated for only a few high-time individuals.[12] It is fitting that BuAer's successor organization, the Naval Air Systems Command (NAVAIR), today operates from a headquarters complex named for William Moffett.

The 1920s, then, were a period wherein naval aviation made enormous strides toward solidifying the early gains of the prior decade and swaying hard-set perceptions about its warfighting utility to the fleet. Those early naval aviation pioneers—the men whose effort and sacrifice set the course for its growth—were largely cut from the same cloth. They were nearly all Naval Academy graduates, many of them classmates, whose identity and loyalty to the Navy were annealed at Annapolis where service traditions were inculcated. They had all served years at sea acquiring first-hand experience at a deckplate level in division and department leadership under way. Where they differed from their seagoing peers was in their collective grasp of the importance of the new science of aviation and its potential role for the Navy. Their names—Towers, Chevalier, Bellinger, Whiting—are legend today, and many of the Navy's air fields and ships bear their names. A few of them proved of inestimable importance in leading naval aviation through its greatest challenge and its most complete victory in World War II. An even smaller sample of those former pioneers and wartime leaders—Mitscher, Sherman, and Stump—were sources of inspiration for a young Ernie Snowden and directly fostered his career progression, mentoring him at critical junctures along the way. Ernie's younger brother Mac was inspired and mentored by a later generation of leaders, most of whom came of age as junior officers and new aviators in World War II. That group was the product of its wartime experience and later service in the postwar transition to jets and super carriers, but the members of that group, in turn, drew inspiration from the early pioneers from the 1910s and 1920s.

Stanley "Swede" Vejtasa was one of those individuals. He was among the many pilot trainees drawn directly from enlistments in the darkening days just before the war. Earning his wings in 1939 only a year after joining the Navy, Vejtasa was flying SBD-3s in Scouting Squadron Five (VS-5) from *Yorktown* when the Japanese attack on Pearl Harbor drew the United States into the war. Part of the early offensive against the Japanese, *Yorktown* brought her air group within striking distance of Makin and Mili atolls in the Gilbert chain of islands for attacks in early 1942, the same island group that would occupy Ernie's energies two years later. In early May 1942, intelligence indicated that a Japanese seaplane base was under construction at Tulagi, prompting new strikes from *Yorktown* by Vejtasa and VS-5. Roving American and Japanese fleets collided in the Coral Sea that May, and Vejtasa was credited with dropping one of twelve direct hits on the Japanese light carrier *Shoho*, sinking her in less than seven minutes. While on antitorpedo patrol over *Yorktown* the next day, Vejtasa and his flight were jumped by as many as a dozen Zeros. Several American aircraft were shot down. Vejtasa maneuvered his SBD hard to take on a swarm of seven Zeros, flaming three in just minutes of hard twisting maneuvers. After the loss of *Yorktown* at Midway the following month, he returned from a brief refit and training evolution stateside as a member of VF-10 flying the Grumman F4F Wildcat in *Enterprise* (CV 6). Vejtasa was in an elite company of aggressive and highly adroit fighter pilots—although their exploits were yet to be on full display—that included Ens. Edward "Whitey" Feightner, Lt. (jg) Butch Voris (future founder of the Blue Angels), Lt. William "Killer" Kane, and squadron skipper Lt. Cdr. Jimmy Flatley. In the final days of October 1942, Vejtasa "intercepted a squadron of enemy dive bombers screaming down on USS *Enterprise* and quickly shot down two. The enemy bombers scattered, but almost immediately Vejtasa sighted 11 Japanese torpedo bombers making a run on the Big E and again he charged in. This time he shot down five and broke up the attack, quite possibly saving one of the war's most famous carriers from destruction," for which he received a third Navy Cross.[13] Swede Vejtasa assumed command of USS *Constellation* in November 1962. He "was a favorite with junior officers but occasionally ran afoul of more senior officers, mainly because he spoke his mind and did not suffer fools no matter how senior they have been to him."[14] In his VF-10 days, Swede was nominated for the Medal of Honor but saw that citation reduced; speculation was that "the reduction might have come because Swede had angered senior officers by an outburst during a ready room briefing several weeks earlier."[15]

As Ernie Snowden was crossing the country to his first duty assignment in USS *West Virginia* after graduation from the academy in 1932, rising first-class midshipman Tom Connolly was already in Los Angeles taking the bronze medal in gymnastics in the summer games of the Tenth Olympiad. Graduating in 1933, Connolly would complete graduate studies in aeronautical engineering at the Massachusetts Institute of Technology and go on to enjoy a highly dynamic and sometimes controversial thirty-eight-year career that combined engineering acumen with increasingly senior flying jobs. In the view of Mac and Ernie Snowden in the early 1970s, there could not have been a more illuminating and clarifying moment for naval aviation than Connolly's testimony before a Senate committee in 1966 wherein he denounced the lack of available thrust in the F-111B. Connolly arrived at that moment having accumulated a stellar record of achievement commanding two aircraft carriers, a carrier division, and Naval Air Forces Pacific Fleet. For an officer clearly marked for positions of greater importance to have publicly rebuked the testimony of his civilian leaders brought the curtain down on an exemplary career. Connolly retired at the end of his tenure on the chief of naval operations staff, forever earning the admiration of naval aviators for standing his ground. For Mac, it would be another lesson in leadership style—a foundational influence.

Another giant in the history of naval aircraft design—one who never served in uniform or manually worked with stick, rudder, and throttle as an operational aviator or test pilot—was George Spangenberg, who rose to director of BuAer's evaluation division by the late 1950s. Spangenberg had started in naval aircraft design in 1935 at the naval aircraft factory in Philadelphia, and by his retirement in 1973, he was the iconic embodiment of the aero engineering sage and arbiter of viable new aircraft designs. As the evaluation division director, he was responsible for establishing overall design requirements for all new naval aircraft and missiles, setting the evaluation factors for design competitions, and selecting the most viable candidates to meet the Navy's needs. His daughter noted that his "abiding desire was to see that our Naval Aviators were flying the best machine possible; he never faltered from that mission up to the time of his death." He once remarked that he "had a very high regard for the Navy, its people, primarily its people. I didn't know enough about the equipment but the people were sure first rate."[16] In his time at BuAer (later NAVAIR), he served as the leading configuration analyst and spokesperson for the Navy, Office of the Secretary of Defense, and Congress on the suitability of several generations of new designs for meeting the service's needs, including the S-3 Viking, the E-2 Hawkeye, the F4H Phantom, the P-3 Orion, and the F-14 Tomcat. Mac would come to know him personally through frequent contact on the TFX, VFX, and eventually F-14 programs from his position as the program coordinator of those designs on the chief of naval operations staff. As a final coda to Spangenberg's remarkable achievements and contributions to naval aviation, he was among the few nonaviators to be selected as an honorary naval aviator in 1973.

In each generation since its founding in 1911, naval aviation has produced distinguished leaders who established examples of excellence in flight, innovation in tactics, foresight in adopting new technologies, aggressiveness in combat, and forbearance in disciplining subordinates. In its first half-century, a new crop of dazzling leaders exemplifying these characteristics took center stage about every fifteen years to shape the course of naval aviation and particularly to assume the mentorship of the rising group of junior officers entering the fraternity that would carry the community forward. Those first pioneers—Ken Whiting, John Towers, Patrick Bellinger, and Bill Moffett—tutored a second run of inspirational leaders that moved the fraternity through the 1920s and early 1930s. Ernie would be the beneficiary of their leadership example along with colleagues Ralph Ofstie, Forrest Sherman, Felix Stump, and Marc Mitscher. Fifteen years later, younger brother Mac would profit from the leadership example of the next wave of leaders— including Swede Vejtasa, Tom Connolly, and George Spangenberg—whose experiences in Pacific combat or in the acquisition struggles in the Pentagon had tempered their maturity and leadership styles. If, however, there was one influencing agent that proved the most determining spur to Mac's lifelong commitment to naval aviation, it was Ernie. As much surrogate father and mentor as older brother, Ernie instilled in Mac from boyhood a devotion to flying and to the naval service that would sustain his total absorption in and commitment to naval aviation that carried well beyond his almost thirty-five years in uniform.

3

Preparation

An institution compounded not alone of seas, ships and salutes, but a domain athrill with widely varying duties[,] privileges and opportunities, with moments of sudden tense drama and unsung deeds of heroism and self-sacrifice inspired not by the heat of martial emergency, but by the dictates of that unsleeping naval alter-ego which makes us ever a part and protector of . . . the SERVICE.

—1932 *Lucky Bag*

Pensacola, Florida, is well situated geographically as a natural, defendable harbor, a fact not lost on the U.S. Navy and recognized immediately by military governor Andrew Jackson when the Gulf coast came under U.S. control in 1821. Navy activity in and around the old Spanish fort at San Carlos de Barrancas surged and waned in the following years. Navy Secretary Josephus Daniels, and later his assistant, Franklin D. Roosevelt, toured the abandoned Navy yard in 1913 and returned to Washington convinced they had found the ideal hatchery for the nascent aviation arm of the Navy. The headline of the February 2, 1914, edition of the *Pensacola Journal* read: "World's First Naval Aeronautical Station Opens Here Today with Flights over Pensacola Bay and the Gulf by Ensign Chevalier and Other Aviators."[1]

Ernie's arrival at Pensacola in February 1936 coincided with sweeping changes to the flight training program. A significant ramp-up in the number of student pilot inductees necessitated major expansion of facilities and modification of what had been the regular course of instruction for at least the prior five years. The influx of new

trainer aircraft, changes derived from fleet experience with a growing number of aircraft carriers and operational aircraft, and rapidly
darkening world affairs all stimulated the adoption of a syllabus that
required three hundred hours of flight instruction augmented by
thirty-two weeks of academic training. Students were moved sequen-
tially through phases of instruction at five training squadrons, VN-1
through VN-5, around the Pensacola area. Ernie's progression through
the syllabus began with seaplane fundamentals in the Consolidated
NY-2, a biplane on floats, followed by primary landplane training at
Corry Field. By late spring when Ernie moved to Corry Field, transition to a new trainer aircraft was well under way, and his landplane
experience would begin in the newer NS-1, an early iteration of the
Stearman Kaydet. Here, Ernie learned "precision spins, slips, fishtails,
small field emergencies and 'shooting the circle,' a precision landing
to a 100-foot circle outlined on the ground. Students were required
to make a full-stall, three-point landing within the circle. Aerobatics
consisted of loops, wingovers, figure-eight turns over pylons at 500
feet, barrel rolls, single-and-double snap rolls, split S's, falling leafs, and
Immelmann turns."[2] Flight time in VN-1 through VN-3 was supplemented by a half day of ground school that included hands-on practical instruction in engine and airframe maintenance, principles of
aeronautics, and basics of meteorology.

Moving through training squadrons VN-3, -4, and -5, Ernie began
to get his first exposure to the kind of flying that closely replicated
what he would see in a few months in the fleet. At the main side Pensacola landing strip, which would soon be named Chevalier Field,
Ernie was introduced to the O3U, a Vought Corsair of an earlier era
but easily a more complex aircraft than what he had flown since the
NY-2. He would launch on training flights designed to introduce
fleet procedures: forming up in nine-plane formations for air-to-air
gunnery exercises, then detaching for individual cross-country and
radio navigation routes. Returning to Corry Field for final instruction in the F4B, Ernie continued work in three- and nine-plane formations performing aerobatics, gunnery, and dive bombing. Before
completing his tutelage in VN-5, he would become practiced at skip-
ping the rope, "power-off, precision landings over a rope with flags
on it, held up by two 7-foot poles that could be lowered," designed

to simulate the rigors of carrier landings.[3] With his winging in March 1937, Ernie's naval career took a markedly different course, one that would place him at greater risk but also bring him much gratification.

As a newly winged aviator on orders from the training group in Pensacola— but already having four years of commissioned service as a line officer in the gunnery department in USS *West Virginia*—Ernie reported to his first squadron in April 1937 shortly before it went to sea in USS *Lexington* to join Fleet Problem XVIII. Squadron designations and logos evolved quickly in these times to create a nearly unfathomable lineage, with numbers and patch designs changed seemingly every time the squadron rotated to sea on a new carrier. The 1937 Chief of Naval Operations directive changing the naval aeronautic organization would simplify designations by aligning squadron numbers with carrier hull numbers.[4]

In his first weeks at sea in a squadron whose reputation was already established throughout naval aviation, Ernie got his first exposure to, and quickly became adept at handling, the Boeing F4B-4 fighter, flown by the High Hatters of VF-1 as they prepared for their role in Fleet Problem XVIII. It was a testament of Ernie's skill that he could so quickly master the transition from more forgiving trainers to the F4B-4. Its short-coupled airframe design and quick control response made pilot-induced oscillations a challenge in all flight regimes for the neophyte. But Ernie, with his excellent hand-eye coordination, learned quickly to use those design traits to advantage in fast-moving snap rolls common in 1930s mock aerial combat.

The F4B-4, entering the fleet in 1933, was the last in a series of Boeing fighters in the F4B family procured by the Navy, only seventeen years after the Boeing Company's founding as the Pacific Aero Products Company. And the F4B-4 was among the last aircraft procured by the service that went by only an alphanumeric designation, lacking the popular name—such as Dauntless or Wildcat—that would become standard practice in just a few years.

The F4B family enjoyed a highly successful run of more than six hundred aircraft in several variants for the Army and Navy, all tracing their origin to Boeing's prototype model eighty-three, which advanced the state of fighter design by replacing wood framing with metal and welded steel with bolted aluminum for weight savings. Additional improvements in the "Four" series included a broader vertical tail of corrugated aluminum with an enlarged ventral "turtleback" spine housing an emergency rubber life raft behind the pilot's headrest. A most important design enhancement for a carrier aircraft was the F4B-4's tapered engine housing that permitted greater pilot visibility over the nose on approach. Excellent performance for its day in speed, payload, and available G-force, combined with rugged dependability, made it the most advanced carrier fighter of the mid-1930s. The Navy procured ninety-two "Fours," generating the longest production run to date of a single model and series Navy fighter.[5]

Just as fighter aircraft were nearing the limit of aerodynamic performance that could be wrung out of wood and fabric biplane designs, a period of relative peace through the 1920s and into the 1930s allowed the Navy to involve most of its capital ships and aircraft in twenty-one large annual maneuvers called Fleet Problems. Perhaps the most beneficial and enduring lesson from the Fleet Problems was the development of carrier battle group operations and carrier air doctrine.[6] As Fleet Problems progressed, there was nothing near consensus on the utility of the aircraft carrier and its air group. Throughout most of this period, aviators had not risen to flag rank with the benefit of having spent an entire career in aviation. Only in 1926—with more than one-third of the total run of Fleet Problems completed—did Congress pass a law requiring that commanding officers of aircraft carriers, seaplane tenders, and major aviation shore establishments be aviation- or aviation observer–qualified. Regular line officers then in command of such ships and facilities were rushed off to Pensacola for a cram course in stick-and-rudder flying so that their command tours would not be interrupted—among them Capt. Ernest King, commanding officer of seaplane tender USS *Wright*, and Rear Adm. William Moffett, BuAer chief. Although they lacked the years of flying experience, these officers and others like them were nonetheless visionaries who advanced the standing of aviation. Such was not the case throughout the senior Navy ranks then organizing and conducting the Fleet Problems. Those senior positions were still dominated by line officers steeped in the dogma of battleship preeminence in war at sea. These leaders could conceive of no utility for carriers and their aircraft other than as airborne scouts and observers calling shot for the battle line.

"Dive-bombing, introduced in the mid-1920s, had [a] revolutionary implication: for the first time aircraft could reliably hit rapidly maneuvering targets such as warships."[7] As this capability began to influence Fleet Problem outcomes, "U.S. doctrine increasingly detached the battle line from the carrier so as to allow it to concentrate, at the outset, on destroying enemy carriers."[8] The series of twenty-one Fleet Problems revealed that not only could carrier-based aviation operate beyond the protection of the battleships, it also was capable of inflicting harm on an enemy's surface forces.[9] As fighter design evolved through the 1930s and 1940s, carrier design and tactics kept pace—to a point. By contrast, in the years immediately following World War II, technological progress in aerodynamics and the resulting advance of fighter design outpaced the carrier's ability to effectively operate them. In the 1930s, however, aircraft and their seagoing bases were being tested together as an integrated warfighting system, with the technological advances of each proceeding roughly in parallel.

Fleet Problem XVIII in the spring of 1937, which ranged over most of the eastern Pacific, involved more than four hundred carrier- and land-based aircraft in mock attacks on Hawaii. The High Hatters, in intricately coordinated operations with other squadrons of their *Lexington* air group and those of *Saratoga*, mounted air attacks on assigned Navy and Army installations and then pressed mock attacks on the opposing force, which included USS *Ranger*. From *Lexington*'s air group, five-hundred-pound bombs borne by Vought SBUs and one-thousand-pound bombs ferried by Great Lakes BG dive bombers did most of the heavy work on mock surface targets. Ernie's squadron worked out top cover and strafing tactics that in later conflicts would be characterized as target combat air patrol and flak suppression.[10] At the conclusion of Fleet Problem XVIII, *Lexington* was detached and steamed westward across the Pacific with some haste to join the search for aviatrix Amelia Earhart. In a move viewed in hindsight as an effort to proliferate promising junior and mid-grade pilots with Fleet Problem experience, the Navy detached Ernie from VF-1 in *Lexington* and transferred him to VF-4 to be embarked in USS *Ranger* the following year for Fleet Problem XIX.

Reporting to the VF-4 Red Rippers at the end of June 1937, Ernie would now climb into the more powerful Grumman F3F-1 biplane that his new squadron would be flying for three more years. The F3F was the most modern and capable dogfighter then in the fleet, even if it lacked the streamlined speed of the monoplane F4F Wildcat that fleet squadrons would have within a couple of years. The F3F could throttle up to a fifty-mph top end speed advantage, and aerodynamic efficiencies and a larger fuel tank volume increased range by more than three hundred miles over the F4B-4 that Ernie had flown with VF-1 in the previous year's Fleet Problem XVIII.[11] The switch in planes was straightforward and required no more transition training than a verbal orientation from the squadron executive officer peering over Ernie's shoulder as he sat facing the instrument panel. From a Boeing to a Grumman product, the instruments changed little—a basic cluster of six to seven flight instruments with two or three engine monitoring gauges mounted to the lower right or left of the instrument cluster. Both cockpits presented the pilot with a gun-charging handle to the upper right or left of the instrument cluster for the forward firing machine guns. The similarity in cockpit layout actually helped a pilot with Ernie's skill to readily discern the differences in aero performance between the Boeing and the Grumman planes. Beyond upgrades in the top end speed and rate of climb, the Grumman aircraft was not designed with as much short wing-to-empennage distance, alleviating some of the pilot-induced control sensitivity but still preserving its superb high-G turning ability. Decades later, pilots in modern jet aircraft pulling 9 Gs were sensitized to the perils of G-force loss of consciousness, but F3Fs stressed for 9 G maneuvers were already in service in the late 1930s and were routinely stressed to their limits.[12] By the time the Red Rippers and USS *Ranger* joined the next Fleet Problem, Ernie and most of the squadron had benefitted from almost a year of intensive training and familiarity in their F3F-1s.

Fleet Problem XIX in March 1938 again encompassed a large area of the northern Pacific Ocean, from the West Coast to Hawaii to the Aleutians. Moving into Phase V of the fleet tactical exercise, the "Defense of Hawaii," the scenario was set for the Red fleet (United States), having suffered a major defeat by the Blue fleet (acting as surrogate for Japan), to reconstitute and prevent Blue from rolling over and taking possession of suitable advanced bases. Blue fleet included *Saratoga* and *Ranger* and accompanying surface combatants. Simulated landings at Lahaina on Maui were covered by VF–3 from *Saratoga* and VF–4 from *Ranger*, successfully fending off counterattacks by land-based aircraft. Moving into the next phase of the problem, "Air Attack on the Fleet," on April 5, the planners intended to exercise the carrier air groups in coordinated attacks on a postulated Blue fleet position, and alternatively, repel Blue fleet counter–air attacks.[13]

This would be an important phase of the Fleet Problem for Ernie and his VF–4 squadron mates. Now a senior lieutenant, department head, and division leader, Ernie would participate in planning squadron-, group-, and fleet-level maneuvers that involved aircraft from *Ranger*, *Saratoga*, and *Lexington*. With Butch O'Hare and Jimmy Thach from sister squadron VF–3 in USS *Saratoga*, Ernie would fly and perfect squadron and group strike tactics that would make a critical difference in the early phase of the air combat in which these aviators would soon find themselves.

Beyond the obvious benefits accruing to their large-scale maneuvers, Fleet Problems were frequently used to field-test promising new black box inventions. Before Fleet Problem XIX concluded, Ernie's squadron would be designated the exercise unit with an experimental technology that held great promise for enabling extended overwater flights far from the carrier. He and selected squadron pilots flew with specially configured aircraft that mounted radio homing devices called ZB adapters.

Built by Western Electric, the ZB adapter clipped onto the loop antenna of a standard ARB radio set. The aircraft carrier would broadcast over the lower part of the very high frequency (VHF) band a Morse code letter as a modulated tone, with a different letter and tone for every thirty degrees off the carrier's heading. In practice, Morse code letters would be changed every day as a guard against compromise. Additionally, using a double amplitude modulation scheme with the transmitter ensured that a casual listener could overhear only a single carrier signal unless equipped with the demodulator in the receiver. The signal emanating from the aircraft carrier was mostly line-of-sight, so if the pilot could detect one or two broadcast letters, he would know his position relative to the carrier. The ZB adapter was, then, a relatively simple VHF receiver that would demodulate the received signal back to the lower portion of the broadcast band, with the signal then picked up by the ARB set. The ARB set's most recognizable feature was the "coffee grinder" tuner knob that the pilot would manually rotate to find the right frequency coverage. Results of VF-4's exercise with the ZB were modestly successful, but the technology, with further enhancements, would prove invaluable in the years ahead for pilots returning from long searches for the enemy fleet.[14]

Other neophyte naval aviators who would later establish indelible reputations for their combat prowess were beginning to enter fleet squadrons and gaining foundational experience that was increasingly shaped by the Fleet Problems. Lt. David McCampbell, who had graduated from Annapolis a year later than Ernie, joined VF-4 about three weeks too late for Fleet Problem XIX. McCampbell would become a favorite of Ernie's, and the two were often paired on the flight schedule as Ernie mentored McCampbell through initial checkout in the F3F and then in squadron section and division tactics. That McCampbell learned these lessons well is evidenced by his later war record as commander of VF-15 and of Air Group 15, leading to his standing at war's end—never matched—as the Navy's highest scoring ace in the Pacific.

In the summer of 1938, Ernie's brother Mac was one of fifty-seven rising juniors at Beaufort High School, which was graduating classes after the junior year for lack of resources and available teachers. Mac, like Ernie, was an accomplished sailor. He was especially proficient handling the Marconi-rigged runabout owned by his closest high school friend, Graydon Paul. Graydon was the grandson of Beaufort's only aviation pioneer, William Luther Paul, inventor of the Bumble Bee. Mac and Graydon made a well-practiced and unbeatable team in pick-up races between the western edge of Shackleford Bank and the eastern terminus of Bogue Bank beneath the old Civil War fortress, Fort Macon. Their affinity for the water foretold an adult life made full by work on the ocean.

Mac's father, Macon senior, had retired from captaining the steam packet ferry service and was working his farmland daily when he was struck down by a heart attack as Mac entered high school in 1935. These years were difficult emotionally for Mac, then just twelve. He probably transferred much of the pride and admiration he had in his father to his older brother Ernie, the Naval Academy graduate and Navy fighter pilot. After Ernie's squadron returned from Fleet Problem XIX in 1938, his commanding officer granted him permission to sign out a squadron aircraft, which was by then en route to an East Coast home base at Norfolk, for a short cross-country flight to visit home. Beaufort was a tranquil, even bucolic village in the mid-1930s, with only the occasional backfire from a Model A or the low diesel chug of a returning menhaden boat on Taylor Creek breaking the relative quiet. That tranquility was disrupted with Ernie's arrival. While still airborne, he flat-hatted down Taylor Creek at an altitude of about one hundred feet in view of late morning activity on Front Street, made a high-speed pass, then returned for a low-speed pass to give townfolk, frozen in slack-jawed bewilderment, a good look at the most modern of Navy biplane fighter aircraft. He turned at the end of Taylor Creek and landed at the small dirt airstrip near the high school that served the town. When Mac walked the half-mile with his high school classmates to the airstrip to witness this first-ever visit by a frontline fleet fighter, Ernie called him over and sat him in the cockpit for an orientation and some none-too-subtle career counseling.

This was a clarifying moment for Mac. He could imagine his own future and was now resolved to follow his older brother—to earn his gold wings and fly Navy fighters. It would be four more years before he would take the first step by entering the Naval Academy in 1942. As a graduated junior, Mac lacked the age and coursework to enter the academy immediately. Two years at the University of North Carolina and a third year at prep school waiting for his second try at a congressional appointment placed him in the entering class of 1946 (which, due to wartime exigencies, would graduate in June 1945). His close friend Graydon went immediately from Beaufort to North Carolina State to pursue an engineering degree and then a Reserve Officer Training Corps commission in the Navy. When war came, Graydon outranked Mac and entered the Pacific theater a year sooner than Mac as the catapult and arresting gear officer on USS *Sargent Bay* (CVE 83). Mac would reinvest his brother's good counsel by inspiring and encouraging another Beaufort High School student, Michael Smith—future Naval Academy graduate, naval aviator, and space shuttle Challenger command pilot for whom the small Beaufort airstrip would be named. For now, both Snowden brothers were set on paths that would consume their energies and test their spirits within just four years as they became participants in a far-ranging and savage Pacific war.

Before the referees had sifted through scorecards for Fleet Problem XIX, orders arrived from the Bureau of Navigation—predecessor of the bureau of personnel—assigning Ernie to Cruiser Scouting Squadron Six (VCS-6), a composite unit of floatplane detachments dispersed among combatants of Cruiser Division Six in the Fleet Scouting Force. Allotted the standard delay of one week's travel time to present himself with orders in hand at his new duty station in San Diego, and without the possibility of recompense from the Navy for commercial transcontinental DC3 service, Ernie booked the more circuitous but less expensive passage by train. From Washington, D.C., by the Capitol Limited, connecting in Chicago with the Santa Fe Super Chief, he maintained Pullman-style comfort most of the way. Once in San Diego, where he found an affordable used Chevrolet, his only connection to his duty station at North Island was by car ferry to Coronado.

The Navy discovered Coronado's favorable geography in 1846 when a shore party of armed sailors and Marines routed a Mexican garrison in the Old Town settlement of San Diego, seeking to establish a base of naval stores for further sorties up the coast. Not technically an island, Coronado, situated in the center of San Diego Bay, conformed perfectly to the cartographer's definition of a tombolo—a large land mass connected by a narrow isthmus to the mainland nine miles to the south. The land mass at the north end of the isthmus featured a shoreline indentation that came to be called Spanish Bight, dividing North Island from South Island. With California annexed at the end of the Mexican-American War, the natural benefit of a protected anchorage between Coronado and San Diego was lost in the Navy's corporate memory until the early twentieth century, when local citizens inveighed upon Navy and political leaders in Washington to add a port visit for the Great White Fleet then circumnavigating the globe.

The Great White Fleet weighed anchor off Coronado with much fanfare and heightened appreciation for the hospitality shown by San Diegans. In contrast, the arrival of innovator and entrepreneur Glenn Curtiss from New York two years later went largely unnoticed. Attracted to the isolation, flat topography, and fair weather of Coronado, Curtiss secured a rent-free lease on North Island upon which to tinker with his hydroaeroplane designs. Commuting daily from a rented space on South Island by punt across Spanish Bight, Curtiss matured his configuration until, confident of its airworthiness, he lifted off from Spanish Bight to record the world's first seaplane flight. Ever the free-market mercantilist, Curtiss immediately began to build on his achievement by offering free flying lessons to Navy and Army officers in an attempt to sell additional numbers of hydroaeroplanes to the military. The Navy, taking the long view and fully exploring this new technology, detailed Lt. Ted Ellyson to North Island for instruction, earning him the designation of naval aviator number one in the process. Within weeks, the Navy contracted for its first aircraft from Curtiss, thus officially marking naval aviation's birth. Encouraged by this upturn in his business prospects, Curtiss bought a parcel on South Island, Coronado, and constructed a Craftsman-style bungalow at 301 Alameda Boulevard for his family, a building still extant today.[15]

North Island thrived until, by Ernie's arrival twenty-seven years later, naval aviation's footprint was pervasive and well established, with permanent administrative and maintenance buildings constructed in the Mission Revival style evocative of the Panama-California Exposition complex at nearby Balboa Park. Spanish Bight had largely disappeared under landfill tailings piped over from dredging operations on the floor of the harbor to permit deeper draft warships unobstructed access to safe anchorage.

Hollywood discovered Coronado in due time, drawn by the temperate weather for location shoots, the ample and luxurious quarters for crew and cast at the Hotel del Coronado, and the Navy command hierarchy that clearly saw an opportunity to showcase naval aviation to a wider moviegoing public. Producers and directors were exhorted to use North Island, with its rows of aircraft and jaunty, uniformed pilots as props, by chief promoter Frank "Spig" Wead. Despite adversity and setback, Spig was never one to be held back; he always had a scheme or connection that could be worked to his advantage. Medically retired for a nonduty injury, he had spent the early 1920s at North Island as a naval aviator in command of VF-2, a composite fighter squadron of several types of early biplanes. When retired, he turned to writing aviation stories for the screen, drawing on his own experiences. By dint of his enthusiasm, aviation knowledge, and writing talent, he fashioned a new alchemy that combined realistic sets and heroic characters to yield rip-roaring film entertainment. His first two screenplays became *The Flying Fleet* in 1927 with Ramon Novarro, and *Hell Divers*, with Clark Gable and Wallace Beery, in 1931. A half-dozen feature films followed throughout the 1930s with other writers, directors, and actors, culminating in Wead's seminal naval aviation adventure, *Dive Bomber*. Directed in Technicolor by Michael Curtiz and starring Errol Flynn and Fred MacMurray, *Dive Bomber* began filming in 1939 on North Island. True to his reputation, Errol Flynn devoted considerable off-set time to drinking with aviators at the North Island Officers Club and at the "Hotel Del." At about that same period, Ernie returned with VCS-6 in USS *Minneapolis* from Fleet Problem XX. Since Ernie and Errol Flynn frequented the only two popular drinking establishments on base and off almost nightly in roughly the same months of 1939, Ernie very likely persuaded Errol Flynn to hoist more than one toast to the Navy, to naval aviation, to *Minneapolis*, and to VCS-6.

When not at sea with the cruiser squadron, VCS-6 planes and crews bivouacked ashore at North Island, their Curtiss SOC aircraft made serviceable for takeoff and landing on the oil-damped loam of North Island's expansive airfield by means of attachable, trunnioned landing gear assemblies. Near-perfect flying conditions year-round, partially interrupted by a mid-morning marine layer of low clouds in summer, normally resulted in a full pattern that took some getting used to for new arrivals. VCS-6 shared the airspace over North Island with fighter, torpedo, and scouting squadrons from *Enterprise*, *Ranger*, *Lexington*, and *Saratoga* when in port, in addition to Fleet Marine Force squadrons and PBY Catalinas of patrol squadrons operating from North Island's seaplane ramps.

Before putting to sea in *Minneapolis*, Ernie had to go to school for floatplane flying. Even allowing for his stick-and-throttle time in the training command in seaplanes, nearly every aspect of flight operations with VCS-6, from launch to recovery—even the mission itself—was a radical departure from his prior two years of carrier experience with VF-4 and VF-7. The transition was eased by the unfamiliar Curtiss SOC-1 floatplane having an instrument cluster common with most naval aircraft of the day and by Ernie's deft hand on stick and throttle—though the performance drag of pontoon and under-wing floats necessary for water landings denied him the kind of acrobatic pirouettes he mastered in fighter maneuvering. Reintegrating into shipboard routine on *Minneapolis* was effortless. Four years as gunnery officer in *West Virginia* as a client of target spotting calls by the battleship's observation squadron from its O3U pilots had inculcated precious insight into his new mission role.

Throughout the 1920s and 1930s, as carrier and patrol plane operations matured and fostered their own distinct communities, naval aviation curried greatest favor for itself by remaining closely integrated with the more traditional Navy of battleships and cruisers. Even before naval aviation's official birth in 1911, traditional Navy leaders who were raised in battleships and cruisers foresaw utility in harnessing aircraft to serve the battle line. In an age before radar was effectively employed at sea, they comprehended that aircraft could provide the range and elevation that permitted surface combatants to see and seize opportunity beyond the visible horizon. Aircraft could not only provide timely alert of the composition, disposition, and course of an enemy surface force but also could restore greater accuracy to large caliber shells sent over the horizon by gunfire spotting adjusted from aloft. The floatplane secured that association, but remedies had to be found for vexing integration issues.

Initially, the limiting factors for operating aircraft from surface combatants were inadequate takeoff run for launch and the need for an effective recovery scheme that did not impose too great an operational penalty on the ship in the midst of combat operations. More than a decade of innovation and experimentation yielded a workable compressed air turntable catapult and a recovery mechanism closely resembling the davits used to recover ships' small craft.[16] Standardization of catapults, recovery hoists, and floatplane design progressed such that by June 1938, when Ernie reported to VCS-6, both battleship observation squadrons (VOs) and cruiser scouting squadrons were routinely putting to sea with a full complement of three to four Curtiss-built SOC floatplanes.

Paradoxically, after more than a dozen years during which Fleet Problems had revealed the efficacy and potency of carrier-based aviation, Navy leadership—still dominated by officers with battleship and cruiser backgrounds—was wedded to the primacy of the battle line, an institutional bias that would persist into the coming war with Japan. In that environment, assignment to an observation or scouting squadron for a naval aviator was not a career aberration but rather a fairly common duty rotation that brought aviators into regular contact with their ship-serving peers to get "re-blued." Prospects for career advancement in aviation were neither jeopardized nor diminished for regular rotation back to carrier flying, as Ernie would do the following year.

Relations between VO and VCS detachments and their respective ship's company were generally amicable. VO and VCS pilots, despite any initial misgivings about missing carrier flying, quickly embraced their new circumstance, and Ernie was no exception. Author William T. Larkins cites a comment from a near contemporary of Ernie's, Ens. Lionel McQuiston, upon his assignment to VO-1 in *Nevada*:

> Originally, I was disappointed at being assigned to the "unglamorous" ship aviation. In retrospect, I was quite fortunate. Far from being dull, our activities were varied and interesting. . . . We seriously practiced dive-bombing, fixed and free machine-gun firing, and strafing. We towed targets for the ship's machine-gun battery and provided aerial spotting via Morse code to the ship's main battery. We, of necessity, became proficient in dead reckoning navigation when ranging long distances from the ship in mid-ocean. Despite posing an unavoidable conflict for some ship operations, we enjoyed relatively good relations with the "black shoes." Inasmuch as we were closely related to the ship's combat operations, and since we stood OOD [officer of the deck] watches under way when not flying, we matured as "Navy" first and "aviation" second.[17]

Curtiss SOCs were still new to the fleet when Ernie began flying with VCS-6, having won their design competition only three years before. In the twenty years since the first Navy floatplane was acquired in 1911, the Bureau of Aeronautics had established an uninterrupted pipeline of new floatplane types until, in 1933, a replacement was solicited for the Vought O2U and O3U floatplanes. A fly-off of prototypes from Vought, Douglas, and Curtiss resulted in BuAer's selection of the Curtiss XOC3-1. The Curtiss plane was favored in no small part due to the innovation of aero-activated wing leading edge flaps (similar in function to slats seen years later in the Douglas A-4), working in combination with trailing edge flaps, which gave the aircraft very controllable low-speed flight without the penalty of a larger wing. The only noticeable changes to the prototype ordered by the bureau for production versions, termed SOC-1s, were the inclusion of a folding wing for stowage aboard ship and an enclosed cockpit. By June 1938, VCS-6 operated fourteen SOC-1s and one SOC-2 dispersed among ships of Cruiser Division Six: *Minneapolis*, *Astoria*, *New Orleans*, and *Indianapolis*.[18]

Launch sequences for SOC pilots departing from battleships and cruisers had been fairly well standardized by the time Ernie began flying with VCS-6, and they were not too dissimilar to the routine he learned flying from the carrier. A catapult officer—normally a non-flying member of the aviation detachment positioned nearby on the quarterdeck—initiated actuation of the catapult, but approval and signal to launch rested with the commanding officer or the officer of the deck acting in his behalf by means of flag signals and ship's intercom from the bridge. The pilot would wave his right arm from the cockpit in a circular manner indicating that his engine checks were satisfactory. With the catapult officer's acknowledgment, the pilot extended his right arm, moving it backward and forward indicating he was ready for launch. This signal was analogous to the right-hand salute initiated by pilots taking a catapult launch from the carrier deck in later years. A red flag from the bridge held the catapulting sequence short of actual launch until a green flag was flown, sending the SOC down the rail.

Recovery was a more complicated ballet of ship maneuver and air-manship by the SOC pilot that was fraught with much greater risk of going awry. The cruiser would fly the Baker (now Bravo) flag at half-mast, indicating that all aircraft were to return to the vicinity of the ship. When two-blocked, or fully hoisted up the mast, the Baker flag indicated to pilots and to ship's company that recovery operations would shortly commence. The cruiser would take a heading thirty to sixty degrees off the relative wind line and then raise the Cast (now Charlie) flag to half-mast, telling the pilot that the ship was about to start its turn across the wind line. When the Cast flag was two-blocked, the cruiser started its turn with the intention of creating a pocket, or "slick," of undisturbed water on the downwind side of the hull for the SOC to land as close as possible to the ship.

The cruiser deployed a mat, or "sled," that trailed a webbed net, with the entire mechanism extended by boom away from the cruiser's hull to provide adequate separation for the approaching SOC from the side of the ship. The SOC pilot nudged his throttle to provide enough headway to engage the sled, and a grappling hook under his pontoon would snag the net. With the SOC held in trail on the sled, the rear seat radioman would climb out and stand on the fuselage in front of the pilot to grab the ship's hoist as it was lowered. Once the radioman connected the hoist's hook with the loop on top of the SOC's upper wing, the aircraft was lifted aboard.[19]

When mishaps occurred, they generally involved the aircraft becoming entangled in the sled or forced out of position by wave action and either capsizing or suffering damage from contact with the ship's hull. The most serious mishap for Ernie during his VCS-6 tour was coming in direct contact with the hoist hook in heavy seas, resulting in a deep laceration and contusions about the head. This would not be the last time he would suffer physical injuries in the landing sequence. Five years later, landing a battle-damaged F6F Hellcat aboard *Lexington*, he would again suffer serious contusions when the aircraft up-ended in the arresting gear.

During his downtime the year before while not deployed, Ernie had met and begun courting Lois Arnold. Lois was no stranger to San Diego in general and Coronado in particular. Her father, Maj. Henry "Hap" Arnold, had assumed command of Rockwell Field, the Army's early aviation camp on North Island on the upper end of Coronado, when Lois was a child. Having left behind an idyllic childhood in Coronado with her father's reassignment east, she returned to escape the regimented military discipline at home. She was drawn back to Southern California when she came of age and worked a short distance from San Diego's downtown as assistant editor of the nearby Consolidated-Vultee aircraft factory newspaper. By the time Ernie and Lois met, her father, now Brigadier General Arnold, had risen to assistant to the chief of the Army Air Corps. Hap Arnold's parochial feelings for the Army Air Service were well publicized. He was a vocal adherent of positions advanced mainly by Gen. Billy Mitchell that advocated for greater independence for the nascent Army Air Service. Among those views was a call for restricting naval aviation and making it subordinate to a consolidated air service under the Army.[20] Not yet well known publicly were the views held by Ernie and his peers that resolutely maintained that naval aviation had yet to prove its worth as a mainstay of global reach and power for a maritime nation, transcending the dominance of the battle line that held sway. Lois would draw these two committed personalities into each other's sphere when she called her parents in the fall of 1937 to make a startling announcement. Lois' brother and nephew, Col. W. Bruce Arnold and Robert Bruce Arnold, recorded that conversation in their work, *From Vision to Victory, General Hap Arnold's Journey Creating America's Air Force*:

> "I've met the most wonderful guy in the world," she [Lois] shrilled into the phone.
>
> "He's a commander in the Navy and we're going to go across to Mexico and get married immediately unless you promise to come out at Thanksgiving and see us married in a real, honest to God military wedding."
>
> "What's his name?" asked Pop [Hap].
>
> "He's absolutely wonderful and I don't care if you like him or not, we're going to get married in Mexico tonight, if you don't promise to come out at Thanksgiving."
>
> "What's his goddamn name?" Pop yelled into the phone.
>
> "He's absolutely wonderful ... The Class of '32 at Annapolis ... Flies off carriers ... Fabulous man ..." Lois babbled on.

"What's the poor dumb bastard's name?" yelled Pop.

"He's not a bastard! You already don't like him because he's Navy!"

Lois' mother joined in the call, and it continued along this line until Lois put Ernie on the phone for his first direct exchange with Hap:

"Hi, General," he said cheerfully. "What d'you think of your daughter deserting the Air Corps and joining the Navy? But don't worry," he continued more seriously, "even though you're the Chief of the Air Corps and I'm only a little Indian in the Navy, I promise to take good care of her."

"Well, as long as you put it that way," Pop broke in. "Do you know that in American Indian tribes a brave has to give the Chief one hundred white horses before he can marry his daughter?"

"Don't worry, sir. I'll get right on that," was Ernie's reply.

Within a week, Ernie had made a down payment on his obligation by sending General Arnold the first two horses—the small plastic white tokens that came attached to bottles of White Horse Scotch. Thus began a years-long tradition of exchanging practical jokes and good-natured kidding between father-in-law and son-in-law that would occasionally include actual bottles of White Horse. When General and Mrs. Arnold arrived for the wedding, Hap discovered he'd forgotten to pack gold buttons for his dress blue uniform. Ernie, in an obliging gesture, took the dress uniform coat for the Navy to take care of in time for the ceremony. When Hap received the coat at the last minute, he discovered that no attempt had been made to affix regulation gold buttons; instead, silver Navy buttons festooned Hap's uniform. All he could do was laugh and say, "A typical sleazy, swabby trick! Won't I ever learn not to trust 'em?"

In the summer of 1938, Lois' brother Hank visited the newlyweds in Coronado. The Snowdens, Hank discovered, held a party every night: "The drinking was so heavy and noise so loud that the police would sometimes drop in uninvited, but Ernie always seemed able

to charm them, or, at least almost always. One night his commanding officer, a party guest, was arrested, and the Snowdens, to avoid the
same fate, had to flee up the coast to Laguna Beach. But they were
back home the next night for another party."[21] Hank and the Arnolds
may not have grasped the nearly ritualistic place that hard partying
held as the fulcrum of social culture of naval aviation. Flying from
carriers or cruisers statistically diminished prospects for a long life,
and cutting loose after a physically and mentally demanding day of
harrowing close calls was the norm; it was sanctioned immoderation.
Ernie's habit of tippling well into the early hours and then performing on cue the next morning owed much to his inherent skill and
his experience. But he navigated a very fine line between acceptable
behavior and compulsive excess, and in later years after long periods
at sea, he sometimes stepped over the line.

4

Peer Rivalry

By the late autumn of 1941, the Japanese naval air arm constituted the most potent offensive force of any of the three major navies. By the first week of December 1941, this naval power was deployed in deadly array.

—Mark R. Peattie

*A*kagi trundled thunderously down the ways, the freshly riveted steel ribs and plates groaning as she slipped into a calm Seto Inland Sea facing the Kure naval arsenal. That event in April 1925, noticed but lightly regarded by Western navies, denoted a seminal benchmark for the Imperial Japanese Navy (IJN) in its thirty-year progression to a naval aviation force of first rank by the opening of hostilities with the United States in 1941. Often derided from afar as mimicry, the Japanese course was defined by a deliberate process of observation by their navy's foreign exchange officers and naval attachés; selective import and adaptation of aircraft design and employment that suited their strategy and culture; experimentation that melded the best of foreign technology and practice with their own; and finally, vetting in combat in their expansionist war with China begun in 1937.

At her launching, *Akagi* embodied a compromise in design: a battle cruiser hull modified while still in the shipyard to accommodate flight deck and aviation appurtenances that put the ship in compliance with limitations imposed by the Washington Naval Treaty of 1922. Japan was a signatory to the treaty limitations, as were the United Kingdom, United States, France, and Italy. The treaty's terms set a cap on the displacement tonnage of battleships, battle cruisers, and aircraft carriers and also set limits on the caliber of guns carried on those classes of ships. Each signatory was allowed to use two existing capital ship hulls for aircraft carriers with a displacement limit of 33,000 tons each. For the purposes of the treaty, an aircraft carrier was defined as a warship displacing more than ten thousand tons constructed exclusively for launching and landing aircraft. In an important strategic concession to Japan, the treaty also prohibited Britain, Japan, and the United States from constructing any fortifications or naval bases in the Pacific Ocean, essentially eliminating a foothold that Britain or the United States might obtain in the western Pacific beyond Hawaii that might place Japan at a disadvantage in the event of a future war.[1]

A second fleet carrier joined *Akagi* when *Kaga* was converted and launched a year later. The most distinctive external trait shared by the two sister ships was a tiered, three-stage flight deck design that was thought to improve the efficiency of flight operations. The top deck was sloped forward from amidships to ease takeoffs and downward toward the stern to facilitate landings for lighter aircraft. The shortest midlevel deck provided for straight-through takeoff runs for additional lighter aircraft, while the lowest deck, somewhat longer, provided for an uninterrupted takeoff run for more heavily laden torpedo bombers. These and other features reflected a level of uncertainty attendant to untried flight operations, further complicated by the rapid advance in aircraft sophistication and performance.[2]

For the United States, the Washington Treaty likewise forced the conversion of battleship and battle cruiser hulls already laid down that would become the first fleet carriers in U.S. Navy service. Launched that same year and subsequently commissioned as USS *Lexington* (CV 2) and USS *Saratoga* (CV 3), the two American carriers differed from their IJN counterparts, *Akagi* and *Kaga*, in several fundamentally important ways: their single topside flight decks were more than three hundred feet longer than the Japanese carrier flight decks; the maximum range of the American carriers exceeded the maximum range of *Akagi* and *Kaga* by more than one thousand nautical miles; and *Lexington* and *Saratoga* could each accommodate an additional squadron of approximately eighteen more aircraft than could *Akagi* and *Kaga*. The importance of these differences could not be immediately foretold when these ships were commissioned into service, but in the practical exercise of the ships and their air groups in

Fleet Problems over the coming decade, their operational relevance would be borne out.

At the opening of the twentieth century, the IJN, in comparison to the major naval powers of the time, lacked a long history of naval development. The Japanese concentration on rapidly modernizing was evident by their astounding annihilation of the Russian fleet at Tsushima in 1905, showcasing their brilliant success in exploiting technology and tactical innovation. When aviation debuted in those years, the IJN decided to further develop the capability in a bid to put the service on equal footing with the other naval powers. The IJN embarked on a path that diverged from army aviation advocates by empaneling a committee for the study of naval aeronautics. Not by chance, many of the committee members were among those dispatched to learn flying first-hand. So it was that these Japanese lieutenants, including Yamada Chuji, Kono Sankichi, and Nakajima Chikuhei, would join U.S. Navy Lt. Ted Ellyson at North Island in 1911 to undergo flight training personally conducted by Glenn Curtiss. The officers were to become some of the principal naval aviation pioneers of the IJN. One of their number, Lieutenant Kaneko Yozo, after his airborne training wrote presciently in 1912 to Commander Yamamoto Eisuke on the General Staff: "There would be nothing to prevent aircraft from entering a harbor fortified against surface attack and strike enemy warships from above."[3]

These novice aviators correctly assessed that among the naval powers coming out of World War I, only Britain was emphasizing carrier aviation, while the United States was focused primarily on seaplane development. This conformed well with Japan's strategic view of the carrier as offering the most unqualified method of subduing the vast geography of the Pacific. Japanese naval leadership requested advice from the British Royal Navy and were granted the services of Sir William Sempill, former Royal Air Force officer, and his cadre of Royal Navy and British industry technicians. British tutelage greatly accelerated Japan's aviation training and technology. By the end of its one-year tenure, the Sempill mission had advanced Japanese naval aviation considerably down a learning curve in grasping the basics of carrier flight deck operations. Japan was also unique among rising naval aviation powers in husbanding development of land-based aircraft operations. Its trans-Pacific view foresaw island airfields radiating outward from the home island as defensive outposts that could blunt assaults on Japan itself. A tenet of the emerging Japanese naval strategy held that carrier air groups, retaining their inherent freedom of movement, could position themselves nearby these island airfields to aggregate swarms of sea-based and land-based fighters, dive bombers, horizontal bombers, and torpedo bombers to concentrate and overwhelm any approaching naval threat. Everything would depend on available pools of ready, competent pilots and logistically robust aircraft support operations, ingredients that would become increasingly difficult to sustain under the debilitating stress of wartime attrition.

Carrier numbers and the growing technological complexity of IJN carrier aircraft provide only one dimension of a more holistic view of Japanese naval aviation as compared to U.S. naval aviation. When training, aptitude, and even culture are considered, what appeared to be commensurate capabilities entering the 1940s are revealed to have been less so for the kind of war that would be fought. To meet the demand for trained cadres of carrier pilots backstopped by a pool of reserves, the pipelines for sourcing and training new aviators were marked by key differences. At one level, the comparative scale of industrialization of the two nations was starkly uneven. Historian Eric Bergerud highlights the predominantly agrarian society of Japan in 1939 by noting that the prototype Zero fighter had to be disassembled at its design shop and its parts hauled by oxcarts to a nearby naval air facility for reassembly and first flight. Nothing in Japan at the time could begin to compare with the breadth of the U.S. aircraft industry, the large aircraft research and development activities at Wright and Patterson Fields in Ohio, or even the relatively nascent test center at Anacostia in Washington, D.C., which would by 1942 transition to Patuxent River Naval Air Station in Maryland. At that same level of comparison, the societal trend in the United States toward fundamental understanding and familiarization with heavy industry, mass production, and the design, operation, and maintenance of machinery was not as deeply and broadly inculcated in Japan. This machine-age mentality was more widespread in the more open, egalitarian United States than in the rigid, hierarchical, and essentially feudal social arrangement in Japan, thus diminishing the available cohort of technically oriented pilot and maintainer trainees to the IJN. In both navies, a primary source for

educated and motivated pilot trainees was their respective naval academies. In the IJN, these candidates were augmented in the 1920s by
both a pilot trainee program, which inducted serving enlisted members, and a flight reserve enlisted training program, which reached
further into the high school ranks for qualified candidates that could
be oriented toward pilot training. These programs did not regularly
result in the commissioning of pilot trainees, meaning that by the
time of the Pearl Harbor attack, fully 90 percent of serving Japanese
naval aviators were enlisted members. This alone was not a determi-
nant of flying aptitude; however, U.S. naval aviation included a much
greater percentage of academy graduates with several years' service
in the fleet who had been groomed to exhibit resourcefulness and
innovation. Bergerud notes that many U.S. naval aviators in the first
months of aerial combat observed that Japanese effectiveness in the
air declined precipitously when the more senior officers and flight
leaders were shot down. The percentage of Japanese academy graduates never changed appreciably, partly because traditional surface navy
officers continued to be selected for carrier and aviation ship command. The prospects for promotion at the more senior ranks were
thus much lower than in the U.S. Navy, where, by statute, carrier
command was available only to designated naval aviators. However,
as measured by flight time, Japanese naval aviators were well experienced: approximately 1,500 carrier pilots averaged between 800 and
1,000 hours. The IJN entered conflict with the United States in 1941
with 1,000 pilots who had more than 600 hours of flight time. This
number held constant until attrition began to take its toll in the Solomon Island engagements beginning with Guadalcanal in August
1942, and it steadily declined until Japanese naval aviation practically
"ceased to exist as a skilled force" in the aftermath of the battle of the
Philippine Sea in June 1944.[4]

By December 1941, U.S. naval aviation's standing had been greatly
improved through robust support from Congress, which in 1935 had
passed the Aviation Cadet Act authorizing and encouraging recruit-
ment directly from U.S. college campuses. These recruits were commissioned upon winging and spent three years in the fleet; by the time
of Pearl Harbor, half of serving naval aviators were reserve officers

from this group, with many of their number holding reserve commissions in private life ready for call-up. At the beginning of hostilities when reservists were activated to fill out unmanned billets in newly stood-up squadrons, some squadron commanding officers remained in the front-line squadrons to guide their preparation for combat. Many of the more experienced squadron officers were rotated stateside—sometimes as a result of losing their carrier to Japanese action—to form and train new squadrons of trainees and reservists that would be needed for newly launched carriers.[5]

The IJN's carefully drawn plan for aircraft and carrier development was thrown into disarray in the summer of 1937 when simmering discord with China erupted into open bloody war, the second such contest in a little more than a generation. Unresolved tensions between Nationalist Chinese and Japanese troops occupying the Peking perimeter immediately drew Japanese naval aviation forces, reputedly the best trained and readily available, into direct conflict. Initially, the navy's land-based bombers delivered punishing attacks by penetrating the Chinese mainland from offshore in Taiwan and Kyushu to support the army's advance on the ground, while navy fighters, redeployed from carriers to captured forward bases, contested Chinese defenders for air superiority. An overly confident assumption that fighter escorts would not be needed resulted in horrific bomber losses to the Chinese, who were flying mostly in aircraft procured from the United States. A more advanced fighter that had the range for escort and greater firepower was urgently needed, yielding the A6M Type 0—bearing the Allied code name "Zeke" but commonly referred to as Zero in recognition of the year it was introduced into IJN service (1940)—within three years. Navy dive bombers shared provisional airfields with the fighters but typically were assigned to battlefield targets and troop concentrations rather than the enemy fleets for which they had assiduously trained. A beneficial outcome for the dive bomber units was the transition from fabric-covered biplanes to metal monocoque single-wing aircraft. Going from the D1A2 Type 96 bomber to the Aichi D3A1 Type 99 Val improved survivability and lethality over the Chinese mainland and familiarized dive bomber pilots with the type for the crucial combat test to come over the Pacific.

For navy bombers, fighters, and dive bombers, other shortcomings discovered and soon rectified servicewide were lack of aircraft-to-aircraft communications and standardized training in formation flying for mutual protection and generating offensive mass. Squadrons resorted to *shōtai*, a loose, three-fingered formation that permitted improved tactical flexibility, borrowed from the Sempill mission training.[6]

The IJN's combat debut of a robust naval aviation capability had an undeniable influence on the U.S. Navy's Fleet Problem XIX the following year. Taking note of the geography, order of battle, and observations regarding aircraft performance and concepts of employment by both sides, Navy leaders were mindful to inject corresponding scenarios and assumptions into the Fleet Problem. In Part V of the problem, conducted over five days in March 1938, fleet units took station near Maui as the Red force to prevent the Blue fleet, representing the IJN, from seizing Lahaina Roads as a suitable advance base. *Saratoga*, *Lexington*, and *Ranger* masqueraded as a Japanese carrier force, conducting air raids on Hickam, Wheeler, and Pearl Harbor naval air stations with good effect. Ernie's squadron in *Ranger*, assuming the role of Mitsubishi A5M Type 96 fighters, covered amphibious landings at Lahaina, beating off attacks from land-based aircraft.[7]

Part XI of Fleet Problem XIX, played out over three days in April, varied the scenario to pit the surrogate Japanese force (Purple) against the U.S. West Coast. After successful raids on Mare Island shipyard, the Purple force retired in a feint to draw the remnants of the U.S. force (Green) into a deadly trap. The game was called before a decisive victory—clearly for the Japanese—could be declared.[8] The lesson that Ernie assimilated from his part in and the outcome of XIX— assuming scenario assumptions were not overly doctored to ensure a preferred outcome—was that the question of victory versus defeat in this set piece dominated by naval aviation forces was determined by the novel employment of the Purple force carriers. Their commander's decision to permit his carriers more autonomy from the battle line, to freely concentrate air power across the exercise area, presaged the coming of the fast carrier task force that would dominate naval campaigns in the warfare to come. Ernie's confidence in the preeminence of U.S. naval aviation was not diminished in the least, but he assumed a new wariness and respect for the putative capability that the IJN might bring to future conflict.

If Ernie Snowden had an opposite number in Japanese naval aviation—a peer professional as measured by experience in the cockpit as section, division, and group leader in the air and an incessant drive for innovation and excellence in dive bombing and tactical proficiency in carrier operations—that officer was Takahashi Sadamu. The two graduated one year apart from their countries' respective naval academies, Takahashi going on immediately to complete flight training two years ahead of Ernie. Ernie's first aviation assignments in carrier-based fighters and cruiser floatplanes were paralleled by Takahashi's experience in land-based navy squadrons. Takahashi entered the dive bombing community earlier and became immersed in its tactics and protocols from the beginning of his flying career, tested under duress in combat as a junior sub-lieutenant and as a flight leader. When assigned to the dive bomber unit in IJN carrier *Ryujo* in 1938, he applied his growing mission expertise toward documenting and standardizing dive bombing doctrine, particularly against more conventional ship targets. The standard formation he described was twenty-seven aircraft in three divisions, with the lead division of nine in the van and the other two to port and starboard slightly set back. Final approach to the target began at ten thousand feet from dead ahead or astern of the target (ideally an enemy carrier); at twenty-five miles from the target, a ten-degree dive would be commenced to gain top speed, peaking to a sixty-five-degree dive when over the target, at which point dive brakes would be deployed and the bomb released toward an aim point slightly ahead of or astern the target ship. At the push over to the sixty-five-degree dive, the other aircraft would follow in succession. Ideally, multiple divisions would make their runs from different lines of approach to confuse return fire. These procedures were disseminated and practiced rigorously throughout the fleet, yielding marked improvement from two years prior in dive bombing accuracy in the combined fleet exercises of 1941. Results were so spectacular that of 123 bombs dropped on the underway target ship *Settsu*, fleet dive bombers scored 66 direct hits, an accuracy rate of 53.7 that was unequaled in the United States or Britain.[9] Takahashi, to whom much credit is due for standardizing the mechanics of carrier-borne dive bombing, was rightly regarded throughout Japanese naval aviation at this point as an emerging authority on the practice. In U.S. naval aviation, meanwhile, Ernie strove to build flight time, perspective, and reputation in his first five years, not entering the dive bombing trade until his assignment as executive officer of an SB2U squadron near the end of 1941.

Less than a year later in August 1942, Ernie Snowden, leading his scouting squadron of SBD-3 Dauntless from USS *Wasp*, and Takahashi Sadamu, leading his squadron of Type 99 Val dive bombers from IJN carrier *Zuikaku*, would course over the same patch of the southern Pacific Ocean within a few hundred miles of each other. Each aviator was desperately eager for the opportunity to slam a five-hundred-pound armor-piercing bomb into the other's flight deck. They would never get that chance. Within weeks, *Wasp* would meet another fate at the hands of cool, detached, and unseen Japanese submariners.

5

Total War

The President of the United States takes pleasure in presenting the Navy Cross to Lieutenant Commander Ernest Maynard Snowden, United States Navy, for extraordinary heroism in action against enemy Japanese forces on Guadalcanal, Solomon Islands, on 7 and 8 August 1942. His superb airmanship and courageous devotion to duty, maintained with utter disregard for his personal safety, were in keeping with the highest traditions of the United States Naval Service.

—Frank Knox, Secretary of the Navy

World War II opened for the United States with the shock of near-total surprise and devastation at Pearl Harbor inflicted by Japanese naval aviation forces. The global scope of the war proved a test for U.S. naval aviation in both the European and Pacific theaters. The disruption to peacetime routine was immediate: Ernie had been detached from flight instructor duty at Pensacola in November and was on temporary orders at the Bureau of Navigation in Washington, D.C., staffing assignments of reserve naval aviators. One of the calls he fielded within days of the attack on Pearl Harbor was from a concerned inactive naval aviator reservist and Vought test pilot, Boone Guyton. Boone's recollection of that call revealed something of the disorder and commotion of the initial days after the Japanese attack but also suggested his high regard for his former shipmate:

> I knew him [Ernie] as a straight-talking, no-nonsense officer, and also the one who, in a wardroom poker game before shore

leave at Honolulu, had openheartedly relieved me of spending money. There was no time for idle chatter. Since the declaration of war, his position was a super-active hot spot and he endured a score of calls like mine each day. I asked him what he wanted me to do. "Where do you want sea duty," he joked as an instant response. There was a crackling of paper in my ear while he hunted for my file. "Stay put for the moment, Guyton. . . . If we want you, you'll get the message. . . . Right now your job at Vought is priority. Roger? Gotta go. Out!" With that, he had settled my immediate future, and I learned the same had occurred to other military test pilots around the country.[1]

Boone would gain notoriety later as the principal test pilot for Vought's F4U Corsair, destined for frontline service in the Pacific. But now, as 1941 closed, Ernie was acting with some haste with new orders in hand to proceed straightaway to Norfolk to report as executive officer of Scouting Squadron 72, then preparing for immediate embarkation in USS *Wasp* (CV 7).

Capt. Forrest Sherman in the same month took command of *Wasp,* setting the conditions for their relationship to mature. With his elevation to command of *Wasp*'s scouting squadron only months after reporting on board, Ernie set the tactics, schedules, and training for his group to work effectively as the ship's aerial screen, providing critical over-the-horizon surveillance and targeting. This brought the squadron commander and ship skipper in close, daily contact when air operations were conducted at sea. The working relationship they established was without equal for its two-way professional exchanges from which both benefitted. Their time together lasted only a few months until events in the Pacific separated them from their commands earlier than planned. After that separation, the two had no direct contact again until after the war, when Ernie hosted a formal dining-in banquet for veterans of *Wasp* duty preparatory to his rotation to Sherman's staff in the office of the Chief of Naval Operations.

But in early April 1942, *Wasp,* with VS-72, was standing off Scapa Flow in the Orkney Islands, forming up with the Royal Navy Home Fleet as part of Task Force 39. Answering a British request to employ

Wasp in urgent ferry duty, she was soon en route to the island of Malta to replenish Royal Air Force fighters lost to relentless pounding by German aircraft. Ernie took the squadron's fifteen SB2U Vindicators and squadron personnel ashore (one squadron aircraft was lost off Greenock, Scotland, in the North Atlantic in mid-April with both aircrew missing) to the Royal Naval Air Station at Hatston to make room in *Wasp* for forty-seven Supermarine Spitfire Mk V fighters. Joining VS-72 in the ashore detachment were nine F4F-4 Wildcats of VF-71, nine Douglas TBD-1 Devastators of VT-7, and another fifteen SB2Us of sister squadron VS-71. *Wasp* retained only a minimal number of VF-71's Grumman F4F Wildcat fighters aboard to provide a covering combat air patrol. Ernie remained with his squadron and the rest of the air group at Hatston while *Wasp* completed two runs to Malta. Dispersal of their SB2Us at the airfield was a routine practice, as Hatston had been the target of aerial attack by German Ju-88s and He-111s on several occasions (although no major attacks occurred within eighteen months of VS-72's arrival).[2] Much more frequent and predictable was the foul weather that VS-72 and the other *Wasp* squadrons would endure in late spring in the Orkneys. This made the schedule for daily flights—urgently needed for combat readiness—a problematic roll of the dice. Low overcast and drizzling rain dominated the forecast, averaging more than 35 percent of the useful daylight in May and June, with the average maximum temperature in the mid-50s.

Word of a decisive naval action halfway around the globe in the Coral Sea reached Ernie while still at Hatston. VS-72 operations and intelligence officers digested the information about the battle available to them in classified dispatches, taking particular note of the performance of the newer Douglas SBD-3 Dauntless in carrying the offensive to the Japanese carriers. It was plain to Ernie and his squadron pilots that their SB2U Vindicator, derisively called "Wind Indicator" by the squadron, would be woefully inadequate by comparison to the SBD-3 and, critically, to most of the front-line Japanese naval aircraft:

The SB2U . . . had been designed in 1934, but it didn't go into production until 1936. In addition to the normal 1,000- or 500-bomb armament, the SB2U had outboard wing racks for either two 100-pound bombs or 32 anti-personnel bombs, which weighed 3 or 4 pounds each but produced a lot of drag. It was also armed with a .50-caliber and a .30-caliber machine gun in the starboard wing root, firing outside the arc of the propeller. The rear-seat gunner had a .30-caliber machine gun. His gun used cans of 95–100 rounds each, so that he had about 1,000 rounds in the 10 cans he carried. The SB2U was a slow plane in level flight, and a lousy bomber. Up until then, dive-bombers had been biplanes, and they produced enough drag to keep down the speed in a dive, but with the 750-hp Pratt & Whitney engine driving a cleaned-up monoplane like the SB2U series, you'd easily see 390–400 knots on your airspeed meter in a dive from 8,000 feet. It was like riding a rock! You could hardly maneuver—the ailerons became stiff as a board. In comparison, SBDs with perforated dive brakes could hold their speed down to 280 knots coming down in a 70-degree dive from 8,000 to 3,000 feet.[3]

En route to the Pacific area, news of the sinking of *Yorktown* at Midway, coupled with the loss of *Lexington* at Coral Sea a few weeks before, meant that *Wasp* would be making all haste to get to the central Pacific. By mid-June, *Wasp* was in San Diego, where—much to the satisfaction of Ernie, his squadron mates, and all the air group aviators—VS-72 and VS-71 traded in their SB2U Vindicators for the SBD-3 Dauntless, and VT-7 exchanged its Devastators for Grumman TBF-1 Avengers. In late June, word was passed that *Wasp* would sail from San Diego as part of Task Force 18 under command of Rear Adm. Leigh Noyes. Ernie knew Noyes passingly, though separated by Naval Academy classes twenty-five years apart. They graduated in the same flight school class in March 1937—Noyes by then a captain but required to undergo and pass flight training at his advanced grade before he was permitted to take his next assignment as commanding officer of USS *Lexington*. Both Ernie and Leigh Noyes, upon their winging in Pensacola, proceeded to *Lexington* in late March 1937, Ernie to report to his first squadron, VF-1. By summer 1942 Ernie had progressed beyond his initial VF-1 assignment to successive postings with VF-4 in USS *Ranger*, VCS-6 in USS *Minneapolis*, and VF-7 in USS *Ranger* once more before VF-7 was reassigned to USS *Wasp*, finally culminating in flight instructor duty in

Pensacola. He was, by July 1942, a well-experienced pilot, mature flight leader, and able administrator and mentor, highly suited for command of VS-72 in USS *Wasp*.

On July 1, Task Force 18 with *Wasp*, cruiser USS *Quincy* (CA 39), and light cruiser USS *San Juan* (CL 54) assembled off Point Loma Light and was soon making flank speed to rendezvous with Task Force 11 built around USS *Saratoga* and Task Force 16 centered on USS *Enterprise*. In transit to the southwest Pacific, *Wasp* "took station astern of the rest of the ships, making it easier for her and her plane guard destroyers to conduct flight operations."[4] Ernie had now assumed command of VS-72, and his squadron pilots were flying multiple training sorties a day underway at sea to familiarize themselves with the SBD-3's performance, to snap in bomb sight settings, to strafe and bomb the sled behind the task force's destroyers, and to practice aerial combat maneuvering. The Douglas prototype for the SBD had flown for the first time only four years prior as Ernie and his fellow Red Rippers of VF-4 were just standing down from Fleet Problem XIX with their Grumman F3F biplanes. The SBD-3 now flown by VS-72 was a low-wing monoplane incorporating the latest advancements in the type to include a more powerful R-1820–52 powerplant (nearly twice the horsepower of the Vindicators they had just traded in), a bulletproof windshield, armor protection, self-sealing fuel tanks of greater capacity, armament of two .50-caliber forward firing fixed guns and two .30-caliber trainable tandem guns operated by a rear gunner, and 1,200 pounds of ordnance under the fuselage and 325 pounds under the wings.[5]

Individual flying skills—gunnery, bombing, and proficiency around the ship—were critical, but no less so were formation tactics and multi-aircraft attack profiles. SBD squadrons typically organized in three plane sections, further aggregating by threes as numbers built up to as many as full squadron strength of fifteen to eighteen aircraft, depending on the size of the flight deck. These formations of threes stepped down on the section ahead into a *V*-shaped formation when transiting to and from a target area. Cascading sets of these formations were not optimal for going into an attack profile but did serve flights well for mutual protection. If the years of squadron and air group level rehearsal in Fleet Problems before the war had a shortcoming, it was the lack of emphasis on efficient integration of multiple carrier air groups that denied the task force commander the offensive mass of large, well-synchronized numbers of fighter, bomber, and torpedo aircraft. That lesson would be learned under the unforgiving strain and urgency of combat operations in the Solomons.[6]

In the first year of war at sea and in the air, U.S. seamen and airmen learned and relearned hard lessons, often at terrible cost. In the Pacific theater, the Japanese proved to be a relentless foe, possessing a disciplined fanaticism and being well rehearsed in the employment of then-superior weapons and tactics. The force-on-force engagement at Midway was a singular moment in June 1942 when intelligence, surprise, and selfless sacrifice converged to achieve for Americans a defining victory. Yet in many lesser encounters throughout the Pacific, the margin of victory for the U.S. Navy was not as clear-cut, and naval aviators brawled with their Japanese counterparts fiercely to just hold the line. The Fleet Problems conducted during the prior two decades had undeniably helped rationalize order and operational application of the growing numbers and capabilities of naval aircraft and carriers, but they could not provide naval aviators with first-hand knowledge of Japanese aircraft performance and tactics. Initially, the Japanese pressed a clear advantage in aircraft, position, and initiative in most encounters.

Chastened by their stinging defeat and loss of face at Midway, Japanese naval strategists shifted attention to shoring up gains in the Bismarck Sea. In the Solomon Islands, their flank was exposed by the presence of an Australian base that was quickly evacuated on word of the approaching Japanese, who occupied the former Australian facilities on May 3. Establishing their own anchorage at Tulagi, primarily for hosting Nakajima A6M2-N Rufe float plane fighters and supporting facilities at the neighboring islets of Gavutu and Tanambogo, the Japanese put their energies into constructing a more capable airfield on the much larger island of Guadalcanal immediately to the south. Here, the United States would make its stand, a violent and sustained confrontation that began the long, arduous rollback of the Japanese empire. In waters adjacent to Guadalcanal, the Navy would fight six major engagements more bitter and bloody than any naval battle in American history since 1814. There were fights almost daily between the Imperial Japanese Air Force and U.S. flyers; some thirty occasions when land-based airplanes attacked ships; a fair number of submarine battles; and almost continual ground fighting by U.S. Marines and soldiers against Japanese troops.[7]

On July 26, the carrier task forces earmarked for the Guadalcanal offensive assembled about 350 miles south of Fiji and became identified by their aggregate command grouping, Task Force 61, supporting amphibious landings by units under Task Force 62.[8] By sunset of August 6, "the south coast of Guadalcanal loomed only 85 miles northeast and Tulagi another 50 miles beyond. After dark crews began spotting first-wave aircraft on blacked-out flight decks, while below . . . bedding was piled on deck in the middle of compartments, and flammables placed in steel lockers and cabinets."[9] Although Guadalcanal's dry season lingered into early August, the humidity remained oppressive. For Ernie, pausing on *Wasp*'s bridge wing before the pre-launch briefing, the on-shore breeze at first carried an unmistakable scent of coastal pine and honeysuckle reminiscent of mid-summer in Beaufort. As the breeze intensified, the faintly familiar scent was soon overtaken by the sickly-sweet scent of late season orchids and hibiscus—now beginning to decay—mixed with noxious odors rising off the swamps. This overpowering musk was more akin to the days-old decomposing menhaden that he remembered from the fishing piers in Beaufort. But Ernie's thoughts were on VS-72's assigned targets and possible air opposition for that day: Japanese defensive positions on the beaches and inshore on Tulagi, Tanambogo, and Gavutu some twenty-five miles north of Guadalcanal across the Sea Lark Channel.

The U.S. amphibious invasion force, composed of the 1st Marine Division, escorts, minesweepers, and fire support ships forming Task Force 62, approached its landing beaches from due west of Cape Esperance on August 7, 1942. The geography of Guadalcanal loomed black against a breaking dawn to starboard as the force took an easterly heading. "Aircrews manned planes around 0500, as idling engines dotted the decks with bright blue exhaust flames. . . . Clouds towered northeast toward Guadalcanal and the seas were rough."[10] The first wave of U.S. Marines went ashore on Guadalcanal shortly after 0600.

Incredibly, there was no evidence that the landing force or its escorts had been detected, and the landings continued that morning on Guadalcanal unopposed. From the opening bombardment, planes from *Saratoga* stood by for close air support over Guadalcanal, with planes from *Wasp* allocated to the area north toward Tulagi. *Wasp's* F4F fighters of VF-71 opened the aerial offensive with strafing runs on seaplane moorings around Gavutu and Tanambogo and were later credited with destroying thirteen flying boats and seven float fighters.[11] The landings on Tulagi commenced at 0800, followed at noon by landings on Gavutu and Tanambogo. From *Wasp*, Ernie led elements of VS-72 in relieving VS-71 mid-morning to provide air support against targets on Gavutu and Tanambogo. Three companies of the U.S. Marines 1st Parachute Battalion, attached for this operation to the 1st Marine Division, moved ashore in successive waves at Gavutu, encountering an alerted and ready Japanese opposition. Highly practiced and sighted Japanese shore battery fire was exacting an increasing toll in U.S. casualties and checking the Marines' advance.[12] The naval bombardment had dismantled a seaplane ramp that was the object of the landing, forcing the Marines' landing craft into a more exposed position on a small sandy beach. Japanese gun emplacements on Gavutu and nearby Tanambogo were set to unleash flanking enfilade fire on the nearly four hundred Marines rushing onto the open beach.[13] Ernie, leading three dive bombing attacks against those batteries and their ammunition storage bunkers, silenced the enemy guns opposing the landing.

A lingering concern from the early planning and throughout the offensive on and around Guadalcanal was the Japanese advantage of having airfields in range of Guadalcanal from Rabaul. The nearest American land-based air support was more than 600 miles away, making the aircraft carriers of Task Group 61.1 the only practical air cover for the amphibious operation and the only effective response at a distance to enemy surface combatants or carriers sent to challenge the landings. Providing responsive air cover to the Marines ashore while also preserving the freedom of movement at sea to respond to Japanese air and submarine attacks stretched U.S. carrier planes dangerously thin. Much depended on adequate resources being allocated to long-range reconnaissance to cover wide tracts of ocean to generate as much warning as possible.[14] On August 8, Ernie led twelve SBDs northward in the general direction of Rabaul in a wide-area search for enemy carriers. Reconnoitering a sector from 280 to 040 degrees, ranging outward to 220 miles, Ernie encountered and splashed an Aichi E13A1 Type 0 floatplane—popularly known as a "Jake"—from the Japanese heavy cruiser *Kako*, part of Cruiser Division Six, lurking some distance to the northwest. Ernie made short work of it using his fixed forward-firing 50s, using aerial tactics that by now were second nature from six years of squadron drills in VF-1, VF-4, and VF-7. What Ernie could not have known then was that *Kako* would launch a second E13A1 that night to illuminate unsuspecting Allied ships at anchor or barely making way near Savo Island. *Kako*, in company with others in her cruiser division, would level devastating large-caliber gunfire and torpedo attacks on those illuminated targets, resulting in the loss of three heavy cruisers and causing heavy damage to a fourth that later had to be scuttled—for the exchange of minor damage to three Japanese ships. At 0300 on August 9, with the Japanese flotilla beginning its retirement up the slot, a flash message circulated among U.S. ships indicating "some type of surface action in the Tulagi-Guadalcanal area."[15] *Saratoga*, *Enterprise*, and *Wasp*, at the time just clearing San Cristobal about one hundred miles southeast of Guadalcanal, received the message simultaneously. Capt. Forrest Sherman on *Wasp*, aware that Ernie had trained his VS-72 pilots in nighttime attack, urgently requested Rear Admiral Noyes to permit *Wasp* to launch an intercept of the retiring Japanese—but was refused.[16]

Ernie's VS-72, with sister squadron VS-71, acquitted themselves with great distinction: while working over Japanese targets near Guadalcanal, the two SBD squadrons shot down seven Japanese aircraft before the ship's fighters could score a victory.[17] As the Marines consolidated their gains of August 7–8, a desperate struggle ensued on Guadalcanal in the following weeks as the Japanese mounted a determined opposition with the intent of throwing the Marines back into the sea. The Japanese notion of their own invincibility was dashed as they were awakened to the prospect of having their Solomons flank turned back on them. They responded almost immediately by pouring troop reinforcements into Guadalcanal to dislodge the Marines, covered by air and naval presence in force to clear the surrounding sea areas. The United States reinforced its newly gained foothold by ferrying in more Marines, with steady infusions of air-craft based ashore at Guadalcanal. For weeks, U.S. and Japanese carriers probed and pawed at each other in brief but intense encounters with neither securing a clear advantage. Japanese light carrier *Ryujo*, set afire and torpedoed by aircraft from *Saratoga* and *Enterprise*, capsized and sank on August 25. At the end of the month, *Saratoga* was forced to retire to Pearl Harbor for repairs to torpedo hits, and by mid–September, *Enterprise* followed suit. Rear Admiral Noyes' Task Force 61 now comprised 154 planes on *Wasp* (CV 7) and the newly arrived *Hornet* (CV 8) compared to 129 planes on *Shokaku*, *Zuikaku*, and *Zuiho*. He ordered a force disposition that put in motion a tactical scouting group of VS-72 SBDs carrying armor-piercing five-hundred-pound bombs to reconnoiter ahead of the *Hornet* strike group, while the remainder of *Wasp*'s airborne F4Fs from VF-71 and SBDs from VS-71 flew combat air patrol and antisubmarine surveillance over the task force. At 1315 on September 14, Ernie, acting on earlier sighting reports, launched in the lead of fourteen VS-72 SBDs to search a northerly sector bounded by 306 degrees to 354 degrees out to almost 280 miles. His flight reached a point fifty miles short of actually sighting the Japanese carrier force that was retiring smartly for refueling. *Wasp* and *Hornet* recovered their aircraft and spent the night anxiously awaiting a probable dustup the next day.[18]

Task Force 61 was still loosely tied to its escort mission for the movement of Marines to Guadalcanal, and on the morning of September 15, *Wasp* and *Hornet* were positioned well south of Guadalcanal but in range to support arriving reinforcements with the 7th Marines. *Wasp*, responsible that day for combat air and antisubmarine patrol, turned into the wind at 1420 and slowed to recover and launch aircraft for the afternoon cycle. Ernie was piloting one of three SBDs that recovered in that flight deck evolution, and after his aircraft was chocked, he headed for his stateroom. As *Wasp* returned to her base course, Japanese submarine *I-19* launched a spread of six torpedoes, three of which struck with tremendous force. Ernie was thrown from his bunk and immediately found his way to the flight deck, where fires from ruptured fuel lines were beginning to envelop the ship forward of the island superstructure.[19]

Those closest to Ernie by this time—squadron mates and air group colleagues—were seeing both the unmistakable emergence of a combat leader and more personal behaviors that would become hallmarks: a penchant for hard living and, when ashore, hard partying. Shipmate and assistant navigator on *Wasp* Ens. Mickey Weisner remembered a telling moment about Ernie when *Wasp* had been torpedoed and the order given to abandon ship. Years later, as an accomplished naval aviator in his own right and deputy chief of naval operations for air, Weisner recalled his astonishment and that of his shipmates at seeing Ernie race back across the flight deck near the flaming wreckage in order to reach his stateroom and retrieve personal effects and a sizable cache of poker winnings. Otherwise, on the undamaged side of the ship, evacuation was proceeding calmly. Captain Sherman, by his superb shiphandling, had maneuvered *Wasp* to keep the flames downwind to permit more time for the crew members to manage their exit over the side. When Ernie returned to join the rest of the crew going over the side by rope and by leap, he observed that the extra time had allowed them to take a hasty muster, remove their shoes, and place them in neat rows on the flight deck. An order had been issued to the stewards' mates to retrieve tubs of ice cream and spoons from the pantry, and crewmen were each allocated a few spoonfuls while waiting for their signal to go over. But in the moment, Ernie's almost cavalier disregard of exploding ordnance on a sinking ship displayed a disdain for personal danger, even a kind of recklessness, that fueled a reputation for bravery in the most extreme circumstances.

With her entire complement of aircraft either discarded over the side or consumed by flames and with gasoline vapor touching off a succession of huge explosions above and below the flight deck that threatened to next incinerate *Wasp*'s bridge, the ship and her aircraft could not be saved. Captain Sherman's order to abandon ship came only an hour and twenty minutes after the first torpedo hit, but he and the embarked task force commander, Admiral Noyes, stayed with the ship until 1500 before going over the side. In the oil- and gasoline-slicked water, Ernie swam for about an hour before rescue by *Duncan*, one of several destroyers standing off several hundred yards from *Wasp*. Among those destroyers, *Lansdowne* drew the distasteful

duty of administering the coup de grace by torpedo when *Wasp* settled but would not sink. Four of Ernie's VS-72 SBDs—airborne during the torpedo attack—were able to recover aboard *Hornet*. The rest
of the squadron's aircraft were lost with *Wasp*. About ninety percent of
the ship's crew survived and was rescued. Ernie and his shipmates were
repatriated with great expedience, mainly to San Diego and most with
new orders to squadrons that were standing up to populate new flight
decks coming down the ways. En route to his new assignment, he had
enough time during the customary thirty days of survivors' leave to
visit his mother at home in Beaufort, North Carolina, and to corre-
spond with his in-laws, who were living in Washington, D.C.[20]

Before and during the war, Ernie carried on a light-hearted exchange
with his father-in-law, General Arnold, about trading gifts of spirits
that both euphemistically referred to as the continuation of a long-
standing Native American custom observed between chiefs and braves
who had married their daughters. From their first introduction by
Lois, these quips became an expected and enjoyable part of their rep-
artee. Their correspondence always showed a tongue-in-cheek reference to the frequent exchange of bottles of scotch, even to the point
of Arnold's promise of a bottle of White Horse in his condolence letter to Ernie for the sinking of *Wasp*. By this time, Arnold was dealing
with his own excessive compulsions, and he may have appreciated the
company of a family member with a shared propensity for an occasional scotch. Arnold was dealing with persistent rumors in Washington that "he was, in his own term, a drunkard."[21]

Their constant ribbing, while not always about scotch or whiskey,
most often reflected an abiding care and concern for one another.
They had grown genuinely fond of each other and never let a profound partiality for their respective services' aviation component
interfere with their high mutual regard. None of their correspondence reveals this so much as General Arnold's letter to Ernie, written on War Department letterhead, a few weeks after Ernie assumed
command of Bombing Squadron Sixteen at Naval Air Station Quonset Point, Rhode Island. The letter was in lamentation of the outcome

of the 1942 Army-Navy game, held that year due to the onset of war at Annapolis in 14,000-seat Thompson Stadium. "Inside Thompson Stadium, half of the Brigade of Midshipmen was ordered to cheer for Army and they took instruction from cheer books sent down from West Point . . . which featured humorous illustrations of goats braying like mules and cartoons of midshipmen cheering with fingers crossed."[22] This was the first game played in Annapolis since 1893. Plebe midshipman Mac Snowden was in attendance and cheering for Navy, which won, 14–0. General Arnold's letter to Ernie began and closed with the expected saucy but good-natured mockery:

November 30, 1942

Dear Ernie:

It is not without some misgivings that I enclose herewith check for ten bucks. Were I of the same temperament as some people I know who gloat over taking money away from others, my statement to you would be about as follows:

Mental anguish during the game that took about 10 years off my life	1.69
Penalty for having game in Annapolis when it should have been anywhere else	.23
Rebate for Army playing its first team	3.06
Penalty for your being a graduate of the Naval Academy and midshipmen trying to root for cadets, thereby making many misplays and causing much confusion	4.44
Refund for Navy running in ringers when they played their first team	.13
Total	9.55

Accordingly, I should send you a check for $0.45 but being a generous soul, I realize that those who went down into the sea and lost all their worldly goods and chattels are probably broke and have no where-with-all to provide sustenance and clothing for those who depend upon them for support. Therefore, I am taking the magnanimous attitude and hope it will in part repay you for the bill you must have incurred when you went to the Diamond Horseshoe to see "Stars and Garters."

In any event, hope you are settled up at Quonset and everything is going along all right.

Sincerely,

H.H. ARNOLD,
Lieutenant General, USA[23]

Ernie's relationship with his father-in-law may have involved many sessions of intemperate drinking, but Ernie could keep his tippling within bounds, perhaps because of the resilience of his youth. Before the war, in more tranquil settings ashore where there were less pervasive checks on after-hours activity, the evening cocktail ritual became more the norm. In the absence of the total focus that would soon be imposed by literally years at sea and in combat, Ernie lapsed more easily into a casual pattern of social drinking. Eventually it would place a strain on his career and his health, but not before he added even more luster to his years in service to naval aviation. At the peak of his training, experience, and energy in the hard trials to come, his leadership would be on constant display.

Leadership has been variously defined by academics and observers as situation-dependent but evident to most, particularly in a military community, as proactive problem-solving where the leader enjoins others to readily embrace a common purpose and identity. For Ernie, his brother Mac, and possibly for a great many other naval aviators, it could often be distilled to a mix of unimpeachable flying skill, constant mentoring of that skill in squadron pilots, visible regard for the welfare of squadron officers and enlisted men, and an exuberant sense of purpose to the point of defying personal risk. Already evident to

Wasp shipmates and VS-72 squadron mates, Ernie's leadership would soon be validated by events surrounding a historic engagement in the Pacific, the battle of the Philippine Sea. For a long time after the unfortunate events of September 15, however, he nursed a lingering sense of guilt for having survived the sinking of his ship and felt a growing determination to exact revenge. He would not have to wait long. His survivors' leave was truncated by new orders effective October 13 to report to the senior naval aviator, Fleet Air Detachment, Naval Air Station Quonset Point, Rhode Island, to assume command of Bombing Squadron Sixteen (VB-16) for fitting out and making the squadron ready for deployment as part of Carrier Air Group Sixteen (CVG-16) embarked in the newly commissioned USS *Lexington.*

On a raw early spring day in 1943 at Quonset Point, with VB-16 personnel arrayed in formation, Ernie and four of his peers were called before Rear Adm. Calvin Durgin, commander, Fleet Air Atlantic, for presentation of the Navy Cross. Ernie's Navy Cross citation noted the actions in and around Guadalcanal on August 7–8, 1942, when, in the lead of VS-72 SBDs, he pressed home an attack on Japanese gun emplacements that were impeding the advance of U.S. Marines and later, in aerial combat, shot down an observation float plane that was reconnoitering U.S. ship dispositions around Savo Island for the Japanese surface fleet. Standing with Ernie for presentation of his own Navy Cross as commanding officer of the SBD squadron on USS *Hornet* for action in October 1942 was classmate Lt. Cdr. William "Gus" Widhelm. Ernie and Gus would be reunited a year later in USS *Lexington* when Gus served as Vice Adm. Mitscher's operations officer in Task Force 58 and Ernie commanded *Lexington*'s air group.[24] However, this moment on the tarmac at Quonset Point was a welcome, if brief, respite from the nerve-racking stress of constant combat at sea. It also yielded an endearing and welcome note of appreciation and highest regard from General and Mrs. Arnold at Fort Myer, Virginia, to their son-in-law, both writing: "The ceremony today deepens our pride and admiration for you. Love, Mother and Dad."

Lexington was the sixteenth carrier hull to be laid down and the second carrier of World War II to be named *Lexington.* Fitting U.S.

Navy tradition, she was the fifth warship to be commissioned as *Lexington*, the first having distinguished herself in the Revolutionary War before succumbing to British guns off the coast of France. The first *Lexington* (CV 2) aircraft carrier, from which Ernie had flown F4B-4s with the High Hatters of VF-1, had been sunk in the first carrier-on-carrier battle in the Coral Sea in May 1942. The newest *Lexington*, after her shakedown, work-ups, air group training, and repairs, sailed for Pearl Harbor and then on to combat action with the Japanese by mid-September 1943.

Lexington sailed in company with carriers *Princeton*, *Belleau Wood*, *Cowpens*, *Independence*, and *Essex*, forming Task Force 14, and arrived in the Gilbert Islands for strikes on Tarawa and Wake in early October. Commander L. B. Southerland, commanding CVG-16, was Ernie's immediate senior and was normally addressed in that role as "CAG," an honorific title for the ship's air group commander. Ernie's role as a subordinate commander of the CVG-16 bombing squadron is described best in his summary to CAG Southerland. Ernie led four strikes over two days—the second and third each day from *Lexington*. In the terse language of an official combat action report, he reported the second day's events:

---

6 October 1943

STRIKE TWO—I led Strike Two consisting of 23 SBDs, 19 F6Fs, and 10 TBFs. We commenced launching at 0645, rendezvoused and departed at 0702. Arrived at target at 0802. We ran into heavy rainsqualls and in many places the ceiling was zero over the target. Clouds were heavy in the entire vicinity. I ordered the division leaders (typically a [flight] of four to six aircraft) to take their divisions down on the target. We had only 1,000 feet to 1,500 feet maximum over the target area necessitating shallow glides at low speeds with a dangerously low pullout in order to get on our targets. We completed our attacks about 0850. I bombed a large building and the radio-man reported that we hit it. On the pullout, I strafed in front of me until I could get clear. Heavy weapon anti-aircraft fire was behind me but never caught completely up with me in my return. On our way into the target everybody (Japanese defenders) seemed to be shooting with small weapons. We had 5 planes shot up by anti-aircraft fire in this attack. One fighter failed to return. Two SBDs obtained oblique photographs of the damage to the Island. When I left, 10 large fires were burning furiously. We landed aboard at 0900 to 0915.

STRIKE THREE—I led Strike Three consisting of 23 SBDs, 19 F6Fs, and 12 TBFs, which was the final blow delivered by our carrier group. We commenced launching at 1120, rendezvoused and were over the target commencing attack by 1230. I ordered the fighters to strake their assigned targets just prior to commencing my dive. The dive-bomber division leaders and the torpedo division leaders were ordered to attack assigned targets. I led my 11 planes down in a dive on the heavy anti-aircraft installations on the southeast corner of the Island, and on the pullout observed several columns of smoke and debris caused by the bombs all exploding in our target area. After making the attack, I circled around the Island observing the damage to same. I saw our submarine rescue vessel being shelled by a shore battery. One of our fighters dived into the shore battery and silenced same by strafing. The submarine continued with his rescue operations. Three SBDs took oblique photographs. On our return to base, one SBD fell out of formation and landed in the water. The crew immediately got in their boat and appeared to be all right. I ordered two planes to stand by until forced to leave the scene of the accident due to shortage of fuel. Four planes were damaged on this flight and serious damage was done to the enemy shore installations.[25]

Later that same day, after the two SBDs orbiting the crash scene returned to *Lexington* with low fuel, Ernie made his third launch of the day in a desperate bid to find the crew and cover the crew's position before they drifted out of contact with rescue vessels. He reported that flight in the same terse manner: "I led a search flight for and found Lieutenant (jg) McCarthy and ARM2c Bonilla, 102 miles from the ship. I kept one plane down low circling the boat (life raft) while I climbed to 8,000 feet and turned on my emergency IFF [identification friend or foe] and also got communication with the ship on high frequency. I then broadcasted to the rescue vessel the latitude and longitude of the rubber boat. I was ordered to return to the ship and did so."[26]

Admiral Durgin, a future deputy chief of naval operations for air who had presided over Ernie's VB-16 assumption of command and Navy Cross ceremony at Quonset, took a special liking to Ernie and followed reports of his exploits with VB-16 from USS *Lexington*. Durgin penned a personal note to Ernie in late October:

----

26 October 1943

Dear Snowden

When I pinned the last medal on you shortly after you arrived at Quonset, I remember saying that I hoped before very long I would have [the] chance to pin another medal alongside that one. Well, it looks as if somebody will have that privilege because from all accounts it looks as if your squadron did a bang-up job on the Japs at Wake.

My staff and all of the Fleet Air, Quonset Point are proud of the Lexington Group, and we know we are going to hear more of you before so very long.

Please remember all of us to the rest of your squadron and with kindest personal regards.

Sincerely yours,

C. T. Durgin

When *Lexington* retired for replenishment in mid-November, Ernie used the pause to write to Mac. The brothers connected by letter often in the years before the war, but letters during these months were rare given constant movement and frequent action that *Lexington* and her task force were engaged in. Ernie used his pen at this pause in a desultory ramble that revealed to Mac the passions that were foremost on his mind and, not coincidentally, again stoked the imagination and desire—even envy—of the younger brother to emulate Ernie's experiences in this great naval aviation adventure:

17 November 1943

Dear Buddy,

Sorry I haven't answered your letter before but I have been busy as hell of late working over my dear friends, the [Japanese] bastards! Certainly have had a lot of fun this time Buddy. I went from squadron commander of eighteen planes to all the bombers—thirty-six planes—and have been promoted air group commander and have all ninety-three planes on this bucket. I now fly a "Hellcat" all rigged up pretty like and it certainly is good to get in the 400 mile per hour class. My three squadron commanders are swell people and we have the *best damned group in the Navy*! Our ship's captain even says so. Have been recommended for another Navy Cross and also the Silver Star medal. If I don't get some metal in my hind end on this trip I'll probably get something else. This is a grand show out here and we are gunning the bastards something to remember—if any of them can live to remember.

Haven't heard from mother for a long time and won't hear from anyone for a while. We'll be back in soon and then maybe celebrate Xmas—too damned far from home! Tell her to write. You write *too* Buddy. I'll get your letters even though you may not hear from me for long intervals. Come on you short fellow and write your *little* buddy. When do you graduate? It's too much for me to even try and figure out what class you are in or when you'll be out.

Can't get over being an old Fudd 3-striper. Sure does seem funny to have everybody all at once jump up and *give* every time. Hell, I don't like it. I'm a fighting man, not a stripe-toting bastard with his feet on a desk—which, thank God, I am not behind yet!! Maybe this sounds a little strong buddy, but it's the way I feel. I'm out here because I want to kill these bastards. Whereas a lot of naval officers are at home behind a desk and you couldn't budge them with a hot rod. Don't let them give you the old stuff about reserve officers being no good. I have four Academy men in my group of 130 officers, counting me. There are nineteen out of 126 officers on the ship. Figure this out for yourself: who's fighting the war? The Reserves. There's nothing wrong with them. Take a broad outlook and you'll do ok. The only Academy man in my squadron (each) is the skipper. In my last squadron—on the Wasp—I had ten. This group is *twice* as good as *my old one*. I brought this baby up from a pup.

Well, Buddy—don't know much more to say—been talking about myself too much. Don't take it wrong. I haven't done right by you in writing! When and if I get in next time, I'll write you a better letter. Tomorrow we'll be under the enemy's planes and the next day we will be giving him hell for a while. If you get this without a frill saying all's well on the front of the letter, you'll know I had a helluva good time while I lived, Buddy. Best luck and good hunting. You're a damned good kid.

Your Buddy

Ernie undoubtedly had knowledge of specific imminent combat action when writing this letter to Macon. Within two days, on November 19, preparatory to U.S. Marine landings on Tarawa, Air Group 16 mounted a maximum effort against a large Japanese airfield on the nearby island of Mille to deny any air support to the defenders on Tarawa. Ernie led strikes with strafing of the one hundred Japanese fighters and bombers on the airfield on November 19, 20, and 22. His side number sixty-nine Hellcat suffered enough damage from ground fire on the last day that his control effectiveness was seriously impaired. He made a difficult approach to *Lexington*, ultimately crash-landing into the barrier rigged beyond the arresting wires. His Hellcat upended and came to an abrupt stop with the tail in the air and the propellers mangled in the barrier, but he was still strapped in and not seriously injured. Nonetheless, the ship's medical personnel assisted in extracting Ernie from the cockpit, forming a cradle with their interlocked arms and giving him a "chair carry" down to sick bay. The Hellcat was damaged beyond immediate repair and pushed over the side by the flight deck crew. A second Hellcat was assigned from VF-16 as the CAG bird and repainted as number sixty-nine. Ernie was directing strikes and flying combat air patrol again by December 2. In raids in the Marshall Islands on December 4, Ernie's group arrived over the target at 0755 when he saw one Japanese cruiser and a large cargo ship at anchor south of Roi. He ordered one element of his group to attack these ships and sent another element after another cruiser he could see in the distance heading out to sea. Direct hits were made on both cruisers and the cargo ship, leaving the latter burning furiously. Torpedo hits were seen on all three. He led the flight thence to Kwajalein where he could see ten large ships and six medium-sized ships at anchor or dead in the water from earlier attacks. Three or four of the large ships were settling by the stern, and many were burning. The air group made several runs to finish the work, and Ernie turned them toward home by 0830. Passing Roi, he could see that the two cruisers were trailing oil, listing, and possibly sinking. As he gazed on the burning cargo ship, it erupted in a huge fireball, with flames shooting one thousand feet into the air and a pillar of smoke reaching ten thousand feet. He was able to estimate the heights "because I was flying my Hellcat at 5,000 feet and I had to look way up to see the top of the smoke. It probably was an ammunition ship."[27]

Ernie, in command of *Lexington*'s air wing, CVG-16, and Felix Stump, commanding *Lexington*, formed a tight professional relationship and a close personal friendship. The nature of their relationship was on full display in a personal note from Stump to Ernie, reporting on a visit with Ernie's in-laws, the Arnolds, during a brief excursion to the East Coast while *Lexington* underwent repairs:

USS LEXINGTON
Fleet Post Office,
San Francisco, California
January 11, 1944

Commander E. M. Snowden
Commander Air Group SIXTEEN
c/o Fleet Post Office,
San Francisco, California

Dear Ernie,
I went to see General Arnold at his office and gave him a copy of the summary of what you boys had accomplished in two

and a half months. I went over and took Commander Steichen with me to Fort Myers and had dinner with General and Mrs. Arnold consisting of: 1. Quail, 2. Pheasant, 3. Fresh home grown chicken, 4. Boiled rice, 5. *Fresh* peas, 6. Ice cream made with real cream, 7. Cake with celery and all the other fixings, preceded by good whiskey—which the General did not touch. It was a delightful home-like evening.

Commander Steichen took over one picture of you and is going to send over more.

I certainly hope you people are staying put and not going on any other ships. We are going to be a lot better ship after we leave the navy yard than we ever were before.

Admiral Pownall forwarded my recommendation for citations on the ship, recommending approval, and also for the Air Group. He forwarded my recommendations for Presidential Citations to the Group and to Fighting SIXTEEN, two separate recommendations, stating that the work of the Air Group was outstanding and he forwarded those recommendations for consideration.

I think General "Hap" Arnold is pretty proud of you and I think he is a swell gent.

Best regards to the gang.

Sincerely,
FELIX B. STUMP
Captain, U.S. Navy

Roaring into late spring of 1944, naval forces composing the U.S. Fifth Fleet were in full stride across the central Pacific in Adm. Chester Nimitz's push toward the invasion of Saipan. In the van was Task Force 58 commanded by Vice Admiral Mitscher, who broke his flag in *Lexington*. She had rejoined the task force on March 1 after repairs to the hull from Japanese torpedo damage were completed at Bremerton Naval Yard in Washington. She was placed under the subordinate command of Rear Adm. J. W. Reeves in Task Group 58.3, steaming in company with carriers *Enterprise* (CV 6), *Princeton* (CVL 23), and *San Jacinto* (CVL 30). Reeves had formerly commanded *Wasp* until late spring 1942 when relieved by Capt. Forrest Sherman. Ernie had operated with Reeves before, as executive officer and then skipper of VS-72 in *Wasp* when Reeves commanded the carrier, and both were known to each other and confident of each other's experience and judgment in their current positions.

Since late November of the previous year, Ernie had been in command of *Lexington*'s Air Group 16 and had become a trusted adviser on air group capabilities, limitations, and tactics to Vice Admiral Mitscher and his staff, including the newly assigned chief of staff, Capt. Arleigh Burke. This was the same Marc Mitscher who had earned fame in naval aviation circles a quarter-century before, made nationwide headlines, and captured a young Ernie's imagination for his heroics in the attempted Atlantic crossing with the NC-1 flying boat; two years before, he had skippered *Hornet* while delivering the Doolittle raiders to their launch point. According to historian E. B. Potter, Mitscher "looked anything but a warrior, and the baseball-type cap on his bald head failed to add a sporting touch. In a less warlike setting he might have passed for a village grocer. His speech was mild, unassertive, and not much above a whisper."[28] But, "Mitscher got the best out of his men. He stayed close to his pilots and made their concerns his own. They were 'his boys.' He talked to them constantly. In every decision he made, their well-being was foremost in his mind. Mitscher would cultivate in his second life [as a senior flag officer] a relentless culture of competitive performance among flag officers in command of his task groups."[29]

In the few months they served together in the spring through early summer of 1944, Mitscher, Burke, and Snowden took the measure of each other and formed a very fast working collaboration based on professional respect and admiration that would last well beyond the coming action.

Burke's arrival as chief of staff to commander, Task Force 58 was not met with exuberance, at least initially. Burke recalled: "When I first reported aboard *Lexington* to be Admiral Mitscher's chief of staff, I was a chief of staff he didn't want, and it was a job I didn't want. The reason why both Admiral Mitscher and I were unhappy was that Admiral [Ernest] King (then Chief of Naval Operations) had ordered aviation flag officers then in combat at sea to take surface sailors as their chiefs of staff. Mitscher refused. He knew carrier and aviation operations inside out, and had grave reservations that any surface sailor could be helpful—especially as his chief of staff."[30] Burke sensed immediately that if he was to weather this assignment and have any expectation of a successful Navy career, he had to get up to speed quickly by immersing himself in the standing orders, procedures, daily routine, and the aviators' professional idiom. In Burke's memory, he "went into the ready rooms, to talk to the pilots, the squadron commanders and the air group commander. I got wonderful help from men like Ernie Snowden, Ralph Weymouth, Paul Buie, Hugh Winters and dozens more."[31]

Besides Mitscher and Burke, Ernie was under the scrutiny of his squadron skippers and the aircrew of Air Group 16. Already somewhat of a known quantity from the air group's stand-up at Quonset Point as skipper of VB-16, Ernie earned high marks for planning and leading VB-16's early strikes in the fall of 1943 in the Gilbert Islands. His penchant for well-planned and -conducted strikes continued after taking over the air group in late 1943 and well into the spring of 1944. By his example of visible leadership in the preparation, in the air over the target, and in the quality of poststrike assessments and retargeting on every major enemy engagement, he secured for himself immutable loyalty and praise from all hands, not least of all from his squadron commanding officers. Perhaps the greatest measure of his impact on air wing cohesiveness and tactical efficiency was his habit of involving his squadron commanders and their executive officers in the planning and execution of strikes, assigning one of them the lead role. Ernie would typically ride high perch over a strike in his F6F number 69, observing and occasionally, though sparingly, offering words of encouragement, correction, or compliment. Late in life, when interviewed about Ernie's example at a Tailhook reunion in Reno, Nevada, VF-16 ace Alex Vraciu unhesitatingly remembered Snowden as a "fearless combat leader" and strike planner for whom he had the utmost regard.

As a remedy to the strain of constant drill and actual combat, Ernie had taken to organizing down time with equal parts horseplay and hijinks aboard ship to lighten the intensity for the air group. By his eighth month in command of the air group, morale could not have been higher, as noted by *Life* magazine in their feature story "Life Goes to an Aircraft Carrier Party" published on June 3, 1944. The party in question was the founding of the "West of Tokyo Missionary Society" on board *Lexington* to commemorate the Navy's first attack (by CVG-16) on Japanese positions west of Tokyo. The founders' honorable and virtuous purpose, as set down in their high-sounding manifesto, was to celebrate this "zealous attempt to convert the reluctant and retiring Japanese fleet. . . . The missionaries by their enlightening bombs converted over 30 heathen ships—to scrap iron."[32] Honorary membership was accorded Jimmy Doolittle for his raid on Tokyo two years before. Marc Mitscher was designated "chief ministering missionary" in part for delivering Doolittle to his launch point and in part for overseeing the recent havoc wreaked on the Japanese as commander of Task Force 58. Next senior in the Missionary Society hierarchy was "chief evangelist," the title conferred on Ernie as commander of Air Group 16.[33] *Life* photographer J. R. Eyerman captured the horseplay with a series of images that began with Ernie reading the manifesto in mock seriousness to the assembled Air Group officers and enlisted men, and then descended into ritualized pranks that were borrowed from the traditional hazing of pollywogs by shellbacks in an Equator-crossing ceremony. Inside a month of these well-organized antics, Air Group 16 would face its greatest test at sea.

The sweep of strategic maneuver in which Ernie, Air Group 16, and the entire Fifth Fleet would find themselves engaged in June 1944 is difficult to portray. The Japanese desire to maintain the Marianas and the U.S. desire to seize the islands for air bases would collide in the Philippine Sea. The Marianas island chain constituted sizably more acreage than previous amphibious objectives, encompassing Tinian, Saipan, and Guam. And among those islands, the Japanese had invested heavily in fortifications and airfields with supporting infrastructure. Dubbed Operation Forager, the scope of the U.S. commitment and the scale of operations at sea to adequately cover the invasion force demanded correspondingly large naval force components. Carrier forces consolidated under Mitscher's command were allocated to four task groups totaling nine large deck carriers and seven light carriers operating more than nine hundred aircraft.[34]

Moving to block Task Force 58, the Japanese mobile fleet under Vice Admiral Ozawa Jisaburo sortied from anchorage in the Philippines. Ozawa, aware of his disadvantage in numbers, organized a complex operation that relied on island-based aircraft to attrite and degrade Task Force 58 until his carrier aircraft could be brought to bear. Task Force 58 intelligence staff correctly interpreted Ozawa's plan from signals and observed movements. With that knowledge, Ernie sketched out a quick action brief and ran to the flag bridge for an audience with Mitscher and Burke, mapping out a characteristically aggressive counterplan to open the engagement on the afternoon of June 11 with a surprise fighter sweep that would practically eliminate air opposition over Saipan. These strikes were followed by intensive and repeated strikes over the next four days, culminating in the landings on Saipan on June 15.[35]

U.S. naval intelligence, though spotty in some details, was sufficiently discerning to fathom the Japanese moves, prompting Admiral Mitscher as early as June 16 to signal his task group commanders: "Believe Japanese will approach from a southerly direction under their shore based air cover close to Yap and Ulithi to attempt to operate in the vicinity of Guam. However they may come from the west. Our searches must cover both possibilities."[36] Anticipating that the Japanese might use the larger island facilities as a stopover for shuttle bombing runs, Mitscher also directed his force to undertake a special strike against Guam airfield to destroy aircraft and crater the runway. By the night of June 18, however, Mitscher informed the force that no more strikes would be made on shore targets and to be prepared for strikes on enemy surface forces.[37] The full weight of U.S. and Japanese forces finally crashed headlong in a thunderclap on June 19, with the Japanese aerial order of battle bringing to bear 450 aircraft of which roughly half were Zeke fighters, 100 Judy dive bombers, and 90 Jill torpedo bombers, with another 40 Val and Kate dive bombers. In the melee that followed, extending into June 20, U.S. naval aviators scourged their Japanese counterparts in an epic contest known in the official annals as the battle of the Philippine Sea, but thereafter and forever known by the naval aviators as the Marianas Turkey Shoot.

The most intimate, first-hand retelling of those epic two days of battle may have been recorded by *Sunday Star* reporter George

Kennedy just two months later. He opened his report by noting that Ernie was in Washington where they were meeting for lunch, "driving around in the shiny new automobile his mother gave him for coming back alive. He is a quick-moving, brown-eyed North Carolinian with dark hair and a ready liking for company. With his wife, who is General Arnold's daughter, he spent two days at the Ritz in New York—two days in which he got to a press conference and a radio interview that the Navy's public relations let him in for, and on his own to *21* and *Larue's*—spent a lot of money and had a swell time."[38]

Kennedy, drawing a segue from his reference to Ernie's wife to set his theme, noted that some of the Army pilots who had been bombing Germany in Fortresses and Liberators were amazed at being home again, speculating on their chance of earning a furlough by going unscathed through the remainder of fifty missions. "Navy pilots, by contrast, don't accept the death of one of their number as a necessary happening in major air battles. When one is lost in a brush with the Japs, the remainder go into a huddle over it in the ready room once all is secure, wanting to know: Could it have been prevented? Was the protective team work maintained?"[39] With Kennedy prompting and transcribing replies, Ernie began to recall events on the morning of June 19.

Kennedy: Morning found Task Force 58 in one of those paradoxes of aerial naval warfare, steaming away from the enemy but into the wind so it could launch its planes. It was west of the Saipan–Guam line.

Ernie: They were too far away for us to reach them. We could hear our search that went out before dawn reporting an empty sea. Then about 9:30 observers began to report bogeys. We knew then what the Jap was up to. He was too far away to strike us and get back to his carriers. He was figuring on striking us, then landing on Guam nearby. Guam was still held by the Japs. I wanted to go out, but Commander Leonard "Sheik" Southerland, the air officer, said I had better stay. For miles fore and aft, planes were taking off our carrier decks. Commander Ralph Weymouth took off after the fighters with his dive-bombing squadron (VB-16).

Kennedy: Why did you launch the bombers with the Japs beyond range?

Ernie: Because they are so dangerous to the carrier during an attack if they are standing there on deck all gassed up and with their bombs in them. When Ralph got up he decided to go over to Guam and roughen up the landing strips for the Japs before they arrived. He and his boys had a lot of fun strafing the flying fields, and caught some planes on the ground.

The first Japanese planes were intercepted at a considerable distance. We began to hear squadron leaders making reports over their radios like, "Splashed 15 out of 16." Reports of what was going on were coming out of the loudspeakers throughout the ship constantly. You see, only about seven hundred of the approximately three thousand men on one of our big carriers are above deck. It's pretty tough on the rest during an action if you don't let them know what's going on.

Kennedy: The fellows in the engine room?

Ernie: No, it's the damage and fire control parties. They have to wear their flash suits and helmets and it is hot below decks in the tropics. Only the ready rooms for flight personnel and plot are air-conditioned. And they have nothing to do until there's a hit or a fire—it's toughest on them. Off the record, one day everyone was ordered to stand by for dive-bomber attack. The boys of the damage and fire control parties went down on their knees per instructions to brace themselves for the shock. You're much more likely to be useful after a hit if you haven't been thrown against a wall or some tubing. The attack petered out but no one told them about it and two hours later they were found still on their knees.

The search did all right. It was two TBFs and a Hellcat. They were jumped by twelve Zekes. The Hellcat pilot hollered for help and while another fighter nearby was coming to him, he knocked down three of the Zekes. When the other arrived they knocked down three more and drove the rest away.

By this time we could see vapor trails of planes coming in with tiny black specks at the head. The sky was a white overcast and for some reason the planes were making vapor trails at a much lower altitude than usual. That made it much easier for our boys to find them. The air was so clear that you could see planes eight or nine miles away, tiny specks tangling in the sky. Then a flamer would go down. We would hope it was a Jap and from the radio chatter we could hear from the pilots, it seemed that it was the Japs who were getting it.

I went to Sheik Southerland again. "How about my getting into 69? That was the number of the fighter plane I had been using. He gave me an ok. I led a fighter flight off the deck. When I first looked down after feeling secure about the take off, I saw green in the water where a couple of planes had crashed. Our planes have green markers that float in the water and show rescue parties that an American plane has crashed there. I thought: "They're knocking our boys down!" Later I realized that the green effect came from the engine fluid of Jap motors that broke open when they hit the water.

One of my problems coming back was to stay away from the battle fleet in our task force. The AA [antiaircraft] gunners on the battleships don't

look to see who it is in a combat like that. They
fire at every plane in sight.

On my way back I saw three Judys coming
in. They are the Jap torpedo planes. They were
just skimming the water. I dived after the first
one. I figured the pilots following me would take
care of the other two. I gave him a working over.
The tracers seemed to be going right on to him,
but still he didn't blow up. I wiggled the nose of
the plane a bit to be sure he was getting it all over.
My speed was taking me over him and out of
range. Just as I got over him, he blew up—right
under me. Gave me a jolt. Shook me up.

Kennedy: How long was this after you took off?

Ernie: About four minutes. I talked to Commander Joe
Eggert (by radio), the fighter director on the flagship. Joe told me to go up to 20,000 feet and orbit.
I did. At first I was alone, but then my wingman
came along. We were still joining up. The sky
was full of planes and I was ducking them. They
were our planes but unless you make the proper
approach they start shooting.

We were circling up there when we heard
from Joe that there was an attack coming in, but
it was a fighter job—they did not want the group
commander to lead the attack. I turned the flight
over to Elmer Kraft, our fighter executive officer,
and hung on in the formation. However, nothing
happened.

We came down. When I stepped out of my
plane, everybody around me—the men of the
deck crew—were wearing tin hats. Warning had
just come through to stand by for a dive-bomber
attack. I like to have been scared to death! I ran
over to the island and stood under it, donning my
own tin hat.

But the dive-bomber attack never happened. Instead, there was an attack by low flying torpedo bombers a few minutes later. Things were terrific as the automatic antiaircraft guns on the starboard side let go—a gun every few feet down the rail and all going at once. The Judys were all knocked down before they could successfully launch their torpedoes.

Later in the fighter squadron ready room everything was horseplay—kid stuff. Lieutenant Alexander Vraciu of Chicago, the Navy's top ranking ace with nineteen kills to his credit, was being ragged endlessly and unmercifully. "How many did you get?" was asked when he came into the ready room. "Only six!" the boys kept repeating sarcastically. He had come upon a string of Judys coming in and started working over the last one, going up the line. They all blew up.

It was an unbelievable day. From the reports from other carriers we realized that Task Force 58 had knocked down several hundred Jap planes. On our own carrier the score was forty-three for the fighters. There were two more from the bomber and torpedo squadron who had taken off only to get out of the way. The score was forty-five Japs splashed and we had lost only one plane. That was from motor trouble—not from enemy action, and the pilot was fished out.[40]

After mauling the Japanese air arm on the first day, June 19, Task Force 58 was in the hunt for the wounded. The Japanese mobile fleet was retiring on a westerly heading in some haste, but its commander, Admiral Ozawa, was not yet fully cognizant of the extent of the Japanese aircraft losses. The U.S. Fifth Fleet was three hundred miles astern, but the prevailing easterly wind would cause it to have to turn away from the pursuit to launch aircraft, opening the gap. By early morning on

June 20, the Fifth Fleet commander was sifting through the day's intelligence and making known his intent to run up the score and extract
the most favorable outcome of the engagement, sending to Mitscher a
message at 0800: "Damaged *Zuikaku* [remaining Japanese carrier] may
still be afloat. If so, believe she will be headed northwest. Desire to push
our searches today to westward . . . *Zuikaku* must be sunk if we can
reach her."[41] In mid-morning, Ernie huddled with academy classmate
Gus Widhelm to conceive another aggressively bold plan and proposed to Admiral Mitscher a long-range search by bomb-laden F6Fs
well beyond their maximum range. That Gus was serving as Mitscher's
operations officer after recording his own impressive combat record as
an SBD squadron commander on *Hornet* lent credence to their petition. In an audience on the flag bridge, Mitscher considered Ernie's
proposal and "looked him over admiringly. 'They're a long way off.'
Ernie replied unhesitatingly: 'I'll use volunteers.' Mitscher pondered
the offer for a few seconds and decided: 'I've got a search out that
should be back about 1100. If I don't get anything, I'll send you out.'"[42]

Historian Barrett Tillman recorded Ernie's bravado in mounting
this risky mission in his thorough account of the battle of the Philippine Sea, *Clash of the Carriers*:

> Snowden trotted off the flag bridge, headed for Fighting 16's
> ready room to find eleven volunteers. Addressing the Airedales
> [fighter squadron VF-16's popular name], he said, "Chances are
> less than fifty-fifty you'll get back." He chalked a dozen numbers
> on the blackboard with his name in the first spot. Thirty min-
> utes later he returned to find every slot taken. Ernie Snowden
> was part of the reason for *Lexington's* sky-high morale. . . . When
> the regular search teams turned up empty-handed, Snowden
> returned to flag country, suited up for flight. Confirming orders
> for the longest U.S. carrier-based search of the war to date, he
> headed below to man up and launch. As insurance, he had eight
> VF-51 escorts from *San Jacinto*.[43]

Hours later, Ernie brought his search flight back to *Lexington* empty-
handed. Before entering *Lexington's* landing pattern, he could make out
faint radio calls from *Enterprise* pilots who had spotted the remnants of

the Japanese carrier force. At that moment, Air Group 16 made immediate preparations to assemble a ready strike group, striking below Ernie's returning fighters to clear the deck for the first of two planned strike groups.

For Task Force 58, *Enterprise*'s scouting plane reports were the initial sighting of an enemy fleet at the far western reach of his search at mid-afternoon on June 20, revealed by following surface furrows of high-speed wakes tracking to the western horizon. Fueled and armed, Air Group 16's fighters, bombers, and torpedo planes sat in readiness with flight deck crews close by and Air Group 16 pilots with flight gear donned, awaiting intelligence updates in their ready rooms. With acknowledgment and go-ahead for pursuit obtained from Fifth Fleet commander Adm. Raymond Spruance, Task Force 58 commander Mitscher calmly ordered, "Launch 'em." Chief of staff Burke started the order down the command echelons by broadcast on the talk between ships (TBS) net: "All task group commanders from Commander Task Force 58 . . . Launch first deckload as soon as possible . . . Prepare to launch second deckload."[44] Teletypes clattered as the printed strike order was projected on illuminated screens in each squadron ready room. The reconnaissance picture became more refined as fresh reports added enemy fleet disposition, composition, and heading, prompting Burke to again broadcast over the TBS: "All task group commanders from Commander Task Force 58 . . . There are two, possibly three groups of enemy ships. . . . One group, ten to fifteen miles to the north consists of one large carrier, two or three heavy cruisers, and eight destroyers. . . . A southern group has two carriers, two tankers, and a destroyer on a course due west. . . . The third group consisting of one carrier and many other ships is sixty miles west of center group; the primary objective is the carriers!"[45]

On *Lexington* and the other Task Force 58 carriers, the Fox flag was closed up on the yardarm and the green light was turned on, signaling the launch of aircraft at 1630. Ernie positioned himself abeam the flight director, leaning over the railing on the island catwalk to observe the launch and to be clearly visible to departing aircrews. Lt. Henry Kosciusko of VF-16 roared down the flight deck at full throttle to lead the fighter escorts off in advance of *Lexington*'s attack aircraft. Air Group 16 had scheduled thirty-three planes for the strike: eleven

F6Fs, seven TBMs, and fifteen SBDs; one TBM, one SBD, and two F6Fs turned back after launch for mechanical problems. Ernie's group and squadron staffs had organized his remaining squadron aircrews for a second strike launch that would necessitate an attack in waning light with recovery not possible until well after dark. Reasoning that the command responsibility for that second launch should fall to him due to the added risk and uncertainty, Ernie held himself back to assume the lead for the second strike. As the first deckload cleared, Admiral Mitscher paused to consider both the likely range to close on the reported sightings and the hours remaining of usable daylight for recovery of returning aircraft in the first launch. Finally, he quietly said, "Hold that second strike. . . . There's no telling how many we'll lose from this flight. . . . We've got to have something left to hit them with tomorrow."[46]

Ernie had assigned group lead for the first launch to the VB-16 commanding officer, Lt. Cdr. Ralph Weymouth, in whom Ernie had utmost confidence because of the discipline and maturity Weymouth had demonstrated since taking over the squadron from Ernie when fleeting up to CAG. Weymouth, like nearly all the pilots and aircrew of Air Group 16 in general and VB-16 particularly, were plankowners, having labored under Ernie's exacting tutelage in the initial nine months of hard stand-up training in squadron and group tactics and endured the prior eight months of combat through campaigns in the Gilberts and Marshalls under his close in-air leadership. Only four months before this action, Ernie drew singular praise from the commander, Air Forces Pacific Fleet operations staff, observing that Air Group 16 had the "best night rendezvous they had ever seen," a well-rehearsed practice for the group that would prove astoundingly prescient for the coming action.[47] Ernie deliberately apportioned responsibility for leading strikes among his squadron commanders in those early campaigns to hone strike-planning experience and to afford them a visible leadership opportunity at the head of multiplane, multisquadron strikes. Weymouth had performed admirably as strike leader in the Gilberts campaign and only the day before had led strikes by VB-16 and VT-16 on Guam's airfields to render them less useful for Japanese fighters in the current action.

From his catwalk perch, Ernie looked down on the flight deck as Weymouth taxied into position, mentally reviewing the sequence of pre-takeoff checks he knew Weymouth was absorbed in: stowing his navigation table and plotting board beneath the instrument panel; cowl flaps—OPEN; carburetor air—DIRECT; mixture—AUTO RICH; prop—2,600 revolutions per minute (rpm); supercharger—LOW blower; finally, throttle—open to 46.5 inches of manifold pressure, standing on the brakes as he waited for the director's flag to point toward the bow.[48] In the first of the bombers to take off, Weymouth began a gradual turn over the carrier at 1,500 feet to permit an easier join-up for the aircraft taking off in sequence behind him. Air Group 16's aircraft, fully weighted with fuel and ordnance, clawed for altitude, rising from *Lexington* to join their formations holding shallow circling turns over the ship. Three-plane vees joined on their squadron leaders in one massed strike formation that, on Weymouth's cue, singled up on a west by northwest heading to an intercept point projected from the last known enemy sighting. Formation discipline and communication doctrine, regulated and standardized by Ernie over those preceding months of aerial combat, were evident.

SBDs and TBMs settled into familiar formation in three-plane vees behind Weymouth to his right and left. Gently raising his nose, Weymouth started his climb to the group's initial cruise altitude of 9,000 feet, retarding the throttle slightly to 45 inches of manifold pressure, switching the supercharger to HIGH, and picking up his best cruise climb airspeed of 130 mph. At altitude, he closed the cowl flaps, further reduced the throttle setting to around twenty-eight inches, set the prop at two thousand rpm, and gradually increased airspeed to his best cruise speed for the long flight ahead. Lieutenant Kosciusko's fighters took a high perch to the front of the bombers and to the right and left of the SBD squadron. The fighters began weaving in shallow S-turns approximately two thousand to four thousand feet above the bombers to hug the main formation while maintaining speed and altitude advantage for the coming fight. VT-16 skipper Norm Sterrie, leading the TBM flight, was new to command, having replaced Lt. Bob Isely when he was shot down and lost only a week before, but Sterrie had been in the squadron long enough to know his aviators and become familiar with the group's formation tactics. He took his TBMs into a trailing position behind the SBDs.

Figure 2. Members of Air Group 16

VF-16: Grumman F6F Fighters
1. Lt. Henry Kosciusko
2. Ens. Bill Seyfferle
3. Lt. (jg) Art Whiteway
4. Lt. (jg) John Bartol
5. Lt. (jg) Alex Vraciu
6. Ens. H. Brockmeyer
7. Lt. (jg) Jim Arquette
8. Lt. Jim Seybert
9. Ens. Ed Wendorf
10. Lt. Don Kirkpatrick
    AOM2c Richard Bentley
11. Lt. (jg) John Reichel
    ARM2c John Landaker
12. Ens. Gene Conklin
    AOM3c John Sample
13. Lt. Cook Cleland
    ARM2c Bill Hisler
14. Ens. John Caffey
    AOM2c Leo Estrada

VB-16: Douglas SBD Bombers
1. Lt. Cdr. Ralph Weymouth
   ARM1c Bill McElhiney
2. Lt. (jg) James Shields
   ARM2c Leo LeMay
3. Lt. (jg) Tom Sedell
   ARM2c Tony Maggio
4. Lt. Tom Dupree
   ARM2c David Dowdell
5. Lt. (jg) George Glackin
   ARM2c Leo Boulanger
6. Ens. Orville Cook
   ARM2c Ted LeMieux
7. Lt. Bill Harrison
   ARM2c Ray Barrett
8. Lt. (jg) Bill Adams
   ARM2c Henry Kelly
9. Ens. Hank Moyers
   ARM2c Bob Van Etten

VT-16: TBM Torpedo Bombers
1. Lt. Norm Sterrie
   ARM1c Klingbeil
   AMM1c Jack Webb
2. Lt. (jg) Clint Swanson
   ARM2 Rene LeBlanc
   AMM2c Bill Smith
3. Lt. Clyde Bronn
   ARM1c Gene Linson
   AOM1c Mike Banazak
4. Lt. Kent Cushman
   ARM1c Francis Fredo
   AMM1c Phil Layne
5. Lt. Warren McLellan
   ARM2c Selbie Greenhalgh
   AMM2c John Hutchinson
6. Lt. (jg) Harry Thomas
   ARM3c Bob Clasby
   AMM1c Grady Stanfill

Confidence was high, and blood was up. Any apprehension about a difficult recovery at mission's end in darkness aboard an unlighted ship was put aside to be dealt with later. Now, all eyes scanned the horizon for telltale signs of a fleet retiring at high speed. To a man, aircrews were resolute in seeking out a punishing action with the Japanese mobile fleet that would strike a mortal blow—even as they anticipated a desperate fight from a wounded but still resilient enemy. On *Lexington*, the order was given to stand down from flight quarters, but ship's company remained at battle stations should an immediate response be needed to resist a Japanese counterstrike. Among the senior officers in *Lexington*, probably Ernie alone imagined himself at the head of the formation, working through attack maneuvers and imparting some telepathic encouragement and mentoring to each of his pilots; he knew everyone in this strike formation—pilots and enlisted aircrew—by name from close association since the earliest formative days of the air group at Quonset Point.

Ernie's confidence in Weymouth proved well placed. As the flight began to overrun random Japanese destroyers and tankers that were lagging the capital ships, Weymouth resisted the lure of easy targets and pressed onward to the west. After two and a half hours since leaving *Lexington*, the flight emerged from cloud cover and light rain to find the southern group of the mobile fleet arrayed around its two *Hayataka*-class aircraft carriers to their port quarter. The few remaining carrier-borne fighters not splashed by F6Fs from VF-16 and other Task Force 58 fighters the previous day were up and on the prowl from the converted merchantmen *Hiyo* and *Junyo*. The Japanese combat air patrol screening the southern group immediately pounced, dropping a TBM and F6F escort and beginning twenty minutes of unrelenting aerial attacks by Japanese Zekes on the Air Group 16 formation. Arcing left around the western perimeter of the fleet, Weymouth put his formation vees into right echelon for the pushover and diving attack as antiaircraft fire from the ships began to sparkle in the fading light. He was well placed on the roll-in with the sun behind his back, into a strong easterly wind and lined up with his targets on the oblique for optimum bomb spread geometry as the big ships began hard defensive turns to port.[49]

In succession, the bombers rolled over into their attack dives, leveling out with several degrees of separation from each other and aligned

**Figure 3. Air Group 16 Strike on the Japanese
Mobile Fleet's Southern Group, June 20, 1944**

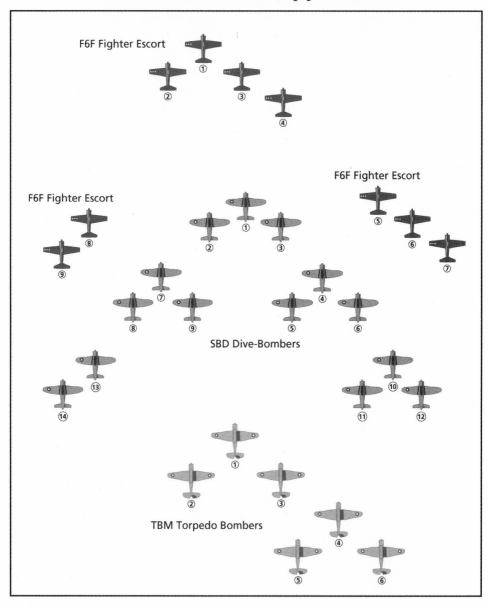

on their attack runs, much like the spokes of a wheel—the better to complicate the aiming solution of the Japanese gunners below. Japanese fighters made firing runs on Weymouth's formation even as they bore down in their bombing runs, the deadly harassment continuing as the bombers banked and jinked away from their targets. Most of the flight concentrated on *Hiyo*, with three SBDs splitting off to take on *Junyo*. When results were compiled from poststrike debriefings of the entire group, Ernie's after action report noted that in less than thirty minutes over the target, his group received sole credit for sinking one large carrier, administering the final blow to sink a second large carrier, and delivering major bomb and torpedo hits to a third carrier—likely *Ryuho*—rendering it ineffective for further flight operations. Air Group 16's exemplary results late on June 20 were not without sacrifice: in addition to the TBM and F6F lost in the initial arcing turn toward the target, a VB-16 SBD with its crew was lost to enemy fire exiting their bomb drop, and at least another TBM, F6F, and SBD were lost while retiring to *Lexington* from fuel starvation or battle damage, although aircrews from the latter three were rescued. That night, in darkness, twenty-two planes groped their way back to recover on *Lexington*'s flight deck, only ten of those belonging to Air Group 16. The remainder recovered on other Task Force 58 carriers, seeking any identifiably friendly flight deck as their fuel neared exhaustion.[50]

Following the battle, *Lexington* retired for refit to the fleet anchorage at Eniwetok, taking on a new air group. Air Group 16 stood down, with aircrews allowed well-deserved leave. Upon his return stateside the following month, Ernie would again find himself pressed into service for the benefit of public affairs and public morale. Escorted by Navy media specialists, Ernie was brought into a Navy public relations branch studio to recount his impressions of the recent action in the Philippine Sea on the "March of Time" radio broadcast. His interviewer prompted him with a short introduction:

> Tonight, a veteran of [the] Marianas campaign from the battle of the fleets west of Saipan to the bombardment of Guam is at our March of Time microphone. He is Commander Ernest M. Snowden, one

of the first air group commanders to return from the Marianas. Commander Snowden's group— Carrier Air Group 16—was based on Vice Admiral Marc Mitscher's flagship in famed Task Force 58 and has a record better than twenty to one against the Japs. Commander Snowden . . .

Ernie: The Admiral's operations officer, Gus Widhelm, offered to bet one thousand dollars that we would have a carrier fight. Gus was quickly covered, I can tell you, and by men who hoped they'd lose their bets. That's how anxious we were to get the Jap fleet to stand up to us. So the fighters and scouts were sent out with orders to watch for carrier planes. One of them spotted a Jap plane, all right, and came up underneath him—close enough to see his tailhook. That meant he was a carrier plane. Then he pulled back and shot him down. We knew we were near the Jap fleet. But first the Japs sent in their best-trained, land-based night torpedo squadron to get our carriers. We shot down all but one of them. A few days later, our planes took off for what turned out to be what we call the Marianas Turkey Shoot. My air group shot down forty-five Jap planes without the loss of a single pilot or air crewman. Altogether, Task Force 58 shot down over four hundred enemy planes that day, the first day of the battle of the Eastern Philippines. However, winning a fight like that isn't just shooting down enemy planes. That's merely the defensive work. It's the dive bombers and torpedo planes that carry the fight to the enemy, and they're under instructions not to shoot unless they're attacked. How well they did their job is shown by the fact that Air Group 16 scored sixteen direct hits on one 28,000-ton Jap carrier, sinking her, and scored two direct hits on another similar carrier, actually sunk by another air group. And those dive bombers and torpedo planes had to fight their way in, and fight their way out under constant attack. But then the planes had to get home. They'd gone some eighty miles farther than expected, and flying back at night, they probably figured they only had a fifty-fifty chance. And then Task Force 58 did a daring thing. They turned on searchlights and any other lights that would help the pilots and told them by radio to land on any carrier they could. Those boys had taken great risks to hit the Japs hard and we were willing to take any risk to get them back. There was a time when a pilot who landed at sea had little or no chance. Now he can be shot down on enemy islands, harbors, or in the middle of the Jap fleet, and we'll go in and bring him back. In fact, nobody in naval aviation is expendable, and our losses have been so much less than the most optimistic estimates, that the Navy has actually had to cut back its pilot training. However, don't let anybody tell you the Pacific war is easy. Personally, I believe we will have to fight every inch of the way to Tokyo, kill each Jap individually, or let him commit hari-kiri [sic]. And that's going to take a long time.[51]

Air Group 16's tally was the destruction of forty-five Japanese aircraft on June 19 and participation in the sinking of a carrier and four tankers—and probably a second carrier, tanker, and destroyer—in raids on the retiring Japanese mobile fleet on June 20. The record shows that, under Ernie's leadership from the month of the air group's commissioning the year prior until his relinquishing of command in July 1944, CVG-16 amassed a spectacularly effective combat record, placing it in the top three of all carrier air groups then operating in the Pacific.[52] Among the group's accomplishments in that period were the following:

- 125 enemy planes destroyed on the ground
- 150 enemy planes destroyed in the air (137 by VF-16; 11 by VB-16; 2 by VT-16)
- Sole credit for sinking one large aircraft carrier and delivering the finishing blow to a second large aircraft carrier, then scoring a major bomb and/or torpedo hit on a third large aircraft carrier
- Sole credit for sinking one large attack transport and delivering finishing blows to eight large and medium transports and one smaller transport
- Sole credit for sinking a fleet oiler
- Credit for delivering finishing blows on a damaged fleet destroyer
- Credit for major bomb and/or torpedo hits on at least eight coastal vessels or large patrol boats. [53]

This illustrious record prompted Task Force 58 commander Vice Admiral Mitscher to fire off a naval dispatch on July 10 to Ernie and Air Group 16, along with his USS *Enterprise* counterpart, Cdr. William Kane and Air Group 10: "YOU LEAVE THE AREA WITH THE BEST WISHES OF THE ENTIRE FORCE X YOU HAVE DONE A GRAND JOB AND DESERVE THE HIGHEST HONORS X HAVE FUN AND DON'T DRINK ROT GUT AND DON'T DO ANYTHING THAT I WOULDN'T DO X GOD BLESS YOU."[54]

Word traveled up and down the chain of command quickly, as commander in chief Pacific, Admiral Nimitz, added his own naval dispatch to Air Group 16 on July 16: "CONGRATULATIONS UPON COMPLETION OF YOUR COMBAT TOUR PERFORMED IN AN OUTSTANDING MANNER X WE ARE ALL PROUD OF YOUR SUCCESS X WELL DONE."[55]

For the action in the battle of the Philippine Sea on June 19–20, Ernie was proud to personally draft citations, adding his endorsement as the air wing commander, for the Navy Cross for his three squadron skippers: Paul Buie (VF-16), Ralph Weymouth (VB-16), and Norm Sterrie (VT-16). He happily added his endorsement to his skippers' nominations for another three Navy Crosses in the torpedo squadron and fifteen for the bombing squadron, as well as the Distinguished Flying Cross for every enlisted aircrewman in both the torpedo and bombing squadrons. For his part in organizing, preparing, and inspiring Air Group 16's successful actions during June 11–20, and particularly for his personal leadership of air group strikes that destroyed warehouses, supply dumps, numerous vehicles, and parked aircraft on the ground on Guam and Saipan, neutralizing much of the Japanese land-based air complement prior to the coming battle at sea, Ernie was presented with the Silver Star by Vice Admiral Mitscher at quarters on *Lexington*'s flight deck before the assembled ship's company and air group personnel.

Following these events closely consumed the little free time that Ernie's younger brother had. By June 1944, Mac was a nineteen-year-old youngster—or second-year midshipman—at the Naval Academy. Life as a midshipman was exacting and academically rigorous, and Mac neither distinguished himself nor allowed his grades to drop to an average requiring an appearance at the "long green table" of a convened academic board. He had lost none of his zeal for aviation and still saw that as his future profession. News of Ernie's exploits only reinforced his ambition to fly fighter aircraft from a carrier deck.

Mac arrived for his Naval Academy induction to an Annapolis little changed in physical appearance from the year of Ernie's graduation a decade earlier. Main Street architecture bore predominantly the same colonial brick facades that would have been an everyday sight for Annapolis resident and signer of the Declaration of Independence William Paca, more than 150 years before. Only the shops' owners and their signage had been updated to cater to mid-twentieth-century consumerism, though wartime rationing of staples had been decreed by the U.S. Office of Price Administration only the month before Mac's arrival. In the words of contemporary Annapolis architects, the town had "charming irregularity, picturesque idiosyncrasy and the messy vitality of over 300 years of human occupancy."[56]

The rhythm of life Mac experienced as a midshipman was little changed from Ernie's time in the yard. Academic standards had undergone wholesale revision in the late 1920s, yielding accreditation for the bachelor of science degree in 1930. Bachelor's degrees would not be conferred until 1933 when, by act of Congress, the academy was permitted to award them to all graduates along with their commissions—Ernie would graduate with only a diploma in 1932. The curriculum, however, was essentially unchanged: liberal portions of calculus, statistics, marine engineering, seamanship and navigation, thermodynamics, physics, and chemistry. The only elective open for both brothers was the foreign language each chose to study. Both had to take instruction in aviation in their engineering coursework, but there would have been substantial differences in content reflective of the rapid advance of aviation science and application in the fleet in the years between 1932 and 1945.

Yet there were marked contrasts in their respective academy experiences, owing to the wartime mood that prevailed during Mac's time as a midshipman. Mac's class would be the fourth accelerated class in a row to miss an entire junior year, graduating in three years. Summer cruise, a regular feature of the midshipman experience between academic years, would, for Mac, not include transoceanic steaming on large surface combatants. Most cruisers and battleships, even those probably too old to risk under fire in the open Atlantic, were needed elsewhere. Perhaps the most visible reminder of the wartime atmosphere during Mac's entire time at the academy was the construction of gun mounts, directors, and a plotting room along the Severn River seawall installed for midshipman loading drills and gunfire spotting practice.

Required reading during Mac's first summer at the academy began with *Makers of Naval Tradition* by Carroll Alden and Ralph Earle, which grounded new students in the legendary icons of the naval profession. From chapter to chapter, plebes were introduced to the likes of Jones, Decatur, Dahlgren, Mahan, and Dewey. It was not lost on Mac that the last chapter, "Makers of Tradition of Our Day," was reserved for the exploits of naval aviators Marc Mitscher, John Towers, and A. C. Read in attempting the first trans-Atlantic crossing by airplane. This comported perfectly with Mac's ideal of the traditional and future winged naval leader, one that he fervently aspired to be.

In April 1943, when Mac was a plebe, or freshman, USS *Lexington* paid a port call on Annapolis, steaming up the Chesapeake Bay and anchoring at the mouth of the Severn River to host midshipman visits. As he had done four years earlier during his own flight to Beaufort's small airport, Ernie—then commanding officer of Bombing Squadron 16 in *Lexington*—made sure that Mac received a personally guided tour of the ship's bridge, of squadron spaces on the ship including the ready room, and of the squadron's factory-new SBD-5 Dauntless dive bombers stowed on the hangar deck.

Mac would spend the better part of that summer commuting daily across the Severn River to further his technical knowledge in non-credit coursework hosted by training squadron VN-8. In classrooms adjoining aircraft hangars, Macon sat raptly through instruction in subjects such as theoretical bombing, aviation gunnery, and aeronautics lessons in airfoil and propeller design, stability, controllability, and maneuverability. Classroom time was augmented by back-seat orientation in VN-8's assigned Curtiss SOC-1 Seagull and Vought OS2U Kingfisher floatplanes.[57]

6

Transition

*In these few years since December 7, 1941, our dauntless Navy has
amazed the world. Bravo, Navy! Hail, Men of '46. The blessings, prayers
and fervent hopes of the entire Nation are with you now.* Godspeed—
and Happy Landings!

—1946 *Lucky Bag*

The members of the class of 1946, one of the shortened wartime
academy classes, bypassed their junior year. Mac went immediately from youngster year to first-class midshipman in his last year
at the academy. In June 1945—just as halfway around the globe Air
Group 87 aircraft from USS *Ticonderoga* attacked airfields on Kyushu,
Japan, to preempt kamikaze aircraft from launching attacks on the U.S.
fleet—Mac escorted his future wife, Evelyn, to the Farewell Ball in
Dahlgren Hall, the largest ever hosted at the academy.[1] "A sea of brilliant colors swayed to the barely audible strains of Lt. Sima's Music-
Makers," in one last relaxed evening before graduation the next day.[2]
Ironically, in another twenty years from that night, Mac would com-
mand Air Wing Five from the deck of *Ticonderoga* in an attack on targets around Hanoi in North Vietnam.

Throughout most of the twentieth century, academy and Navy
policy dictated that graduates serve at least several years at sea before
starting any specialized training such as aviation. So it would be that
Mac would serve upon commissioning as first lieutenant and fire control officer in USS *Caperton* (DD 650), in which he replaced Ens.
Forrest Petersen as the junior officer aboard. Mac, with Forrest and
the rest of the *Caperton* crew, would serve the remaining few months

of the war performing picket duty screening for kamikaze attacks and then, after hostilities ended, in occupation duty in Tokyo Bay. A decade after the *Caperton* tour, Mac would be rejoined by Forrest in class seventeen at the Navy's test pilot school in Patuxent River, Maryland. Months together at sea, at everyday morning quarters and daily meals in the wardroom, as well as during anxious moments at battle stations on the picket line off Okinawa, formed an enduring friendship that would last well beyond that first tour.

From the *Caperton* tour, Mac reported to USS *Knight* (DMS 40) as damage control officer and finally reported for flight training to Naval Air Station Dallas in January 1947. He could not have foreseen the momentous changes that would soon roil naval aviation. Some of the lingering effects of the postwar winddown, mainly reduced funding appropriations for naval aviation, seemed to be overtaken by the appearance of new threats in a changed world order and even more so by the rapid onset of new technologies, from jets to tactical nuclear weapons.

When Ernie entered naval aviation at least a decade earlier, biplanes were giving way to monoplanes, and carrier tactics were rapidly maturing. Now, in the late 1940s, Mac was entering the trade as propellers were making way for jet turbines and carriers were adapting to the generational advances in aircraft performance by reengineering changes such as angled decks to accommodate them.

As surely as the battle of Midway marked the turning point for the United States in the war in the Pacific, the resounding defeat of Japanese naval air forces at the battle of the Marianas indicated that U.S. naval aviation had hit its stride in exercising a new lethal warfighting effectiveness against the Imperial Japanese Navy. The war would grind on at high pitch for another year against a fanatical Japanese navy with diminishing wherewithal to resist, culminating in a massive flyover of the U.S. Navy's air armada to mark the Japanese surrender in Tokyo Bay.

But by July 1944, Ernie's war was over. To be sure, his talents and experience would still be employed while overseeing assigned air groups on the staff of commander, Fleet Air (COMFAIR) in Alameda, California, and later, while preparing and justifying plans for new and modernized aircraft carriers in Washington, D.C. Yet he would not again experience the strain of extended periods of combat at sea or the intensity of emotion in leading naval aviators in aerial warfare. By July 1945, good fortune would bring Ernie and Mac together in the San Francisco Bay area—Ernie on the COMFAIR staff in Alameda and Mac assigned to *Caperton*, then pierside at Hunters Point. Ernie, capitalizing on Mac's proximity just across the bay, made what he thought was good use of one more opportunity to stoke his younger brother's enthusiasm for aviation. Ernie scheduled himself for proficiency flight time in an SNJ trainer assigned to the Alameda air station and took Mac on a two-hour familiarization flight over Alameda, Oakland, and Sausalito. Within days, Mac would ship out on *Caperton* to join the fleet then preparing for invasion of the Japanese home islands. With the announcement of the Japanese surrender in mid-August, Ernie booked himself on naval air transport to the operating area around Japan, ostensibly as part of his staff duties for COMFAIR Pacific. By another stroke of fortune, the Snowden brothers would both be in Tokyo Bay on September 2. *Caperton* was anchored in the bay with the U.S. Fleet for the formal Japanese surrender aboard USS *Missouri*. Ernie had high-lined to USS *Randolph* (CV 15) outside Tokyo Bay. He was then accorded a singular honor of participating as a flight crew member in a 1,200-aircraft flyover, led by 450 U.S. Navy TBMs, SB2Cs, F4Us, and F6Fs. This was the culminating moment of the Japanese surrender ceremony, and Ernie was flying in the rear seat of a VB-16 SB2C Helldiver flown by Lt. Cdr. Roland McMackin. McMackin was one of VB-16's plank-owners who had served with Ernie since the stand-up of the squadron at Quonset, Rhode Island, in early 1943 through Ernie's departure from Air Group 16 in June 1944. McMackin had remained with VB-16 throughout the war and, when the air group transferred to USS *Randolph*, continued flying strikes with the squadron on Japanese airfields until just two weeks before the formal ceremony. On *Caperton,* anchored in the bay alongside an Allied fleet that numbered ten battleships, fifteen cruisers, and four dozen destroyers, the sight of the massed air armada astounded Mac. Knowing his brother Ernie was in the air, he could not have been more proud but was also a little envious. He knew he had to endure another two years of sea duty in destroyers before orders arrived for flight training. But now, in this celebratory moment, both brothers were overtaken by a surge of emotion that was part relief, part joy, and part sorrow for shipmates, squadronmates, and classmates who had been lost over the preceding four years to make this moment possible. Though not immediately obvious by either brother, this was a transcendent moment for both. The naval aviation career of one had plateaued, and that of the other was about to begin arcing upward. Ernie possessed the satisfaction that came from leading a squadron and air group in combat in the Navy's biggest test since its inception. All that followed for Ernie in his professional life seemed perfunctory and lacked that intensity and meaningful gratification. Mac would soon go to flight training and eventually put his own mark on the profession, ultimately experiencing the same fulfillment but also enduring deep disappointment at the conclusion of his career.

Within six months, Capt. Arleigh Burke contacted Ernie, urging him to accept a new assignment with the forming Eighth Fleet. Adm. Marc Mitscher had been picked to command the new fleet and was given the national security policy objective of reasserting U.S. military presence in the Mediterranean. The admiral and Captain Burke were fond of Ernie and impressed by his leadership of Air Group 16 when embarked together in *Lexington*. What they had in mind now was to bring Ernie on to the fleet staff as the air operations officer and principal aviation adviser to Admiral Mitscher. The new Eighth Fleet put to sea for mock battle in an exercise that was observed from USS *Franklin Roosevelt* by President Harry S. Truman, Secretary of the Navy James Forrestal, and Fleet Adm. Chester Nimitz, now Chief of Naval Operations (CNO). The Army Air Forces, determined to embarrass the Navy and bolster its argument that aircraft carriers in the atomic age were an anachronism, timed a heavy bomber assault on the Eighth Fleet for the moment that the distinguished visitors were aboard. The Air Force's anticarrier cabal, eager to discredit Mitscher for his postwar assertions that carrier supremacy won the victory in the Pacific, mounted the mock attack without official notice or invitation, with the expectation of overwhelming the fleet's defenses.

The setting for the Air Force's attack was freighted with particular historic import: near these waters a generation earlier, Gen. Billy

Mitchell had bombed and sunk an anchored battleship, the World War I German prize *Ostfriesland,* to demonstrate the vulnerability of warships to air attack. For the assault on *Roosevelt* and the Eighth Fleet, the bombs were simulated, the ships were moving, and the ship's defenses were themselves airborne. Historian E. B. Potter noted: "The air force planners may have counted heavily on the brevity of its [Eighth Fleet] training. If so, they must have been unaware that the training had been carried out by the Mitscher-Burke-Griffin [Fleet Operations Officer]-Snowden team."[3] Admiral Mitscher was fully briefed on the air plan by Ernie several days prior to putting to sea. As the encounter unfolded, Captain Burke escorted President Truman to the flag plot where he could watch events on radar repeating screens. In his biography of Burke, Potter presented an assessment of Ernie's contribution:"Snowden had drilled his pilots in using a modification of Joe Eggert's [Lt. Joe Eggert, Task Force 58 fighter director in USS *Lexington* in June 1944] tactical plan that achieved the Turkey Shoot. He lacked fighters to build a defensive wall of planes, but those he had stacked themselves at great height, whence they swooped down upon the oncoming, unsuspecting attackers. Had the carrier planes opened fire, the air force planes would have been clobbered, and their pilots knew it. The rules of the game required them to acknowledge defeat by turning back, and they did. Their attack had ignominiously backfired."[4] Scuttlebutt circulated around the Eighth Fleet about what had just happened, but at the moment that *Roosevelt*'s aircraft returned overhead, the party of distinguished visitors congratulated their hosts with some exuberance and cheered the naval aviators' return from the bridge wing. This was one of the opening salvos in an interservice struggle that would go on for several years as a newly created U.S. Air Force overestimated its own importance and maneuvered for dominance over the other services—particularly the Navy—in the defense reorganization of 1947.

The interservice struggle was only one outward eruption of the tremendous tensions and anxieties that settled over the defense establishment in the aftermath of World War II. "Sudden and rapid demobilization of the armed forces resulted in near chaos, uncertainty, and lack of purpose and direction. Within the aviation navy, carriers and squadrons were decommissioned at an astounding rate."[5] The Navy's primary peacetime challenge now became to maintain its relevance by evolving and adapting to a revitalized strategic posture just as new weapons and aircraft were making its recent war-winning Pacific operational doctrine obsolete—and to do that while maintaining a robust overseas presence commitment in a new postwar national security environment. The Navy's battlefield "shifted rapidly from the waters of the Atlantic and Pacific to the halls of the Pentagon and the committee rooms of Congress."[6]

The Air Force's new assertiveness coalesced around the massively large B-36 bomber, which according to Air Force talking points in those years had rendered the Navy's carrier-borne naval aviation irrelevant in the age of the atomic bomb and the means to deliver it by long-range, land-based jet bomber. Not willing to cede its role as a principal means of delivering airpower at significant range—proved over great ocean distances in the war just won—the Navy had started planning for construction of a new aircraft carrier to handle more capable, longer range jet aircraft, the USS *United States*.

In an effort to construct stronger intellectual underpinnings for its argument, the Navy initiated a more comprehensive survey of its role in postwar defense strategy. The General Board, a distant forerunner of today's CNO Advisory Board, was appointed to this task, directed by Capt. Arleigh Burke, recently assigned to the strategic studies cell on the Chief of Naval Operations staff (OPNAV). The General Board concluded that the Navy's initial tasks of control of the seas and attack on forward Russian bases, coupled with the logistical supporting effort for the other services, would place demands on the service well beyond its capacity. The rise of a newly realized Soviet submarine threat added to the complexity of the problem. In part, the study contributed to the Navy's pursuit of a middle ground in justifying USS *United States*, knowing the fiscal environment was growing increasingly difficult. USS *United States* would be commissioned primarily as an instrument for delivery of strategic atomic weapons, but she would have the capacity to achieve a number of conventional objectives as well. The logic seems true today, but in this era, the secretary of defense viewed it as duplicative to the capability offered by the Air Force.

The General Board's work concluded, Arleigh Burke departed for a fleet tour, only to return in some haste to the strategic studies shop at OPNAV by the end of 1948. Under mounting pressure for defense unification and subordination of naval aviation under the Air Force favored by Secretary of Defense Louis Johnson, Burke's task was to deconstruct the Air Force arguments for the B-36 and to prepare the analysis supporting both a primary strategic role and a secondary conventional role for the Navy in general and for naval aviation specifically.

In mid-1949, the air warfare division under the deputy CNO for air produced a report that made the most cogent argument yet for carrier-based airpower, and one that became generally embraced by naval aviation in future force planning:

> Carrier aviation must retain the bulk of its strength in offensive power if it is to support a truly offensive Navy rather than a defensive one. Our Navy must carry out numerous functions other than defensive antisubmarine warfare and must possess the self-contained ability to move at will and wage offensive war against the enemy in the air, on the surface and below the surface. . . . The Air Warfare Division report made clear that heavy attack aircraft and nuclear weapons would play only a minor role in naval aviation. It recommended that heavy attack planes be kept to a minimum in designing carrier air groups and that emphasis be placed instead on general purpose fighter aircraft with offensive and defensive capabilities and on day attack and close air support attack airplanes.[7]

Although Burke was in the strategic studies division of the staff and not the air warfare division, their report clearly benefitted from the rigor of his analyses and bore the hallmarks of his strategic thinking and counsel. Nonetheless, when Secretary Johnson cancelled the appropriations request for USS *United States* in an act of unmistakable bias toward the Air Force agenda, the interservice battle was joined in full. Navy leadership made its case to Congress in defiance of the defense secretary's direction in an act known since as the "Revolt of the Admirals." They argued for the warfighting utility of carrier air and against the shortcomings of the B-36. By testifying before Congress against the Air

Force agenda and for carrier airpower, CNO Adm. Louis Denfield was subsequently fired for making a principled stand on behalf of his service's future. In the purge that followed, more senior Navy officers were cashiered. Burke's name was withheld from the flag promotion list for his part in the "revolt," but the senior civilian leadership stopped short of forcing him into retirement. Burke was all the more surprised because of the central role he played in crafting the revolt's arguments. But in a turn of fortune, the civilian leadership viewed him as the most pragmatic and least dogmatic of the "insurrectionists" and thus worthy of retention. Incoming CNO Adm. Forrest Sherman recognized those same traits and took note that Burke's new immunity conferred on him a degree of cachet with those same civilian leaders.

Inheriting a staff in disarray since Denfield's firing, Admiral Sherman needed to stanch the service's loss of standing with and respect from the Office of the Secretary of Defense and most probably the president. The preservation of a defining role for not only naval aviation but also the naval service as a co-equal branch at the outset of the Cold War was paramount. Sherman understood that Burke was the indispensable man in that undertaking. As Sherman's protégé, Burke was moved through a succession of increasingly visible and career-broadening posts, including as the deputy chief of staff to the commander, Naval Forces Far East. Here, he served in a role of utmost importance to Sherman as his eyes and ears in the planning for the Inchon landings in Korea.

Burke's progression was a calculated part of his grooming for future senior Navy leadership. Intimate conversations between Sherman and Burke would invariably turn to how best and with whom to populate OPNAV to ensure that their design for naval aviation and for the Navy's strategic posture more generally maintained continuity through subsequent leadership changes and challenges from the other services. Critically, they needed experienced and capable officers in key positions that they personally knew would be loyal, energetic, and supportive. That Ernie's name would be spoken often and in laudable terms in these consultations was a foregone conclusion. Both Sherman and Burke knew Ernie well. For months at a time in 1944, Ernie had been a frequent visitor to *Lexington*'s nerve center, working long hours shoulder-to-shoulder with Burke in flag plot, with Mitscher present on the edge of the room observing the dynamic interaction. Sherman was the commanding officer of *Wasp* during the first six months in 1942 of Ernie's command of VS-72 in *Wasp*, and in press interviews that fall he spoke highly of Ernie's skill and the effectiveness of his leadership in combat right up to *Wasp*'s inglorious end. Whatever his personal quirks, Ernie was remembered for his combat leadership, for his ability to grasp and articulate the strategic picture, and for his advocacy of naval aviation bred through a dozen years in cruiser-based scouting aircraft and carrier-based fighters. Sherman was elated to receive Ernie's invitation in December 1949—barely two months into Sherman's tenure as CNO—to a reunion dinner of former *Wasp* shipmates, held at the naval air training base at Corpus Christi, Texas. Applying his hard-earned operational and flying experience as the director of training on the staff of the chief of naval air training, Ernie would not have to wait long for orders to OPNAV in the Pentagon.

In all these interactions, Ernie's personal habits were not known or at least were not considered disqualifying in any way among Navy seniors. On Lois' side of the family, there was some consternation about her and Ernie's hard partying and heavy drinking, which continued at some level after the war. However Ernie might have rationalized rumors of his behavior, a now-retired General Arnold felt enough concern to write to Ernie and Lois in the winter of 1948, counseling: "This must be read as one of those father to son and daughter letters. These letters are not easy to write, but I believe necessary. . . . For some time I have been convinced that you both are drinking more than people of your age should—more than does you any good—so much that it may be detrimental to your future. Won't you both think this over carefully? Everyone in the services that I have met who knows you has spotted you as real outstanding people. I am not preaching— for God knows I am not that kind—but where you have so much ahead of you, why spoil it?"[8] How Ernie or Lois processed this advice is not known. What is known is that Ernie performed admirably in a succession of posts to follow and earned further plaudits for his lasting contributions to naval aviation that would benefit the service in future

conflicts. Younger brother Mac was a singular example of a rising generation of naval aviators behind Ernie that would benefit directly from
the carrier modernization and recapitalization programs that Ernie
shepherded through the Navy staff in the Pentagon.

Wed for just over ten years by then, the patterns of behavior in Ernie
and Lois' relationship were set and readily observed by those close
enough to witness them outside of working hours. Until social mores
changed years later, at least in the 1930s, '40s, and '50s, going to sea
for extended periods of time was the exclusive domain of men, and
women, as their spouses, were called to dutifully observe a support
role, coordinating household affairs while the husband was deployed
and yielding as the head of household to him upon his return. These
were generally accepted roles in American military society of the time
and were even codified to a degree in one of the most circulated and
observed manuals of that time, "Guidelines: Naval Social Customs,"
wherein wives were counseled: "Your attitude will make a great difference in your husband's job, his career . . . in short, his happiness. The
more you give of your time and your efforts, the more satisfaction
you will receive. Realize your obligation to the community of which
you are a part as well as our own Navy."[9] Lois was not unaccustomed
to the ways of military life, and despite frequent moves and consign-
ment to base quarters as a young girl, she was the product of a fairly
privileged life as the daughter of an upwardly mobile career officer.
This offered some insulation from the societal displacement wrought
by the Depression. Most accounts of her personality mention a kind
of irreverence, even rebelliousness, punctuated by dramatic turns. Hap
Arnold's biographer, Tom Coffey, noted that "Lois' waywardness was
becoming a cause for deep concern" before she was of an age to
leave home. But in Ernie, she found exactly the right match for her
need for domesticity spiced with a modicum of revelry. She embraced
her role as the dutiful wife and smart hostess to his frequent partying with squadron members, entertaining classmates, senior officers,
and the occasional Hollywood celebrity on location film shoots. That
they never had children removed them as a couple from the duties

and distractions of parenthood and freed them to pursue a very gregarious lifestyle up until they decided to separate in the early 1950s. Lois spent most of the rest of her life in Sonoma, California, near the Arnold family ranch on the side of the Sonoma Valley, until passing away on September 26, 1964.

Mac married Evelyn Grass in June 1946 in a small ceremony in the base chapel at Naval Station Treasure Island, a landfill of quarried rock piled on top of Yerba Buena Shoals in San Francisco Bay. They remained together for forty-six years until her death in July 1992. Evelyn, the youngest of four children, grew up in a family that was less well equipped than Lois Arnold's to deal with the privations of the Depression. They resided in Culloden, West Virginia, for most of Evelyn's youth, not a prosperous town by any measure and one considerably burdened by the financial downturn in the 1930s. From a young age, Evelyn was expected to tend a family vegetable plot to supplement the family's subsistence. She was energetic and curious but never a problem for her parents, always a well-behaved and generous child, self-aware of her natural beauty but possessed of a modest demeanor. Yet she looked outward in her late teens for the opportunity that could take her beyond the meager circumstances imposed by life in rural West Virginia. The U.S. entry into war in the 1940s unexpectedly brought opportunity—she enlisted in the Navy and was stationed at the Washington Navy Yard as a yeoman performing clerical duties. She met midshipman Mac Snowden and began a relationship that continued after her discharge at the end of the war. Evelyn adapted well to the demands of being a Navy wife and happily provided the support that kept the home in good order during Mac's long absences on cruise. A junior officer, later reflecting on his first squadron assignment, encountered her as the wife of his squadron's commanding officer, commenting: "She was *special*. I thought she was the epitome of what a supportive Navy wife should be." That Mac and Evelyn had three children may have brought a stability to their family life that was lacking in Ernie and Lois' home, but it also ironically served to bring Ernie and Mac closer together over time. Ernie took great pleasure in visiting with Mac's children, which brought Ernie and Mac into a closer fraternal regard. In surveying the brothers' careers, the less visible and less easily confirmed truth is that both were well supported by wives who understood that their husbands' Navy service demanded a constant and conscientious observance of protocol and that their unofficial duties as Navy spouses became increasingly more important to their husbands' careers as they advanced in rank. As the wives of squadron commanders, they were expected to hold together an affiliation of officer and enlisted wives of squadron members as social directors, news reporters, grief counselors, and especially mentors to more junior wives who had not yet fully adapted to the year-long—sometime longer—absences of husbands on cruise, and both Lois and Evelyn met and exceeded that standard.

Aircraft modernization proceeded apace. Jet power rapidly replaced propeller-driven fighter aircraft in the five years after the war. As a new threat to U.S. carriers at sea emerged from long-range Soviet bombers, the need increased for more capable, heavier jet aircraft that could fly out from the carrier deck at greater speed and intercept inbound threats at greater distance from the carrier. The science and engineering of aerodynamic design lurched forward to meet the requirement: "In 1946, nobody knew that a high-performance jet fighter needed such appurtenances as a stabilator (instead of an elevator); irreversible hydraulic flight controls with artificial feel; redundant hydraulic systems; pitch and yaw stability augmentation; ejection seats; air conditioning; and others."[10]

The earliest jet engines were commonly centrifugal flow designs that channeled air outward from the core to an array of burner cans that resembled the radial piston designs they replaced. The centrifugal flow designs were not the most efficient, and because of their girth and large frontal area, they presented a challenge for the fuselage designers. With the adoption of the axial flow engine and a more simplified single-spool compressor, greater thrust could be achieved with a much smaller frontal area, permitting a more streamlined fuselage. Speeds increased greatly, but recovery at the ship necessitated slower approach speeds from which jets struggled if required to wave off due to longer engine spool-up time. For the slow-speed flight regime, new appurtenances such as slats and speedbrakes appeared on jet aircraft.

The carrier itself evolved in design features to accommodate the jets in a safer and more operationally efficient manner. An angled deck was built out to provide more landing area while preserving space forward for parking aircraft that had already recovered or were being readied for the next launch cycle. Perhaps the greatest innovation of this time was the mirror landing system on the port side amidships that provided pilots visual light cues for maintaining the optimal landing configuration. All of these advancements occurred in the short time between the end of World War II in 1945 and the early 1950s. Learning these lessons required a trial and error process that resulted in the fielding and rapid obsolescence of a series of different jets, each reflecting solutions to the defects discovered in earlier models.[11] The result was "near catastrophic accident rates. In 1954 alone, the Navy/ Marine Corps accident rate was almost fifty-five major mishaps per hundred thousand flight hours, meaning that 776 aircraft and 535 aviators were lost."[12]

That naval aviation was able to accommodate these disruptive influences and still emerge from the postwar decade as a dominant aviation force at sea was a testament to the leadership of the war veterans such as Ernie and the character and motivation of the most junior officers then entering the profession. One of these was Mac Snowden, who was taking his first steps toward his own naval aviation career when he reported to the Naval Air Basic Training Command at Naval Air Station (NAS) Dallas in January 1947. In quick succession, Mac progressed through basic and advanced training at NAS Dallas, NAS Corpus Christi, NAS Pensacola, and NAS Jacksonville, amassing forty hours in the N2S Kaydet—more commonly known as the Stearman or Yellow Peril—another two hundred hours in the SNJ Texan, and finally ninety-three hours of advanced training in the F4U-4 Corsair. The F4U-4 that Mac flew in advanced training was the last in the series of the gullwing fighter and had flown in combat against the Japanese in the closing six months of the war. The "Dash 4," arguably the best all-around fighter-bomber in any theater at the war's close, was at the pinnacle of fighter design that began immediately before the war and accelerated during the war years.

The Dash 4 was hugely improved over earlier F4U designs with the incorporation of additional power provided by a Pratt and Whitney R2800–24W—developing 2,450 brake horsepower with water injection—and a new four-bladed propeller. Although more demanding of a new student pilot than the SNJ Mac had left behind, the F4U-4's handling was responsive and predictable. Maneuverability was first rate: when rolling—especially left in the direction of powerplant torque—roll rate was comparable to other top-of-the-line U.S. fighters. Despite its size and weight, the Corsair could outclimb the Army Air Forces P-51 Mustang by eight hundred feet per minute; and when accelerating in level flight, the Corsair could best the P-51 by achieving 2.4 mph/second to the P-51's 2.2 mph/second. And top-end speed for the Corsair—446 mph at 26,000 feet—was 29 mph faster than that for the P-51.[13] Only in very slow speed turns could an adversary such as the Japanese A6M Zero gain the advantage. Yet tactics could overcome even that shortcoming in maneuverability advantage.

With his ninety-three hours in the F4U-4, Mac reported aboard Fighting Squadron 21 at Naval Auxiliary Air Station Oceana, Virginia, in August 1948. There his first taste of operational flying would come in the last in the series of Corsairs to be widely used in fleet squadrons—the F4U-5 Corsair, or "Dash 5," which incorporated major changes based on the knowledge gained during the war years. First, the engine was uprated to the 32W variant, featuring a dual supercharger to further boost engine power. Due to the increase in horsepower, the fuselage was actually lengthened by five inches and the engine angled down two degrees for more stability. "Until the dash 5, the outer top wing panels and the control surfaces of the Corsair had been fabric covered. At speed, the fabric tended to deform and slow the aircraft by a few miles per hour. The F4U-5 had all fabric surfaces replaced with sheet made to minimize this problem."[14]

Mac quickly established a reputation for superb airmanship in VF-21. His squadron skipper, Cdr. H. H. Barton, rated his flying ability above average, underscoring that "he is aggressive as a fighter pilot." Macon attained his designation as a division leader within a year of reporting aboard VF-21, and within twenty-four months he garnered for himself and his squadron special recognition from commander, Air Forces, U.S. Atlantic Fleet (AIRLANT), for achieving the highest fleet individual score in aerial gunnery—scoring 58 hits on the banner with 150 allowed rounds. In one more instance of the older brother paving the way for the younger brother that would reoccur during Mac's career, the AIRLANT commander who sent this special recognition was Vice Adm. Felix Stump, who was the commanding officer of USS *Lexington* in 1943–44 when Mac's brother Ernie was in command of the *Lexington* air wing. In a sense, Ernie's reputation for airmanship and leadership had paved a path for Mac, whereupon favorable name recognition would gain a second look for the younger brother from more established and experienced naval aviators.

As Mac neared the end of his first twenty-four months in VF-21, the squadron would begin its own transition to jet power that was catching up with all Navy fighter squadrons by this time. With the swap of piston-powered F4U-5s for the much faster jet-powered F9F-2s, the squadron's newly adopted sobriquet, Mach Busters, took on a very immediate and literal import. Before detaching, Mac would complete the squadron's first jet cruise from January to May 1951 in USS *Franklin Roosevelt*, during which he added more than two hundred hours of jet time to his logbook in the F9F-2 Panther—and furthered his growing reputation as a superb fighter pilot and master of squadron administration, "knowing all the men and all the answers."[15]

Mac had little knowledge, though, and probably no expectation of flying jet-powered fighter aircraft when he first reported to NAS Dallas for flight training in January 1947. He could not have known that in that same month, a prototype jet fighter nicknamed Banshee would take to the air for its first flight as the XF2D-1 from the airport at St. Louis. The Banshee's lineage could be traced to a design that originated four years earlier. In January 1943, the Navy turned to McDonnell Aircraft Company to produce the first seagoing jet fighter.

Because the Navy's premier fighter producers, Douglas, Vought, and Grumman, were at near capacity producing front-line wartime aircraft, the McDonnell Company got the nod to build two carrier-capable jet fighter prototypes under the designation XFD-1, denoting an experimental aircraft from McDonnell, or manufacturer *D*. When the first prototype flew in January 1945, it acquired the moniker Phantom. In the vernacular of aircraft alphanumeric designation of the mid-1940s, McDonnell aircraft were reassigned the letter *H* when Douglas returned to fighter development. The later Banshee, a derivative of the Phantom, initially was known as F2D and then later as the F2H.

Satisfied with the early promise of the Phantom, Navy BuAer in 1944 issued a fully specified requirement for a jet-propelled fighter with a demanding set of capabilities for jet aircraft of the time:

- catapult-launched with takeoff speed not exceeding 110 mph
- combat radius of 300 nautical miles
- armed with four 12.7-millimeter (.50-caliber) guns with 400 rounds per gun
- spot factor no larger than the Vought F4U Corsair.

Inside two weeks' time, Grumman, Vought, North American, and McDonnell submitted proposals. Other noted manufacturers of that time all indicated they were not in a position to undertake new designs. Only Douglas was willing to offer a design, but the bureau insisted that it confine its efforts to continuing its line of attack aircraft. In order to save time, the bureau went forward with a fighter program based on only notional concepts ahead of complete evaluations.[16] Strict observance of a level playing field and competitive prototyping would preclude such an approach today. But the exigencies of wartime need permitted a more streamlined and, in truth, more practical and efficient procurement approach.

From McDonnell's eleven different design studies, the Model 24B was selected to become the XF2H-1 prototype, mounting two Westinghouse J34 axial flow turbines that could propel the XF2H-1 to 576 mph at sea level and 552 mph at 20,000 feet altitude.[17] A solid performer in its initial fleet design as the F2H-1, it would be quickly overtaken by the improved Big Banjo, the F2H-3, flying first in March 1952. The "Dash 3" featured a fuselage stretched by more than eight inches to accommodate more fuel, a repositioned horizontal tail with increased dihedral, extended wing chord, a dorsal extension to the horizontal tailplane, and the addition of a superb all-weather radar for the time, the Westinghouse APQ-41 with a twenty-eight-inch dish. A novel but important new feature for the Big Banjo was provision for a large special weapons pylon under the starboard wing. The Navy recognized the need to get atomic weapons to sea aboard aircraft carriers, but options for effective delivery of those weapons from the carrier deck were limited until the Big Banjo provided the requisite lift, speed, and range.

The Big Banjo's long legs made it the Navy's first nuclear-capable tactical aircraft; a single Mk-7 (1,650 pounds) could be carried under the starboard wing. The nuclear warhead was fitted in a more aerodynamic shape called a bombardment aircraft rocket (BOAR). Because of the lack of ground clearance when the rocket was hung in that position, the unit had a lower fin that was stowed in a retracted position on the ground and was extended once the carrier fighter was in the air. Capable of either an air or a ground detonation, the Mk-7 had a yield in the kiloton range.[18]

A shore duty tour to the University of Illinois as head of the Naval Reserve Officers Training Corps seamanship department and freshman class adviser gave Mac time to throttle back and reflect on where he was and where he could be headed in naval aviation. His performance, as recorded in annual fitness reports, was rated in his earliest assignments as exemplary and gradually progressed to exceptional in his aviation billets. His flying skill, his judgment, and his apparent leadership presence among peers and division sailors were establishing him as an officer on an upward track. His return to sea duty would present fresh opportunities to hone an exemplary record.

Mac reported for duty to Fighter Squadron 41, the Black Aces, in June 1953. VF-41 had only recently transitioned to the F2H-3 Big Banjo, but Mac arrived ready to make his mark and advance expeditiously to flight division leader and department head. As luck would have it, he was assigned primary duty as the squadron special weapons and ordnance officer at precisely the time when tactical nuclear weapons had achieved a manageable size and were being introduced into aircraft carrier magazines without much benefit of a practiced understanding of the operational handling of these new weapons.

Delivery of nuclear weapons by small tactical aircraft was not common. Experiences at the close of World War II had shown it could be done successfully from large land-based bombers at high altitude in a fairly benign environment for opposing fighters. However, mounting a successful delivery from a carrier-based fighter now required innovation in planning, flying, and actually dropping the weapon in a way that would yield the desired blast effect and give the single-seat pilot the highest confidence of getting away from the detonation. Other squadrons were just beginning to grapple with the challenge. In characteristic fashion, Mac seized upon the opportunity to meld flying and academic study to develop a detailed process and squadron manual for safe handling by the ordnancemen and for target planning, cockpit "switchology," and recommended flight profiles for the pilots. He researched what technical information was available in classified treatises to understand weapons effects and the recommended delivery parameters. He developed a squadron instruction for nuclear mission planning that walked squadron pilots through the process of determining flight profiles based on assigned weapon yield and burst type. He flew the profiles in the Banshee to record times, airspeeds, and maneuvers to launch an inert BOAR store. For VF-41 pilots, he documented best techniques in a pocket checklist for flying low-angle loft release with wingover egress to high-angle loft with over-the-shoulder release and egress. These were new concepts for naval aviators of that time. Jet aircraft had only been widely operational in fleet squadrons for less than five years. The introduction of atomic weapons added new complexity to the squadron pilot's job but was a hallmark of a historic transition for naval aviation. Now, carriers at sea were the equal of the Air Force's long-range land-based bombers in carrying the important national security responsibility of nuclear response on a global scale.

The leader of the Black Aces was Cdr. Dexter Rumsey, a salty aviator with a colorful background. Rumsey was Navy through and through. He entered the service in 1938 as an aviation cadet, roughly a contemporary of Mac's older brother in terms of aviation longevity, but with a career progression that placed him with large seaplane patrol squadrons rather than carrier-based fighter squadrons. On June 4, 1942, then-lieutenant Rumsey was flying a PBY Catalina patrol plane around French Frigate Shoals northwest of Oahu scouting for Japanese movement as the battle of Midway was unfolding farther northwest.

Prior to taking over the Black Aces, Rumsey was the leader of VPB-211, a patrol bombing squadron flying searches for German submarines in large PBM-3 Martin Mariner seaplanes from primitive bases in Brazil at the close of the war. Fighter Squadron 41 was

Rumsey's first experience in carrier tactical aircraft, but across aviation communities within the Navy at the time, moving from one type and model of aircraft to another was not uncommon and was a generally accepted practice. An aviator who had consistently demonstrated flying competence and innate leadership qualities could move from fighter to bomber to patrol plane with greater ease as he advanced in rank. This practice became less common as the gulf between fighter and land-based aircraft performance widened. As missions became more specialized and aircraft designs were more closely adapted to those mission needs, cross assignments from fighter to bomber (now attack) or from attack to heavy attack squadrons became more a thing of the past. The trend did not really take a new turn until fighter and attack mission design attributes were purposely blended into the F/A-18 in the mid-1980s. Visionaries, safety experts, and Navy leadership would soon make a connection between horrible mishap rates and the lack of standardized career progression in a single type, and lack of standardized procedures in that type, Navy-wide.

Commander Rumsey noted Mac's enthusiasm, persistence, and attention to detail for the task at hand, writing in a performance report that Mac "pioneered in the field of special weapons delivery by light carrier aircraft. . . . Largely through his efforts as the squadron special weapons officer, this command (VF-41) enjoys a service wide reputation as the first carrier based jet squadron to successfully complete an operational readiness test in the delivery of the atomic bomb." That his pioneering effort in this instance contributed significantly to the squadron's battle efficiency "E" award in 1954 was confirmed by direction from the AIRLANT commander to attach his congratulatory letter to Lt. Macon Snowden's fitness report. One recognition led to another as he was designated squadron operations officer inside eighteen months; upon detachment from the squadron, he was assigned to the staff of AIRLANT as the ships' special weapons officer for the entire Atlantic Fleet for his "initiative and zeal."

★ ★ ★

In December 1952, the Korean War, initiated in June 1950, would drag out for another six months until an armistice ended open hostilities. Carrier aviation, still flush with an inventory of twenty-five

Ernie's 1932 graduation photo in the Naval Academy yearbook, the *Lucky Bag*.

Between assignments to carrier-based squadrons VF-4 and VF-7, Ernie was with Cruiser Scouting Squadron Six (VCS-6) attached to USS *Minneapolis*, flying the Curtis SOC floatplane. Here he pauses on deck of *Minneapolis* prior to the cruiser's participation in Fleet Problem XX in 1939.

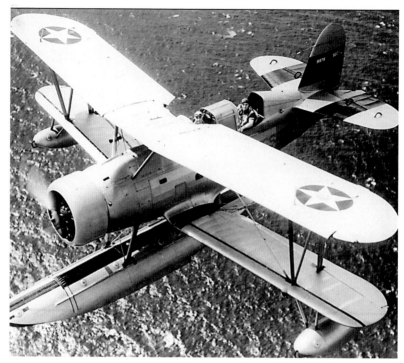

Ernie pilots a Curtiss SOC-1 floatplane assigned to USS *Minneapolis*. The bands on the vertical and horizontal tail would be black, indicating this SOC belonged to Cruiser Scouting Squadron Six. The rear seat radioman is unidentified. *U.S. Navy photograph courtesy of Steve Ginter Publications*

VS-72 squadron pilots exit the flight line after deploying to Royal Navy Air Station Hatston near the Scapa Flow anchorage in Scotland in April 1942. Ernie, soon to take command of VS-72, is second from right.

Smoke rises from Tanambogo Island near Gavutu and close by Tulagi as U.S. Marines consolidate their landings on August 7, 1942. Known for his insistency on photographic documentation to produce prompt, accurate strike damage intelligence, Ernie normally required his rear-seat radioman/gunner to bring a large format camera. This photo was most likely taken from the rear seat of Ernie's aircraft. Note the perforated wing dive flap visible in lower right that was characteristic of the SBD dive-bomber design. *Naval History and Heritage Command*

Officers of Bombing Squadron 16 assemble on the flight deck of USS *Lexington* en route to operations in the Pacific area. Commanding officer Ernie Snowden is seated in the center of the front row. His executive officer, Lt. Cdr. (later Vice Adm.) Ralph Weymouth, sits to Ernie's left. Weymouth would take command of VB-16 when Ernie was elevated to command of *Lexington's* air group in the fall of 1943. *U.S. Navy*

Ernie's VB-16 SBDs are spotted forward on *Lexington*'s flight deck after a successful raid on Tarawa, September 18, 1943. *Photo courtesy of Real War Photos Galleries*

After assuming command of Air Group 16, Ernie flew as strike leader for multiple attacks on the Japanese airfield on Mille in late November 1943. On November 22, enemy ground fire damaged his F6F, necessitating a barrier landing on *Lexington*.

Flight deck medical personnel link arms to form an emergency cradle to remove Ernie from the crash and carry him to sick bay.

Ernie (*right*) and *Lexington* skipper Capt. Felix Stump share a moment on *Lexington*'s bridge wing following Ernie's poststrike debrief. The two had high regard for each other's professional skill, leadership, and aggressiveness.

"West of Tokyo Missionary Society" meeting on *Lexington* flight deck on May 8, 1944. Air Group 16 Cdr. Ernie Snowden reads the society's manifesto to enthusiastic pilots and enlisted aircrew. *Photo courtesy of Real War Photos Galleries*

Docks and port facilities at a Japanese seaplane base on Tanapag Harbor on the west coast of Saipan smolder as they come under a follow-on attack by aircraft from Air Group 16 led by Ernie in June 1944, just days before the climactic Marianas Turkey Shoot. Wreckage of Japanese floatplane fighters litter the ramp, destroyed in an earlier sweep by Air Group 16. *U.S. Navy*

In June 1944, Vice Adm. Marc Mitscher, commander of Task Force 58, presents Ernie the Silver Star for his leadership of Air Group 16 in the battle of the Philippine Sea and the Legion of Merit for an earlier action at Kwajalein leading air groups from four carriers in strikes against air and surface forces.

Commander of Carrier Air Group 16 on USS *Lexington*, Cdr. Ernie Snowden stands with his squadron commanding officers in June 1944 (*left to right*): Lt. Cdr. Ralph Weymouth, USN, VB-16 (SBD dive bombers); Cdr. Ernie Snowden; Cdr. Paul Buie, USN, VF-16 (F6F fighters); Lt. Norman Sterrie, USNR, VT-16 (TBD torpedo bombers). *U.S. Navy*

Massed flyover of 450 Navy aircraft and 800 U.S. Army Air Forces and Allied aircraft at the formal Japanese surrender ceremony on board USS *Missouri* darken the sky. Ernie was accorded the honor of flying in the rear seat of one of Air Group 16's SB2Cs overhead while at that same moment younger brother Macon observed from below on the deck of the destroyer USS *Caperton*. *Naval History and Heritage Command*

Former shipmates of USS *Wasp* (CV 7) reunite at a banquet honoring Adm. Forrest Sherman (*center*), former *Wasp* commanding officer and newly appointed Chief of Naval Operations; Vice Adm. J. W. Reeves, *Wasp* skipper prior to Sherman; and Cdr. Ernie Snowden, former skipper of Scouting Squadron 72 embarked in *Wasp* under both former *Wasp* commanding officers. As director of training under the chief of naval air training, Ernie hosted this dinner on December 28, 1949, at Naval Air Station Corpus Christi, Texas.

USS *Kula Gulf* steams off the Virginia coast in December 1954, just days after Ernie assumed command of the escort carrier. The Grumman AF fixed-wing antisubmarine warfare aircraft populating *Kula Gulf*'s flight deck would be replaced by a squadron of Sikorsky HO-4S helicopters by the end of December for effectiveness trials throughout 1955. In fifteen years, the ship type and mission would evolve to Landing Platform Helicopter and "vertical envelopment" of U.S. Marines to inshore landings, epitomized by younger brother Mac's tenure in command of USS *Guadalcanal*.

Mac's class of 1946 graduation photo in the Naval Academy yearbook, the *Lucky Bag*.

In a scene reminiscent of Ernie's graduation thirteen years earlier, Mac's mother buttons on his ensign's shoulder boards following ceremonies in Dahlgren Hall at the Naval Academy in June 1945. Older brother Cdr. Ernie Snowden looks on as his wife, Lois, snapped the photo.

Mac holds position prior to receiving a signal to launch from the director holding the checkered flag, March 9, 1949. Within a few months the squadron, VF-21, would transition to the Grumman F6F-2 Panther. *U.S. Navy*

In 1950, Mac assumed department head duty as administrative officer in VF-21. Here he prepares for an operational training flight in the Grumman F9F-2 Panther. *U.S. Navy*

During a VF-21 training flight on May 15, 1950, F9F-2 number 107, flown by Mac, closes in tight formation.

A flight of four VF-41 Banshees parades up the starboard side of USS *Randolph* during Mac's 1954 Mediterranean cruise with the squadron. Mac is flying the aircraft on the leader's right wing in the foreground. *National Naval Aviation Museum*

Ernie and Mac share a celebratory moment following the latter's assumption of command of the naval air training unit at Naval Air Station Memphis, March 1957. *U.S. Navy*

Mac Snowden assumes command of Fighter Squadron 91, the "Legendary Red Lightnings," on board USS *Ranger* in Yokosuka, Japan, relieving Cdr. C. E. Rich. The previous year, when Mac was the executive officer, the squadron earned the Pacific Fleet Battle "E" for top West Coast fighter squadron. Mac would lead VF-91 to a second consecutive "E" as commanding officer. *U.S. Navy*

VF-91 pilots assembled for squadron photo in November 1961. Squadron commander Mac Snowden is in center, back row. *U.S. Navy*

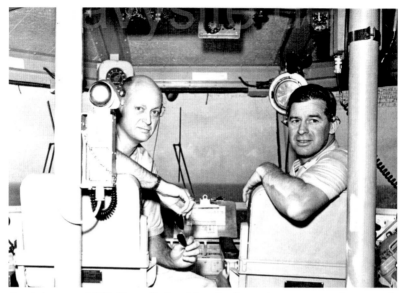

As air boss on USS *Constellation*, Mac sits for an impromptu photograph in primary flight control in June 1964, only weeks before *Constellation* would take part in the Pierce Arrow operation, launching strikes on North Vietnamese patrol boats and port facilities.

USS *Ticonderoga* (CVA 14), with Air Wing 5 embarked, takes on ammunition stores from USS *Mount Baker* (AE 4) during predeployment strike exercises off San Diego on September 1, 1965. At the end of the month, *Ticonderoga* and Air Wing 5 would depart for their Vietnam combat cruise.

Mac Snowden traps aboard USS *Ticonderoga*, taxiing the "CAG bird" out of the wires ahead of other Air Wing 5 aircraft on September 24, 1965. Four days later, *Ticonderoga*, with Air Wing 5 embarked, departed on its first full combat cruise to Vietnam since participating in the Pierce Arrow strikes the year before.

USS *Guadalcanal* (*foreground*), commanded by Mac, steams close aboard replenishment ships participating in exercise "Snowy Beach" off the coast of Maine in January 1972. *Naval History and Heritage Command*

As commanding officer of USS *Guadalcanal*, Mac observes a replenishment ship coming alongside from his vantage point on the bridge wing. *U.S. Navy*

large fast attack carriers at this point, had made itself an indispensable force, "setting the stage for the revitalization that would subsequently occur. . . . When aircraft carriers were able to 'show the flag' in the Taiwan Strait, interdict the enemy's supply lines in Korea, provide crucial close air support to troops on the front lines, and help wrest control of the air from the North Korean Air Force, the future of naval aviation was made secure."[19]

But those twenty-five fast attack carriers were all constructed during or right after World War II and, as a consequence, were designed from the keel up to accommodate radial piston–powered, propeller-driven aircraft—machines limited by the technology of the day. In Korea, the transition to jet-powered aircraft was just beginning to constrain flight deck operations, and with North Korean MiG-15s now the prevailing concern, naval aviation was confined mainly to interdiction and close air support until enough ground could be retaken for surging Air Force tactical fighters from the safety of bases in South Korea. An account by Cdr. Gerald Miller on a carrier group staff operating F9F-2 Panthers off Korea illuminates the consequences of learning to operate jets in a wartime environment:

> We had a lot of these fighters in the air. Then we tried to bring them down and it was a tough job of getting them on board. They were running out of fuel and there was no base on the beach to send them to. We had to get them back on board those two carriers, and we broke up those planes in some numbers.
>
> Well, that was all because of the size of the ship, the nature of the airplanes and straight deck operations . . . Considering the upheaval in the Navy caused by demobilization and the introduction of new technologies, it's amazing that we kept together as much as we did . . . We worried, but we did proceed with the jet program.[20]

Notwithstanding the politically inspired cancellation of the super-carrier USS *United States*, an urgent operational need existed to close the widening gap between carriers designed to accommodate World War II–vintage aircraft and those that would be needed to handle the larger, faster jet aircraft that were now arriving and would soon displace all propeller-driven fighters. Resolving this mismatch was consuming Navy planners in Washington. Ernie was entering a new realm, and his time at sea and leading squadrons and an air group under the strain of constant combat would equip him well for this new combat for appropriations inside the Pentagon and in congressional committee rooms.

Shore duty rotation after several years in the fleet was as a customary part of career progression, performed while looking forward to the next sea duty assignment. Most naval aviators, however, viewed shore duty in Washington, D.C., with aversion, even disdain. Ernie was no exception. Including his prior seagoing assignments on carrier division and fleet staffs, he had spent most of his twenty years on active duty standing watches as part of a ship's company or in the cockpit training for deployment or flying in actual combat, and he did not particularly relish this new assignment. Ernie calculated that only by active intervention in the assignment process could he hope to land a set of desirable orders for a meaningful job in Washington, D.C., that would draw on his considerable experience. In late 1949, when he was director of advanced training for naval aviation at NAS Corpus Christi, he arranged a reunion dinner for past shipmates from USS *Wasp* who might now be in a position to help. With eager collaboration from his boss, Rear Adm. J. W. Reeves, chief of naval air training and a former *Wasp* skipper, incoming CNO (and also former *Wasp* skipper) Adm. Forrest Sherman was invited as guest of honor. Ernie had had the good fortune of working under Sherman twice before in his career and had established a close mentoring relationship. The first time was as a midshipman under Sherman's instruction in the department of seamanship and flight tactics at the Naval Academy in 1931; the second time was ten years later when Ernie commanded VS-72 in *Wasp* under Sherman as the carrier's skipper. In private conversation among the three officers after dinner, Ernie made his wishes known. His standing with these two admirals was such that he achieved a favorable hearing, and the personnel reassignment machinery was set in motion. It would take two years before the actual orders would arrive, by which point Admiral Sherman had passed away unexpectedly on the job.

Upon reporting to OPNAV in 1952, Ernie would embark on a different kind of daily struggle—equally as demanding of his experience and concentration as the most difficult flying—on behalf of the future of naval aviation. As with all his past assignments, Ernie concluded that there was a contribution he could make, and he was determined to apply his accumulated experience to making a difference for the community.

Adm. William M. Fechteler had been CNO for more than a year when Ernie reported to his staff. Fechteler devoted considerable attention to and was perhaps best remembered for his strong advocacy for the service's shipbuilding program that reversed the cancellation of USS *United States* by initiating the Navy's program to build the first large-deck aircraft carriers of the *Forrestal* class.

To appreciate Ernie's pivotal role at this juncture, the larger role of OPNAV must be understood: created in the early 1900s as a kind of general board or permanent body of consultative advisers to the Navy secretary and working under the auspices of the senior Navy four-star admiral, OPNAV coordinated the setting of warfighting requirements, research and development, testing, procurement, and fielding, as well as the logistical aspects of manning, equipping, and training for readiness to sail, fly, and fight. Then, as now, OPNAV was organized around functions or warfighting communities. Ernie, responsible for harmonizing aircraft carrier plans with new aircraft designs and rationalizing budget-constrained priorities before flag-level seniors on OPNAV, played a pivotal leadership role on the staff. Future Navy warfighting posture would be shaped to a large degree by his success in garnering the advocacy of Navy leadership by packaging and advancing the most fiscally executable program that met the operational imperatives for sea-based nuclear weapon delivery and, increasingly, sea-based support of land operations. Navy operations in Korea were an urgent and compelling reminder that, short of all-out nuclear war, naval aviation would still play a vital role in gaining advantage for the conventional land campaign—an advantage that could not always be delivered by the Air Force if tactically relevant airbases could not be secured.

Entering the 1950s flush with an inventory of recently constructed *Essex*- and *Midway*-class aircraft carriers was an advantage for the Navy for maintaining worldwide operational presence in an austere fiscal period, but it was equally a hindrance to further modernization for the jet age. Carrier air groups would, for the foreseeable future, be composed of mixed types of reciprocating prop aircraft and, increasingly, jet-powered aircraft that could, with limitations, be accommodated on the World War II–vintage carriers—but not without substantial upgrades to those carriers, a process that had started in the late 1940s and would continue well into the 1950s. This initially played well with the authorizers and appropriators in Congress who viewed the upgrades as a prudent use of assets already paid for, assets of stout design from which much longer life could be extracted and which could be made serviceable in the jet age even if they imposed a compromise on the immediate and full exploitation of jet aircraft capability.

The extent of the mismatch in operational characteristics between the new jets and the *Essex*-class carriers soon became evident. Ship catapults needed to be substantially more powerful because jets could not attain adequate flying speed off the front end of the ship with a normal rolling takeoff; higher landing speeds required stronger arresting gear; jets consumed more of a highly flammable jet fuel mixture that demanded greater storage volume and reinforced fuel bunkers; and adequate storage for new streamlined, low-drag bombs required sizable increases in magazine volume. These issues drove the Navy to coalesce around a set of design changes coined "Ship Characteristics Board Program 27" (SCB-27), applied initially to USS *Oriskany* (CV 34), then still under construction. A further iteration of the basic SCB-27 yielded the SCB-27A, defined mainly by a new catapult type, and the SCB-27C, which adopted even more powerful C11 steam catapults of British design. The -27C design also added extendable jet blast deflectors, an emergency recovery barrier, and storage for nuclear weapons. The first three carriers to be upgraded to the SCB-27C specification were USS *Hancock* (CV 19), USS *Intrepid* (CV 11), and USS *Ticonderoga* (CV 14).[21]

Further enhancements to the *Essex*-class ships were required to extract the maximum operational utility from their World War II–vintage design. They were embodied in SCB-125, a follow-on to SCB-27C that permitted greater operational efficiencies on the flight deck for handling an air group of mixed prop and jet types. SCB-125 brought the innovation of an angled flight deck, the enclosed hurri-cane bow, optical landing system, repositioned deck-edge elevators, and reinforced flight deck.[22] *Ticonderoga* and *Intrepid* were the last of the original SCB-27C inductees to get the SCB-125 modifications.

Throughout Ernie's tenure as the director of the aviation ships section from late 1952 to late 1954, interservice competition roiled among the senior flag ranks as the Navy asserted the primacy of naval aviation. That advocacy and funding for these critical carrier upgrades continued and even gained momentum were testament, in a smaller way, to Ernie's judgment, doggedness, and skill in a combat arena that was not wholly familiar to him. Less than a decade after *Ticonderoga* emerged from the shipyard with her -27C/-125 modifications com-plete, she would play an integral part in the opening hostilities of the Vietnam war.

More contentious was the Navy's parallel pursuit of a class of super-carriers reminiscent of the cancelled USS *United States* that was purpose-built to host a full complement of jet-powered aircraft up to and including the largest jets capable of delivering atomic weap-ons. Now, however, with the lessons of Korea and naval aviation's con-tribution in that conflict still fresh and with the ongoing introduction of new jet aircraft types, circumstances conspired to propel the Navy down a dual path of robust, steadily paced modernization of older car-riers and slower incremental recapitalization of the carrier inventory with new super-carrier types. That recapitalization started with the lay-down of the keel of USS *Forrestal* in July 1952, six months before Ernie arrived to take over the Navy's aviation ships section in OPNAV.

Ernie would throw himself into the preparing, amending, updat-ing, and refreshing of the justification for the carrier program, refin-ing the funding request, and shaping the congressional testimony to sustain the advocacy and momentum for super-carriers USS *Saratoga* (CV 60) and USS *Ranger* (CV 61), the latter's keel laid down in August 1954. The stability of these nascent super-carrier programs was never ensured once the funding requests passed from the Navy to the Office of the Secretary of Defense and then to Congress. A vigorous defense of the amounts and uses of super-carrier dollars was critical. In precise and impactful phraseology surely edited by if not written by Ernie as an obligation of his staff work, Admiral Fechteler testified before the House of Representatives appropriations committee in May 1953:

> With the advent of jet propelled aircraft, our *Essex* Class carriers became obsolescent. Conversion has delayed the *Essex* Class becoming obsolete . . . These various items that have to be built into the ship [*Forrestal* and subsequent super-carriers] are due to the fact that we are operating heavier aircraft; the ship requires increased fuel capacity; we must have more and higher capacity catapults; you have higher speeds so you must have different arresting gear; you must have additional ordnance capability because these high performance planes can deliver a heavier load; and, finally, you must build into your ship a stronger hull to reduce damage by bombs, torpedoes and other weapons.[23]

Later in the same hearing, Ernie's immediate boss, Vice Adm. Ralph Ofstie, deputy CNO for air, delivered his remarks. Continuing the theme struck by Admiral Fechteler, Ofstie (also employing wording most assuredly drafted by Ernie) told the congressional appropriators: "The carriers must be able not only to launch and recover rapidly the most modern aircraft but they must also be of sufficient size to accommodate increased amounts of ordnance and fuel. We have devised an interim solution in our carrier modernization program, but the ultimate answer lies in carrying through the program of replacement, of which the *Forrestal* is the first."[24]

Ernie may have been one of perhaps a dozen or more captains with long, uninterrupted carrier flying experience and distinguished combat leadership at the squadron, air group, and fleet staff level—peers who might have been assigned this weighty responsibility. But at this moment and in this key position, Ernie validated the confidence placed in him two years earlier by Arleigh Burke and Forrest Sherman by maintaining a firm grip on the process—by working OPNAV to extrude the well-constructed reasoning and the solid fiscal enumeration that kept *Forrestal*, *Saratoga*, and *Ranger* on track toward their ultimate commissioning. What he could not know was that as a result of his labor in OPNAV, he was, even if indirectly, once again giving his younger brother a hand up by ensuring that the fleet's carrier recapitalization to large super-carrier flight decks proceeded apace. Younger brother Mac would, in six years' time, take Fighter Squadron 91 to sea aboard super-carrier USS *Ranger*, first as executive officer and then commanding officer, exploiting to advantage the large deck efficiencies and handling margin afforded F8U Crusaders in the landing pattern and on deck.

In the immediate post–World War II years, what began as a tentative but purposeful trial of small numbers of the experimental jet engines on relatively unsophisticated, boxy airframe prototypes became, by the mid-1950s, a torrent of radically new and different designs that pushed the limits of aerodynamics. The Navy "attempted to reduce strategic risk by letting multiple contracts to different aircraft companies in hopes that at least one of the designs would be viable. On the other hand, it accepted a high degree of operational risk, by ordering series production of various models before flight-testing was complete. The net effect of this strategy was that between 1945 and 1959 twenty-two new type and model Navy fighters made their first flights."[25]

For those naval aviators fortunate enough to be assigned to the Navy's flight test mecca at Patuxent River, Maryland, this flood of new-design aircraft needing to be wrung out was a dream fulfilled. This was the environment to which Mac arrived in April 1955 with orders to report to the test pilot training (TPT) division of the Naval Air Test Center. His request for TPT orders was endorsed by no less a personage than Vice Adm. Frederick McMahon, the commander of naval air forces, AIRLANT, partly as a result of Mac's visibility on the AIRLANT staff, his fleetwide reputation for aerial gunnery scores, and his aggressive promotion of the introduction of special weapons, but perhaps as much for the name recognition that had already become fixed in McMahon's thinking.

McMahon was the skipper of escort carrier USS *Suwannee* traveling in company with Fifth Fleet carrier *Lexington* in late 1943 toward Operation Galvanic to take Makin and Saipan. *Suwannee* formed part of Task Group 52.6 providing air support to the Marine Corps invasion forces, while *Lexington* was part of Task Group 50.1 comprising the carrier interceptor group. McMahon knew of Ernie's reputation with VS-72, VB-16, and now as CAG-16 coordinating air operations with his peers, who included the *Suwannee's* air group commander. More pertinent to the cause and effect of Mac's TPT endorsement was the fast relationship established between Ernie and *Lexington* skipper Capt. Felix Stump in the 1943–44 campaigns in the Pacific. After the war, Captain Stump had risen to flag rank and was McMahon's predecessor at AIRLANT. A call from Ernie to Admiral Stump on behalf of his younger brother Mac set the dominoes in motion for a highly favorable endorsement and orders to test pilot school.

Cedar Point, Maryland, juts into the Chesapeake Bay and is brushed by the Patuxent River on its northern shoreline as it empties into the bay. In the early 1940s Cedar Point, though only about sixty miles from Washington, D.C., presented a remote landscape dominated by a few large farms and several widely dispersed vacation homes set among forested patches of land. When war started, the Navy Bureau of Aeronautics, anticipating a surge in evaluation of new aircraft and weapons prompted by lessons learned in combat, began scouting locations where naval flight testing—then done at NAS Anacostia across from the District of Columbia and at NAS Norfolk—could be consolidated. Cedar Point, with its remoteness and immediate access to open water over the Chesapeake, presented an ideal location. Formal operations began in April 1943. Before the war ended, NAS Patuxent River—sometimes called Pax River—was host to aeronautical evaluations not only of new designs entering U.S. Navy service but also of Allied aircraft and several captured enemy aircraft, including the Mitsubishi A6M5 Type 52 Zero, Mitsubishi KI-46 Dinah, and Nakajima B5N2 Kate. Within a few months of the war ending, Pax River would also receive flying models of the German Focke Wulf FW-190, Dornier Do-335A Pfeil (Arrow), Messerschmitt Me-262 Schwalbe (Swallow) jet fighter, and Arado Ar-234 jet bomber.[26]

In late 1945, the test pilot training division, precursor of the test pilot school, was established at Pax River. This proved quite prescient in preparing a generation of pilots grounded and standardized in flight test protocols to guide naval aviation through the transition to jets, and later into the space program. By the mid-1950s, the jet transition was well under way. For any pilot of high-performance aircraft, this was an exhilarating time to be at Pax River. It was too soon for Mac, arriving for TPT class seventeen in the summer of 1956, to appreciate that his tenure was bracketed by other test pilot classes that numbered among them all of the Navy and Marine Corps *Mercury* astronauts. John Glenn, Alan Shepard, and Scott Carpenter, already TPT gradu-ates, were assigned as project pilots to areas of the air station engaged in aircraft and weapon testing. Mac's Naval Academy classmate Wally Schirra would arrive to join class twenty just over a year later (with classmates Jim Lovell and Pete Conrad). Glenn and Shepard were Mac's neighbors in the newest housing development to break ground in the area, and they would form a small intimate social circle in Town Creek Manor.

Class seventeen in short order became the "Boomers." Their class logo, resembling naval aviator wings superimposed over a mushroom cloud, hinted at some collective association with atomic weapons. In the Boomer class, Mac was reunited with USS *Caperton* ship-mate and good friend from the closing days of World War II, Forrest Petersen, and a diverse mix of twenty-five other classmates arriving from the fleet, from the Marine Corps, from the Royal Navy and Royal Canadian Navy, and from the major aircraft manufacturers, including Vought, McDonnell, Boeing, Convair, and Grumman. The TPT director, Cdr. Loys M. "Butch" Satterfield, newly arrived from command of VF-153, closely monitored class seventeen's six months under instruction. Paul Gillcrist, a student in class twenty with Wally Schirra just months later, penned an apt description of Butch Satter-field in his memoir, *Sea Legs*: "He was a hands-on leader. As such he insisted on flying with each member of our class to check progress and, at the same time, derive some sense of the quality of training his school was providing. At some point early in the academic syllabus, after the stability and control lectures, each student was scheduled for a check flight with Butch Satterfield. Its purpose was to ascer-tain whether we could, in fact, measure certain principal characteris-tics of the airplane's natural longitudinal stability. It was a basic skill, but an important first step in stability and control flight-testing."[27]

Satterfield would tell students: "You must have confidence in your test results. Never let some airplane design engineer talk you out of believing your own numbers. They may be the only real things about some of these new-fangled flight control systems. The measurements you take never lie."[28]

Gillcrist and his fellow students in class twenty would take their check ride with Satterfield in the Lockheed T2V-1, a single-engine tandem cockpit Navy jet trainer derived from the T-33 family of aircraft. The T2V-1 had not arrived at TPT in time for Mac's class, but Satterfield had already settled into his routine of early check rides to gauge student progress. Mac would draw his first check rides inside of eight weeks' time in the multi-engine Grumman S2F-1 and Beech SNB-5. This was a minor challenge after six years in single-seat jet assignments, but Mac had gained some experience with both types of multi-engine propeller aircraft, logging proficiency flight time in between duty stations.

To say that class seventeen felt mildly stressed anticipating their first check rides with Commander Satterfield was an understatement. However, naval aviators in general, and TPT enrollees in particular, had learned to project an outward calm under stress, even a detached composure that belied an intense focus on procedures and checklists. But flight instructors and the TPT director himself were taking note of Mac's distinguishing traits: a superb organization and delivery of technical papers and flight test reports, and an innate feel for the aircraft that went beyond hand-eye coordination of control movements and throttle settings to something approaching a melding of man and machine. Mac's aptitude for test project work was not lost on the class, and his peers readily followed Mac's lead in projects designed to involve student groups.

Forrest Petersen, promoted to lieutenant commander by the end of the course of instruction, edged out Mac for the outstanding student award. But Commander Satterfield rated Mac far and away the number one of four students in the grade of lieutenant and in the naval aviator designator, noting that Mac "contributed immeasurably to the successful completion of these projects by an outstanding ability to work harmoniously with others, and the ability to promote an aggressive group effort."[29]

★ ★ ★

That the Boomer class—and all TPT classes before and since—selected
the very best in naval aviation was a given. Two of the four lieutenants
in Mac's fitness report rating group (those four including Mac) would
progress to command of an F8U Crusader fighter squadron, along
with Lieutenant Commander Petersen. Yet another Boomer classmate,
Frank Austin, the first flight surgeon to graduate from the test pilot
school, would go on to become a project pilot for the introduction of
the Goodrich full-pressure suit, making all of his project flights in the
F8U. Subsequent to his project work, Frank would fly the F8U again
as an instructor pilot in VF-174. Sadly, Vought test pilot Jim Buckner
would be killed in an F8U accident less than six months after graduation from TPT, following a low high-speed pass over the runway during a demonstration at the Vought facility in Grand Prairie, Texas. At
the end of the runway, the aircraft disintegrated due to the structural
limits of the airframe being exceeded.

The North American FJ Fury, the Douglas F4D Skyray, and the
Grumman F11F Tiger were among the iconic new jet fighters debut-
ing in the mid-1950s. Mac flew them all at Patuxent River as an
experimental project pilot. On his reassignment to the armament
test division as a graduated test pilot, Mac specialized in testing the
marriage of airframe and weapon systems. Experimental flights in
the division were more about in-flight performance of aircraft and
weapon, the aerodynamic influence of weapon carriage, and weapon
separation than about the effectiveness of the weapon itself. Intended
missions for these aircraft varied, but the constants were onboard
20-millimeter guns and carriage of the new AIM-9 Sidewinder missile.
The most significant feature of the Fury may have been the designed-
in ability to carry a nuclear weapon on the port inboard store station. Given his background in developing VF-41's tactical procedures
for employment of the BOAR store, flight-testing the Fury's nuclear
weapon carriage was a natural progression. Ultimately, the Fury and
its special capability would populate ten Navy fighter squadrons. The
F11F-1 presented a different test problem. One of the first few designs
to achieve supersonic speed in level flight, the Tiger achieved ever-
lasting ignominy when it shot itself down by running into its own
rounds in flight. Five months prior to Mac's arrival at the armament

test division, Grumman test pilot Tom Attridge, flying the Tiger from Grumman's Calverton site, initiated a shallow dive and fired the fateful two four-second bursts of 20mm. When the speed and trajectory of the rounds declined, the Tiger's flight path intersected. Attridge was startled to see his windscreen shatter and engine RPM decline as the rounds found their mark. He settled into the Long Island pine scrub short of the runway but was able to walk away from the wreckage. One of the priority projects that fell in Mac's lap on his first day was determining the relative flight path of plane and bullet in different maneuvering profiles. Mac would accumulate seventy-five hours in more than fifty-five experimental test flights in the Tiger characterizing its aero-weapons performance. The Tiger design held promise as a successful fleet fighter, but it never attained its potential for lack of an adequately matched powerplant—the regrettable outcome of many early Navy jet designs. Ultimately, the Tiger's production run would be truncated in favor of the widely celebrated Vought F8U Crusader, a beast of a fighter for its day.[30]

At the midpoint of the 1950s, the Navy's aircraft carrier modernization and recapitalization programs were healthy. *Forrestal* was commissioned in October 1955, and *Saratoga*, *Ranger*, and *Independence* were moving down the ways for commissioning before the decade ended. Fifteen *Essex*-class carriers were recommissioned after SCB-27C modernization—three with angled flight decks—all by the end of 1955. At almost any point during the prior decade, this relatively stable situation could not have been predicted with any certainty. Only through the vision, doggedness, and obstinacy of such leaders as Mitscher, Fechteler, Burke, Sherman, and Ofstie was naval aviation—and the naval service—guided through the postwar turbulence fomented by irresoluteness of senior defense civilians and the impolitic, injudicious antics of Air Force zealots. Behind the curtain were a dozen grizzled captains and twice that number of commanders who performed as journeymen staff directors, editors, writers, analysts, negotiators, and proselytizers of carrier aviation as the true course. Not least among those captains was Ernie Snowden. Ernie had played an important, perhaps key, role in his staff duties applying combat-whetted experience and well-honed insights into carrier operations, leavened for consumption by his reporting seniors and congressional committee members with highly impactful data-driven briefings and talking points. By their efforts, these Navy leaders made order from chaos, establishing a fleet force structure centered on the attack carrier (CVA) that would carry the Navy successfully through the next quarter-century and beyond.

Another oceanic threat was emerging from the Soviet navy in the immediate postwar face-off with the United States, one that required renewed attention to the undersea domain. From captured German submarines and from their own technology investment, the Soviets were putting to sea a submarine fleet that could potentially deny, or at least complicate, the U.S. Navy's freedom of operation for its carriers at the start of any conflict. The Navy took a second look at its fleet of World War II–era escort carriers (CVEs)—many mothballed within months of the end of the war—as host platforms for a new class of antisubmarine warfare (ASW)–capable aircraft that could function as pouncers when submarine antennas or snorkels were detected at significant range. Ten CVEs were resurrected from various stages of storage, inducted for a set of improvements that included stronger elevators, enlarged islands, and provision for ASW munitions under SCB-54, and given new life as centerpieces of ASW hunter-killer groups. Ernie's staff in the aviation ships section had begun to assess alternatives for future ASW carriers, when, as recompense for his staff work on large carrier programs, he was selected to command one of the ten CVEs. USS *Kula Gulf* (CVE 108) had been refitted for her ASW task at the Philadelphia Naval Shipyard eighteen months before Ernie assumed command, but the job of integrating a new aviation platform, the ASW helicopter, would become the focus for Ernie and only a few other CVE skippers initially. *Kula Gulf* had until this time operated the fixed-wing Grumman AF Guardian, which was gradually being replaced by the Grumman S2F Tracker—an aircraft too large for CVE operations. Rotary-wing aircraft were the preferred replacement for the Guardian to keep the CVE decks populated but also to provide a swing capability for amphibious warfare when loaded with U.S. Marines for an over-the-beach assault. But the notion of helicopters at sea in any designated mission was still fairly new, and the helicopters themselves did not have a long operational history in the Navy inventory. This was very much a period of trial and error devoted to working out any kinks in the marriage of ASW mission-adapted rotary-wing aircraft and the smaller flight deck of the CVEs. *Kula Gulf*, with Ernie in command, welcomed its first ASW helicopter, the Sikorsky HO4S, followed closely by a second helicopter, the tandem-rotor Piasecki HUP-1 Retriever, for search and rescue operations. Carrier qualifications, ASW, and amphibious exercises kept *Kula Gulf* busy in Ernie's first year as skipper, with two straight-line steamings to Vieques, Guantanamo Bay, and return. On these transits, *Kula Gulf* accommodated at-sea flight tests of two newer ASW helicopters: the tandem-rotor Bell HSL-1, which was determined to be unsatisfactory and never adopted in operationally relevant numbers, and the Sikorsky HSS-1 Seabat, the first of a long run of the type mainly in Army and Marine Corps inventories as the H-34 variant.

Ernie's command tour on *Kula Gulf* concluded after eight months in August 1955, with orders to return to the CNO staff for another five months before his next assignment as commanding officer of the naval air reserve training unit at Memphis. A typical tour of duty as a ship's commanding officer in the 1950s would last at least twelve to eighteen months or longer. For a carrier aviator on a more traditional track to increasingly responsible at-sea command positions, being skipper of a smaller ship such as a CVE could, consistent with Navy practice then and now, be thought of as a springboard to command of a large deck CVA. That would have been consistent with Ernie's background and flying experience. The signs were evident with these last orders, if Ernie was observant enough to see, that his future career prospects were less promising than he would have thought several years prior. There may be a single explanation for this plateauing, or it could have been the convergence of many factors that would now emerge to slow his career progression. His earlier assignments to fleet and training command staffs may have taken him out of cycle with his wartime peers who had already begun transitioning to senior operational commands and were showing good results in a transformational era for the Navy. The unraveling of his marriage to Lois was certainly having a deleterious effect on his mood and self-assurance, which was likely to manifest itself in more frequent bouts of intemperance. A successful career track was not irretrievable at this point, as his class would not be in the zone for flag promotion for another two years. But his first appearance before a flag board would find him in a command that was in some respects second tier and without a major capital ship command. Ernie's initial highly promising career track flattened. His path to flag officer seemed less certain, but he could look on his younger brother Mac's progression with some insight and no small amount of pride. The brothers kept in frequent contact and given the similarities in their carrier aviation jobs (separated by a dozen years) counseled each other on aspects of command in the Navy, shared perspectives on fellow officers that one or the other knew or had encountered, and delighted in recounting experiences in the cockpit of aircraft one had flown before the other. They both grasped that the Navy of pre-war biplanes and empire-beating Hellcats rolling down wooden flight decks was now transforming to the next Navy of supersonic Crusaders catapulting from steel deck super-carriers. Mac's career was going strong as a test pilot school selectee, his days filled with the most exhilarating flying imaginable. At this moment in 1956, it was clear to both brothers that Ernie's career had passed its apogee and was vectoring downward. Mac, meanwhile, was ascending and would soon fly the Navy's most advanced jet in command of his own fighter squadron.

Navy fighter squadron heraldry experienced a rich infusion of whimsy when, in the late 1930s and continuing through the war years of the 1940s, Disney Studios lent their creative output to unit patch designs. Familiar cartoon characters such as Donald Duck and newly drawn caricatures were reimagined as uniformed combatants in fighting poses. Ernie was a department head in VF-7 when that unit became the first Navy fighter squadron to sport a Disney-sanctioned image, an insect in boxing gloves ready to punch and parry. Ernie may have had more than a little to do with the adoption of VB-16's Disney-inspired unit patch of a bomb-throwing bird of prey when he stood up the squadron as its first skipper almost four years later. These caricatures enjoyed wide appeal among pilots and their squadrons during the war years, serving as a visual connection to the popular culture they remembered from home. Theatrical cartoons were a regular part of Depression-era relief for the moviegoing public, and now these familiar animated characters were dressed for battle, an embodiment of high spirit that these servicemen could rally around as an antidote to the rigors and intensity of combat. This practice of adorning aircraft with officially approved caricatures waned to a degree after the war. But starting in the 1950s, U.S. aircraft manufacturers discerned some competitive advantage in identifying their new aircraft designs with cartoon characters or whimsical patch designs, and their marketing staffs eagerly advocated for their own emblems. As recently as the 1970s, Grumman made great use of a preening, cocksure twin-tailed tomcat in its advertising for the F-14 Tomcat fighter. In the 1960s, McDonnell created the image of a smallish wraith in a trench coat and fedora that became the "Spook" to represent the F-4 Phantom. Earlier still, Vought represented the F8U Crusader with the image of a knight with sword drawn, ready to vanquish a malevolent foe. However, Vought's most enduring patch design would prove to be the image of a helmeted fighter pilot with a tear welling up under the banner that read, "When you're out of F8s, you're out of fighters." This was a clear reference to the emergence of the non-gun-equipped Phantom in the early 1960s. The Phantom was bred for a new kind of aerial fight in which long-range missiles would eclipse the need for guns in close. But the F8 would make its name in the skies over Vietnam.

The body of knowledge surrounding high-performance aerodynamics was expanding at an astounding pace in the early 1950s. Well before the initial flight of the F11F Tiger, the Navy's acknowledged first supersonic fighter, a design competition was under way for a true supersonic capability. Specification OS-130 called for a highly maneuverable fighter that could reach Mach 0.9 at sea level and Mach 1.2 in afterburner, and that carried both guns and rockets. Vought's proposed model V-383 was selected over competing models from Douglas, Grumman, Lockheed, McDonnell, and North American, whose proposals were essentially advanced variants of fighters already in some stage of development.[31]

Design V-383 featured four 20-millimeter guns, capability for rockets and Sidewinder missiles, and the most visibly iconic feature of design innovation, the variable incidence wing. The wing leading edge could be raised 7 degrees above horizontal to maintain a desired angle of attack in flight while effectively lowering the fuselage underneath the wing to afford the pilot greater visibility for carrier approaches. Throughout, Design V-383 incorporated the most contemporary aerodynamic innovations with area-ruled fuselage, all-moving stabilators, dog-tooth notching at the wing folds for improved yaw stability, and liberal use of titanium in the airframe. Design V-383 exceeded all the Navy's performance baselines; it flew for the first time on March 25, 1955.[32]

For pilots new to the F8U and its unique variable incidence wing, its operation was usually a reliable source of ready room banter. "Since the wing was doing the flying, aerodynamically the fuselage was raised, and during the auto re-trim the pilot had to fly the fuselage up into the wing. Too little back pressure and the aircraft would settle, too much back pressure and the fighter would climb or porpoise." In formation transitions to lowered or raised fuselage, "standardized signals alerted the wingman and indicated transition execution. If the wingman failed to anticipate a configuration change, or missed the execute signal, the result was vertical separation," requiring an exaggerated maneuver to rejoin. The F8U, with its unique design and exceptional supersonic performance, was known as a challenge to fly. "In all, 1,261 Crusaders were built. By the time it was withdrawn from the fleet, 1,106 had been involved in mishaps."[33] By late 1960, the number of Navy operational or training losses due to ejections was approaching fifty, and the F8U had only been in fleet squadrons for three years. Whether this was due to mechanical failure or pilot error, a contributing factor in the early years was typically a lack of standardized and practiced fleet-wide operating and emergency procedures. Changes were coming, and they bore down on two primary issues: first, the need for dedicated aircraft type training for new aviators before they were thrust into high-tempo squadron operations while simultaneously having to master the idiosyncrasies of a new and unfamiliar jet; and the standardization of procedures that would reduce mishaps due to learned bad habits and individual practices that varied from squadron to squadron and coast to coast. These issues were enormously aggravated by the rapid transition from props to jets throughout the 1950s and also were partly driven by a culture that resisted top-down compliance with "sameness," which was viewed as suppressing a cherished inheritance of individualism.[34]

The first issue was addressed through the formation of aircraft type training in Replacement Air Group (RAG) training units. An earlier progenitor for the RAG—the Jet Transitional Training Unit—stood up in Olathe, Kansas, in 1955 "to orient erstwhile deskbound pilots to jets."[35] Not until three years later did the CNO formalize the concept Navy-wide with language that "provided for a permanent replacement Air Group to be established on each coast and made responsible for the indoctrination of key maintenance personnel, the tactical training of pilots, and conducting special programs required for the introduction of new models of combat aircraft."[36]

Mac reported to the F8U RAG at Moffett Field, California, in late 1959 to begin the course of instruction that would familiarize him with the intricacies of F8U Crusader performance, aloft and in the landing pattern. Having already amassed 188 arrested landings in jet aircraft with two different squadrons over multiple deployments in carriers *Roosevelt, Hornet, Bennington, Randolph,* and *Midway,* Mac felt he had a good grasp and well-practiced eye for the carrier landing environment and the proper technique for bringing a jet aboard.

Remarkably, that technique—relying heavily on cues from a landing signal officer (LSO)—differed little from what he had learned from his nearly seventy prior shipboard arrestments in the prop-driven F4U. More remarkable still, his jet arrestments differed little in technique and LSO cues—except in airspeed control—from the techniques used by older brother Ernie flying the SB2U onto USS *Wasp* in 1942, or, for that matter, the earliest carrier landings made in USS *Langley* twenty years before that. What was changing, and what Mac would soon experience, was the onset of radically new technologies in the carrier landing environment with the addition of angled decks and mirror landing systems.

For the first thirty-five years of carrier landing operations, a successful boarding rate depended a great deal on the skill, experience, and "intuitive feel" of the LSO, positioned on the port side of the flight deck edge. The LSO was the indispensable cog in the landing sequence, and the difference between successful approach or calamity owed much to his ability to discern the minutest variations in aircraft attitude in time to telegraph the right pilot response. The LSO employed a signaling wand in each hand that resembled an oversized, brightly colored fly swatter. Prescribed positions of the wands, called paddles, communicated specific corrections to the pilot so that if his approach was too low, too high, off-center, or off-speed, he could make the appropriate stick or throttle adjustments. Then, in the final seconds of the approach, when the pilot had maneuvered the aircraft successfully over the fantail into the right landing position, the LSO could signal "cut" with his right hand drawing the paddle in front of his neck in a motion that resembled an exaggerated beheading.

For most of those first thirty-five years, pilots entered the land-ing pattern by flying up the starboard side of the carrier at about 300 feet with their tailhook down, then breaking in a hard left turn to slow to 120 knots to lower their landing gear and flaps, steadying up at 150 to 200 feet above the sea on a downwind leg on the carrier's port side. Arriving at a position roughly abeam of the LSO platform, the pilot started his left-hand turning approach, attaining an airspeed roughly ten knots higher than his stall speed by the 90-degree posi-tion and maintaining that approach speed through the remainder of his turn and final approach until getting the cut signal from the LSO. With an acceptable approach by the pilot, the LSO could cut with the aircraft fifteen to twenty feet above deck level, signaling the pilot to chop his throttle to idle power setting. There was no opportu-nity for a touch-and-go if the tailhook skipped over the wires. With aircraft usually parked on the forward end of the flight deck, the straight deck did not permit enough run-through to regain power and lift off again with room to clear the stack of aircraft just ahead. For props and early jets, the only alternative to a hook skip was to plow straight ahead into a fence—or barrier—of nylon straps that could be raised for each approach. Removing aircraft from a barrier engagement could add uncomfortable minutes to recovery opera-tions for other aircraft in the pattern, crimping operational flexibility for the carrier and the air group.[37]

The pilot's scan, in both props and early jets, by the 90-degree position became concentrated on his line-up (rolling out wings level on the landing centerline), his airspeed (maintaining his approach speed until the cut), and on the LSO (for paddle corrections to atti-tude, position, and airspeed all the way to the cut signal). This scan var-ied only in degree for the early jet pilots. The most obvious change in the landing environment on deck was a modification to the barrier to preclude the tendency for more streamlined jet aircraft to penetrate the nylon straps and damage landing gear or endanger the pilot sitting in an open cockpit. Otherwise, the carrier landing approach was unchanged from the earliest days of biplane carrier landings. In time, this intricate duet between pilot and LSO, which had proved to be the most efficient method to get all types of prop-driven aircraft aboard, became known as the flat-paddles approach technique. Approach speeds for prop aircraft varied from sixty to ninety knots, with engaging speeds into the wires quite low. For almost a decade after their introduction, the first jets—the Panthers and Banshees that Mac was familiar with—flew a faster flat-paddles approach at 100–115 knots with engaging speeds at 85–100 knots. The jets would take a cut signal slightly earlier in the approach due to the higher speed.[38]

By the early 1950s, the trend was already clear: as jets grew larger, heavier, and faster, they would impose greater constraints on carrier operations, ultimately stunting their operational benefits as long as the flat-paddles approach was still employed to bring the jets onto a barrier-rigged straight deck. At the same time, the British Royal Navy, still in the business of fixed-wing carrier aviation, was innovating its way out of the problem with two breakthrough concepts: the angled flight deck, which canted the landing center line away from the bow, and the mirror landing system, which removed some of the human error inherent in LSO commands. The mirror landing system, mounted slightly forward of the LSO platform on the port deck edge, incorporated a light source to project an approach path in the sky for aircraft to follow to land precisely at the same point each time. The light source, when reflected along that path to the pilot, created a circular image that became known as the "meatball" or "ball" to aid a pilot in lining up to land. In the center of the mirror are amber and red lights with Fresnel lenses. Although the lights are always on, the Fresnel lens makes only one light at a time seem to glow, as the angle at which the pilot looks at the lights changes. If the lights appear above the green horizontal bar, the pilot is too high. If they are below, the pilot is too low, and if the lights are red, the pilot is very low. If the red lights on either side of the amber vertical bar are flashing, it is a wave-off. Only when the pilot can confidently "call the ball" can he land safely on deck.[39] The LSO then, and now, retains ultimate authority to wave off an approach if the pilot has erred in technique or the deck is fouled.

The U.S. Navy was quick to adopt both innovations and integrate them into its carrier recapitalization and modernization plans. Pilots found that flying the "ball" was actually easier than relying on calls from the LSO. The flat-paddles approach technique gave way to a ball-centered, constant glide slope approach technique. Angle of attack (AOA) became a more reliable indicator of proper approach speed. For Mac, this meant relearning his scan to now focus on ball, line-up, and AOA, to use more measured longitudinal—fore and aft—stick inputs to control AOA, and throttle to control sink rate. The F8U RAG provided ample opportunity for Mac to adjust. He would log another twenty arrestments before completing the course of instruction with mirror approaches to the angled deck on the newly reconfigured *Coral Sea*.

Mac completed the course of instruction at VF-124 by August 1960, graduating with one of the first classes to issue from the F8U RAG at Moffett Field, and headed to VF-91 to be the executive officer. VF-91, "The Red Lightnings," began in 1952 as one of the first jet squadrons flying the F9F-2 Panther. It had transitioned to the F8U only a brief time before Mac arrived, so the squadron was still adapting. The F8U flight manual—developed by manufacturer Vought, fine-tuned in the Navy test program at Patuxent River, and published by the Bureau of Aeronautics—already existed, but an accepted Navy-wide set of Naval Air Training and Operating Procedures Standardization (NATOPS)–compliant procedures for all flight regimes did not.

Within fifteen months of Mac reporting to VF-91 as executive officer, the squadron experienced the loss of four aircraft through ejections, two of those fatal. Whether an F8U NATOPS manual would have provided a qualitative edge over the original flight manual sufficient to mitigate that accident rate is a subject for conjecture. But by the time Mac assumed command, he had already started to reverse the slide through his own rigorous application of lessons learned through a dozen years of flying. By careful attention to his officers' behaviors in the air and on the ground, by minute focus on aircraft maintenance processes and reporting, through steadfast in-close monitoring of pilot performance in the basics of air combat maneuvering and aerial gunnery, and by force of personality, he began to make corrections and redefine the norm. The process really began in the RAG, where he was cited in fitness reports for his special attention to the training of several other VF-91–bound officers. As executive officer, he initially drew scorn in some quarters for his strict grooming discipline and "regimentation extending from monthly personnel inspections to insistence of the highest standards of military bearing and courtesy." But his by-the-book adherence to the flight manual, to techniques retained from RAG training, to preflight briefings and postflight debriefs, and careful tutelage of junior pilots in exploiting the maximum capability of the F8U's early fire control system, he exerted a noticeable improvement in all-around squadron scoring for operational readiness. As executive officer, Mac's unrelenting attention to detail squadron appearance, maintenance records, and flight performance undeniably made the critical difference in VF-91 taking the coveted Pacific Fleet battle efficiency "E" in 1961.

Fleeting up to command of VF-91 in late 1961 was, by any measure, acknowledgment of a successful run of the gauntlet. Mac had negotiated the professional gates by which the Navy measured aviators who screened for squadron command and, to this point, had acquitted himself with a record of extraordinary aptitude and talent for command. To be sure, some junior officers and sailors chafed at the stiff regimentation; some older hands interpreted Mac's command climate as "Old Navy." Squadron command was stressful enough when one considers the inordinate burden of overseeing job performance, even the personal lives, of 20 officers and 176 enlisted people in the daily tempo and routinely dangerous trade of flying, servicing, and flying again. This was magnified several fold when the squadron operated from the carrier. Mac was probably burdened in a less overt way by the added stress of competing against his brother's highly successful record of wartime squadron command—a subliminal spur to one-up his boyhood mentor and idol. The added stress could manifest itself in increasingly brusque mannerisms. He was not a martinet, but he was noticeably intolerant of anything less than everyone's very best effort—from regulation appearance to step-by-step compliance with flight procedures—and he would not countenance any deviation from by-the-book conformance. One junior officer would recall being put in hack, or confined to his quarters, after he responded to Mac's call for the flight to report fuel states with an amount that was a fraction lower than the prebriefed bingo fuel state.

Nonetheless, Mac would continue to garner accolades from superiors. A succession of air group commanders noted his ability to keep morale high, continually attaining the highest reenlistment rate in the group. His last air group commander would cite him for the squadron's unusually high morale, noting that he was "the most enthusiastic and tireless commanding officer I have known. . . . Squadron spirit is as high as any I have ever observed." As evidence of Mac's zealous attitude, the senior officer highlighted with some satisfaction that Mac's squadron was the "first to revive the use of the sword manual of arms during squadron and air group inspections and pass-in-reviews on the west coast."

Mac was accumulating valuable time in the F8U during his tenure with VF-91—valuable in the sense that more time in operational training meant that piloting the aircraft was increasingly second nature when, at his level of seniority, he would be expected to be outside the cockpit leading others, thinking ahead for a flight of aircraft, assessing others' performance in the air, and directing the actions of greater numbers of aircraft in formation against opposing air or ground fire. When his command tour at VF-91 ended, he was not among the high-time Crusader pilots. That distinction generally went to those who came along later when the Crusader had been in the fleet for more than a decade and a career could be built flying a single type and model aircraft. In twenty-seven months as executive officer and commanding officer, he averaged just twenty hours per month in the jet—not a remarkable body of experience but one replete with the kind of flying that stressed pilot and aircraft to the limit. Every hop entailed some aspect of exploiting the aircraft's capability for combat. Every transit, every weapons detachment, entailed one-versus-one or two-versus-two air combat maneuvering to hone an instinctive sense for the aircraft and how to fully employ it against a determined opponent. Mac experienced numerous times when the aircraft would flip tail over nose in a momentary state of uncontrolled flight—valuable lessons in determining that fulcrum where controlled flight gives way to loss of control at high sustained Gs with airspeed bleeding off, and equally valuable lessons in regaining composure and controlled flight in minimal time through sparing use of control corrections. Where it counted, Mac delivered. His fitness report rater, noting his boundless zeal and energy, observed with equal pleasure Mac's unwillingness to concede defeat in the face of what appeared to be almost hopeless odds of repeating the squadron's 1961 win of the Pacific Fleet battle efficiency competition. In the end, VF-91 had the highest number of pilots to receive individual awards for 20,000- and 30,000-foot gunnery and surpassed the high-altitude gunnery record for the Pacific Fleet that they had established in the prior year's battle efficiency competition. Coupled with overall operational readiness scores, VF-91 would take the "E" for the second year in a row, a testament to Mac's impact on the squadron.

Mac reported to USS *Constellation* (CV 64) in November 1962 as assistant air officer, the same month that Swede Vejtasa assumed command of *Constellation*. Within the next year, as one of Vejtasa's departing actions, Mac would step up to become *Constellation*'s air officer. Vejtasa had previously served a tour as air officer in USS *Essex* during the Korean War, and among his department heads and their assistants on *Constellation*, he related most closely with the functions that Mac now performed under his command. Their relationship was always professional as skipper to subordinate, but it became closer to mentor and understudy. Mac had already cultivated and projected his own command countenance and behavioral style in his squadron command tour, but he scrupulously observed Vejtasa for traits that could be readily adopted as Mac contemplated a major command tour in the coming few years. Mac fully comprehended Swede's history, and he readily incorporated the observed behaviors into his own leadership approach. He resolved to stand visibly a bit firmer in front of authority on a few select issues but also to exhibit greater forbearance with subordinates. Perhaps in recognition of Mac's obvious efforts to remodel his deportment, Vejtasa, in his departing fitness report on Mac, two-blocked all his marks outstanding, with particular comment on moral courage, force, industry, and personal behavior, noting the appended award of the battle efficiency pennant as an example of Mac's exemplary performance.

For Ernie, a long career of faithful service was closing. Attendant to provisions of the "Hump Act" of 1959, serving captains who demonstrated the requisite qualifying criteria, such as points for sea service in combat, could voluntarily leave the service and retain the rank of rear admiral in retirement. Ernie was in command of an air reserve training center in Memphis in the late 1950s, but this was not considered a rung on the climb to flag rank on active duty. By contrast, the skipper of VF-16 in Ernie's air group command on *Lexington*, Paul Buie, was now in command of USS *Ranger* (CV 61) and would progress from there to flag rank. Retirement, even with the added distinction of flag rank on a business card, was not a comfortable fit for Ernie. He had difficulty making the transition from a life in uniform at sea and in the air to one in mufti looking for the next investment banking opportunity.

7

Dvinas and Silver Swallows

The entire country and the whole world are behind you every single minute. The nation's destiny totally depends on the air defense soldiers' ability to safeguard Hanoi.

—General Vo Nguyen Giap

"The Tonkin Gulf is one of the world's scenic wonders. Junks and sampans ply its blue waters, silhouetted against a horizon of sharp karsts rising strangely from the sea, their peaks shrouded in gray mist. But this placid picture, depicted in soft brush strokes by painters over the centuries is deceptive."[1] Thus does journalist and historian Stanley Karnow describe the inland sea that lies athwart what was North Vietnam at the midpoint of the last century. That idyllic conception was rent asunder by violent confrontation between the North Vietnamese and the United States in the 1960s. The Gulf of Tonkin incident in the summer of 1964 sparked an indignant but measured response from President Lyndon Johnson. In a speech to the nation on August 4, he projected a sense of resolve, but with a restraint that would come to define a bridled U.S. response to a decade of violent conflict: "The determination of all Americans to carry out our full commitment to the people and to the government of South Viet-Nam will be redoubled by this outrage. Yet our response, for the present, will be limited and fitting. We Americans know, although others appear to forget, the risks of spreading conflict. We still seek no wider war."[2]

With that declaration, he ordered Operation Pierce Arrow strikes by U.S. Navy aircraft on oil storage tanks and patrol boat bases in North Vietnam from carriers *Ticonderoga* and *Constellation* in retaliation for attacks on U.S. destroyers in the preceding days, only one of which was confirmed. Fearing continued hammering by the numerically superior U.S. air forces, the North Vietnamese dug in for the next six months, expecting an onslaught that never fully materialized. What they surmised from the limited U.S. activity was, above all, a lack of war-winning commitment in Washington. The limited response begat another attack on U.S. forces in the south in February, which in turn escalated into Operation Flaming Dart and then into Operation Rolling Thunder, an air campaign meticulously drawn to take down North Vietnamese capacity while carefully skirting any provocation of Hanoi's communist sponsors.

On the morning of April 3, 1965, a new aggressiveness by the Vietnam People's Air Force (VPAF) was on full display, inspired by the militancy of Le Duan, general secretary of North Vietnam's Communist Party. He had been the most persuasive promoter of resistance to a U.S. air campaign, and so on this day the VPAF would engage. Two groups of MiG-17s—"Silver Swallows" in the colloquial Vietnamese—from the 921st Fighter Regiment were fueled and uparmed behind revetment blast walls. The first flight of four, as the intercept flight, would be commanded by Lieutenant Pham Ngoc Lan; the second flight of two, acting as the cover flight, was intended to spar with U.S. escort fighters. Pham Ngoc Lan later recalled that morning: "We were quietly confident at the time and did not have any fear of the Americans, although we respected their experience and more modern equipment."[3] At mid-morning, air defense forces radar revealed the presence of a U.S. reconnaissance flight gauging weather over a likely target in the area of Thanh Hoa. VPAF fighter pilots were ordered to man their aircraft and remain in readiness in their cockpits. At 0948, with ground radar now painting the incoming American flight bearing down on bridges around Thanh Hoa, the launch alert was issued, engines started, aircraft taxied, and takeoff roll started down runway eleven. Once airborne, both the intercept flight and covering flight took a heading of 210 degrees for one hundred miles to the expected encounter. The MiGs were ordered to hug the terrain as much as possible to mask their radar returns in ground clutter; on their way, they commenced gentle *S*-turns in a loose four-finger formation. Pham was in the lead, his wingman Phan Van Tuc to his left and stepped down and slightly behind, with Ho Van Quy flying to his right stepped up and behind, and with Minh Phuong on Ho's wing. After twenty minutes' flight time, they had established visual contact with a group of Navy F-8Es and A-4s already making their strike runs on the Dong Phong Thong bridge nearby the Thanh Hoa bridge. Pham reported his sighting to ground control and was promptly ordered to engage. He scanned right and left, rendering hand signals to his flight to accelerate and gain altitude for as much energy advantage as could be generated before engaging. To his front and right, Phan sighted a section of Navy F-8Es making strafing runs on antiaircraft artillery (AAA) emplacements on the approach to the bridge. The lead F-8E had pulled off his initial run into the target due to obscuration by fog and mist, climbing to ten thousand feet as Phan took the first shot. Pham seeing that Phan had not closed the range sufficiently and his shots were falling off behind the target, immediately crossed in front of his wingman's aircraft and bore in on the same American target. When the distinctive planform of the Crusader filled his reticle at less than four hundred yards, he squeezed off three quick bursts of 37-millimeter (mm) and 23mm cannon fire, scoring hits on the canopy, vertical tail, and wing root near the cockpit, evidenced by the glint of aluminum shards kicking off the F-8E. As a flight of two, the MiG-17s rolled sharply left and nose down, then reversed to their right to engage what they thought was a second aircraft from the rear quarter as Pham passed the lead back to Phan telling him to take the shot. After a short burst, he saw smoke and metal springing from what he assumed was a different F-8E, and he reported he had scored the second kill of the day. In the melee, Pham lost visual contact with his other section of two MiGs; Phan was in trail as the two headed for Phuc Yen airfield, but Pham was forced to make a water ditching when his fuel was fully depleted. His MiG-17 came to rest in soft earth on a bank of the Duong River. Pham was unhurt but disconsolate at losing his aircraft, a valued resource of the people's communist government. In fact, once returned to his squadron, he was feted as a hero of the Democratic Republic of Vietnam. The day was set aside as a national holiday in North Vietnam, celebrated since as "Air Force Day."[4]

Official U.S. Navy accounts of the action confirm that only one F-8E, flown by Lt. Cdr. Spence Thomas of VF-211, was hit by MiG cannon fire and then nursed by Thomas to a field landing at Da Nang. One A-4C in the strike from VA-216 was reported lost to ground fire. But the aerial jet-on-jet combat was a first between the VPAF and the United States and was a turning point in the war, a harbinger of more intensive larger scale air warfare to come.[5] By the closing months of that year, the VPAF would claim fifteen kills of U.S. aircraft. Mac Snowden, who would arrive near year's end on Yankee Station in command of Carrier Air Wing Five (CVW-5) in *Ticonderoga*, was totally focused on preparing his air wing for the worst. The mood among Mac and his air wing pilots was eager but edgy, prompting heightened attention to intelligence briefs on enemy order of battle, recent MiG activity, and AAA and surface-to-air missile (SAM) dispositions.

Increased MiG activity throughout 1965 only complicated an already expanding air defense network of AAA and SAMs assembled by the North Vietnamese. The first indication of an SA-2 Guideline SAM installation—which the North Vietnamese called by the Russian designation S-75 Dvina—in April 1965 went unchecked by U.S. airstrikes until their effectiveness was shown in July by downing an American F-4C.[6] With virtually no modern weaponry on hand until the Pierce Arrow strikes, the North Vietnamese ability to exact these small victories was gaining notice. The unexpected lethality of the North's air defenses surprised many analysts. North Vietnam was viewed as an impoverished country, essentially an agrarian society lacking the sophistication to mount credible opposition to American airpower. By 1965, almost all of the North's fighters, AAA, and SAMs—and the training for those systems—were provided by China or the Soviet Union, often on-site while disguised in North Vietnamese uniforms. The VPAF had only been established five years prior to Pham Ngoc Lan's MiG-17 engagement, initially built around a small inventory of second-hand World War II–era transports and fewer than one hundred pilots trained abroad. In fact, "not many Vietnamese had even seen an airplane before the pilot training program began."[7]

In 1963, the VPAF and the air defense forces were merged, setting the stage for closer integration. Hanoi, with abundant aid from Moscow and Beijing, was able to operationalize air defense command and control by early 1965, anchored by a Chinese-constructed air warning system that could monitor air traffic well beyond urban concentrations of military infrastructure and along observed air routes taken by U.S. aircraft coming from the Gulf of Tonkin. An air operations center, situated at Bac Mai airfield outside Hanoi, digested and parsed data from early warning nodes across its network and passed processed information to a weapons control staff that coordinated engagements through a layered gauntlet of guns, missiles, and fighters.[8]

The emergence of the SAM threat distracted analysts and more specifically aircrew from the much more pernicious hazard of AAA. When the numbers were tallied, the SAMs were by no means as devastating as AAA, with Navy losses due to SAMs at 15 percent and to AAA at 37 percent of all inflight combat losses.[9] The Soviet-supplied SA-2 Guideline had been in service a number of years before the North Vietnamese became familiar with the intricacies of its use in their defense architecture, by then made infamous as the missile that brought down Central Intelligence Agency (CIA) pilot Gary Powers over the Soviet Union in 1960. By the end of 1965, SA-2 sites began showing up with regularity in reconnaissance images captured around Hanoi, Haiphong, and Hai Duong, urban areas that formed a concatenation of transshipment points for war matériel. The nomenclature SA-2 described not just the thirty-five-foot, boosted two-stage, liquid-fuel missile, but also the set of enabling apparatuses that placed the missile next to its intended victim. Prior to flight, the missile rested on a mobile wheeled launcher, rotatable through 360 degrees of azimuth to position the missile in optimal fly-out geometry. Six launchers normally ringed a major SA-2 site, supported by control vans. A Spoon Rest acquisition radar mounted atop a van containing its operators detected incoming airborne threats up to seventy miles away. As the distance closed to around thirty-five miles, the track was handed off to the Fan Song radar for missile guidance and target acquisition. The Fan Song held tracks for as many as four targets, and after launch it could guide up to three missiles to a single aircraft target.[10] Manning each SA-2, a "minimum of five primary crewmen, in addition to maintenance and other support personnel were required: three radar operators, one controller, and a battery commander."[11] These crewmen typically trained as a unit, with the first cohort of about one thousand spending nine months in the Soviet Union in study and practical application of air defense missile techniques. Graduated missileers from this initial class formed the crew of those first SA-2 sites identified in U.S. reconnaissance photos near Hanoi in April 1965. Once more, Soviet advisers in North Vietnamese uniforms were frequent visitors and observers inside the SA-2 sites.

For Navy alpha strikers, getting a visual cue on the SA-2 became critical to getting a broadcast out so that every aircraft in the flight knew where to look. Once a closing SA-2 was in sight, the learned response was for the pilot to maneuver to place the missile in his front quarter view on either side of his nose and watch until it was time to make a hard nose down turn. Climbing would only bleed off airspeed and limit options for responding to a second missile.[12] In time, the North Vietnamese would adjust their SAM tactics as well. Normally launched in pairs when U.S. aircraft were entering a predefined target area, the second missile was delayed slightly to intersect a target aircraft maneuvering away from the first missile. Once the boost stage of the missile burned out, the sustaining stage took over for another twenty seconds of burn, yielding a slant range of around thirty miles up to 60,000 feet. Once on a closing intercept course, the influence of the target would be set to initiate a proximity fuse, detonating the 350-pound high-explosive warhead within a few hundred feet to obtain lethal damage.[13]

For the considerable attention paid to SA-2s in prestrike planning and in prescribed maneuvers for avoiding them, they inflicted relatively few losses overall. In the spring of 1965, SA-2 operations were nascent, although their capability built steadily throughout the year as hardware was delivered and positioned and trained crews began arriving. By year's end, Iron Hand missions, intended to concentrate suppressing fire on SAM and AAA sites, were only beginning to hint at their potential usefulness but were not yet employed fleetwide, and a counter-radar missile would not arrive in theater until the following year. Eight Navy aircraft would fall to SA-2s in 1965, and the lack of a well-practiced, confidence-building tactic to neutralize the SAM threat cast a pall on operations in the waning months of that year.[14]

Despite their fearsome reputation, MiG engagements were much more random and unpredictable. Perhaps the rarity and sudden surprise of actually encountering a MiG in close quarters engendered a collective sense of foreboding that grew in each ready room retelling. In truth, by comparison to the menace of AAA and SAMs, the MiG threat was only marginal, accounting for only 2 percent of the Navy inflight combat losses.[15] Entering the 1960s, the Vietnam People's Air Force had only ninety qualified pilots; fewer than half were qualified in jets, and most of those were consigned to flying obsolescent cargo planes. In 1961, Hanoi selected eighty-two candidates for advanced jet training—fifty-two headed to the Soviet Union and thirty to China for their instruction. Those that graduated—typically one in five that started the training—formed the cadre of fighter pilots who would take on the U.S. Navy and U.S. Air Force in the aerial battles to come. In 1964, the Soviets donated thirty-six MiG-17 fighters and four MiG-15 two-seat trainers to the VPAF. These aircraft and the core group of Soviet- and Chinese-trained pilots composed the first fighter unit for the VPAF established in early 1964 as the 921st Red Star Fighter Regiment at Phuc Yen airfield. The MiG-17C that entered VPAF service was an evolved design of the original MiG-17A introduced in Soviet regiments at least a decade prior. The A model was itself a redesign of the MiG-15 that saw extensive combat against U.S. forces in the Korean War. U.S. airmen were startled in 1950 by the appearance of the swept-wing jet, with its brushed metal sheen and highly raked vertical tail. With an aerodynamic performance nearly comparable to that of U.S. fighters and the throw weight of its heavy guns, it was a fearsome disrupter to presumed U.S. air dominance—especially so in the experienced hands of the many Soviet "volunteers" who flew in those North Korean cockpits. With two port side 23mm guns firing 650 rounds per minute, coupled with a starboard side 37mm cannon firing 400 rounds per minute, the MiG-17 could throw out "70 pounds of shells in a two-second burst—twice the weight of fire of the F-8 Crusader's four 20mm cannon."[16]

The VK-1F Klimov-built turbojet that powered later model MiG-15s was retained in the MiG-17 redesign but was augmented with an afterburner in the C and subsequent models. With the added six hundred pounds of static thrust, MiG-17C pilots benefitted from an available energy surge in tight turns, a doubling of the rate of climb, and a higher service ceiling. A thinner airfoil shape and greater wing sweep opened up top end speed, and fences affixed to the upper wing surface mitigated airflow spillage down the length of the wing for surer high-G maneuvering. In addition, the wings were made dry, eliminating the susceptibility to combustion of wing-encased fuel bladders when penetrated by incendiary rounds. However, a rudimentary gunsight and aircraft instability at high speed conspired to make all but the most experienced VPAF pilots fairly inaccurate shooters.[17]

The first pilots trained on the MiG-17 made up two groups of roughly thirty each—among them Pham Ngoc Lan—that were sent abroad to the People's Republic of China and the Soviet Union for four to six years to complete the course of instruction—first solo through jet qualification. Initial screening for flying aptitude, physical fitness, or technical background weighed much less in the selection process than exhibiting aggressiveness and a correct political attitude. The course of instruction in the People's Republic of China and Soviet Union was a straightforward mix of ground school and inflight progression through increasingly more complex aircraft: an estimated thirty hours to solo in the piston-powered Yak-18 (or the Nanchang CJ-5 in licensed Chinese manufacture), followed by another eighty hours in the Czech-built L-29 Delfin jet trainer, and completing qualification with forty hours in the MiG-17. Training in actual dogfighting was not overly emphasized in recurring MiG training during and after flight school, probably mostly because the communist "way of fighting" relied heavily on strict ground control of engagements and hasty departure if the tactical situation did not favor a quick kill.[18]

About the same time the initial cadre of North Vietnamese MiG-17 trainees had completed their type training in China and moved with their maintenance trainees to Mong Tu airbase in China near the Vietnamese border, Mac Snowden was relinquishing command of his F8U squadron at sea near Japan in *Ranger*. Events unfolding in Southeast Asia foretold an increasing involvement for his naval aviation community and a generation of American servicemen. But at this point in 1963, Mac and his contemporaries could not have forecast—indeed, would not be even contemplating the possibility of—the tempest that would descend on Vietnam in only a few years. His two years as executive officer and commanding officer of VF-91 were, beyond the routine of administration, consumed by airborne training and instruction in the milieu of the Crusader community: air combat maneuvering. All F8 units—VF-91 was no exception—positively thrummed to the rhythm of constant aerial engagement: one on one, two on two, four on four, and four on many. Most often, dogfighting training was a squadron affair, occasionally involving a sister squadron. Fighting an identical aircraft minimized any hardware advantage while teasing out best practices in technique and honing individual skill with the Crusader. What had not yet appeared in any formalized training regimen was the notion of fighting dissimilar aircraft types or replicating the performance of anticipated enemy fighter aircraft in regular training evolutions. The occasional transiting air force fighter might be jumped and goaded into making a few turns, but the organized, monitored Red Flag–like range exercise was still years into the future.

From his time in VF-91, what Mac could not discern with any certainty drawn from first-hand experience was the nature of his opponent in the approaching conflict—the performance of his aircraft, the depth and sufficiency of his training, his motivation and resolve. Crusader training revolved around opposing other F-8s because hard data on a likely future opponent, much less the opportunity to fly against the opponent's equipment, did not exist. What little was known and passed on by the intelligence community and the Air Force about the MiG-17 was postulated from a rare opportunity to wring out a MiG-15 in 1953–54. Shortly after the cessation of Korean War hostilities, North Korean air force pilot No Kum Sok defected to South Korea, landing his MiG-15 at Kimpo airfield after a seventeen-minute flight from his home airbase in the North. The MiG was shipped to Wright-Patterson Air Force Base, where it underwent rigorous evaluation. Other than an approximation of

MiG-17 capability extruded from this predecessor aircraft, the "perceived wisdom on the MiG-17 versus other jet fighters was limited to the assessment of Chinese J-5s in evenly matched combat with Taiwanese F-86Fs in 1960, or Egyptian and Syrian examples fighting Israeli Mystere IVAs in 1956 and 1960."[19]

Not until 1969 was the United States able to obtain first-hand knowledge of the MiG-17. The air war over North Vietnam was in its fourth year, and MiG-17s and MiG-21s had proved to be exceptionally adept at harassing U.S. airstrikes. Yet despite anecdotal observations from pilots who had encountered and dealt with MiGs, little was truly understood about their mechanical makeup and flying qualities that might suggest weaknesses that could be exploited. The CIA initiated a program at Groom Lake, Nevada, that year built around a MiG-17 that was captured by the Israelis in their Six-Day War and offered to the United States. Under the code name Have Drill, the MiG-17 was instrumented and flown in 172 sorties, with a second Israeli-captured MiG-17 following behind with another 52 sorties under the code name Have Ferry. The MiG-17 was spun once, with recovery taking four turns and three thousand feet of altitude, as only the ailerons were hydraulically boosted; the rudder and elevator were manually controlled. Flight evaluation showed that above 0.85 Mach or 450 knots of indicated airspeed (KIAS), high control forces yielded a somewhat lethargic roll rate and pitch response. Above 375 KIAS, the airplane was prone to Dutch roll, and yaw control was always difficult in rough air. The MiG-17 cockpit was characterized as antiquated (in other words, straightforward and uncomplicated) and very cramped for pilots more than six feet tall.[20]

Navy aircrews were invited to participate in Have Drill/Have Ferry and evaluated the MiG-17 performance against multiple Navy fighter and attack aircraft, employing tactics most closely resembling what had been already observed in nearly five years of combat. In sixteen missions pitting the F-8E against the MiG-17, the Navy evaluators concluded that the MiG enjoyed a considerable advantage in roll rate and turn radius over the F-8E when both were below 450 KIAS, but the F-8E outperformed the MiG in acceleration, zoom climb, roll rate, and turn radius above 450 KIAS. At speeds between 300 and 350

KIAS, the low wing loading and 8 G structural limit translated easily to the MiG outturning the Navy aircraft in every encounter. What
most dismayed evaluators was the overconfidence and complacency
aircrews exhibited in set-piece engagements. Although all participants
acknowledged the difficulty of maintaining a visual lock on the MiG,

> Every Navy pilot engaged in the project at Groom Lake lost
> his first engagement with the Fresco (MiG-17C). The Fresco's
> over-performance in the Air Combat Maneuvering environ-
> ment surprised all crews concerned with the project. Recom-
> mendations from the U.S. Navy as a result of this evaluation
> were that Navy fighters should maintain a high energy level:
> 500–600 KIAS; avoid high "g" maneuvers below 500 KIAS; use
> thrust advantage to prevent the MiG-17 from getting into gun
> position; force the MiG-17 to fight above 475 KIAS; engage
> only as a section with strict mutual support; exploit the MiG's
> blind area below the horizontal, its poor roll rate, and marginal
> control effectiveness at high 'g'; use maximum rate/minimum
> radius turns two to three miles from the MiG and reverse base
> on energy and tactical situation.[21]

None of this information was yet available to Navy aircrews in 1965
when MiGs made their first appearance in the battlespace. Consistent
patterns or tactics on the part of the MiGs that could be observed and
retained by U.S. aircrews through the chance encounters of swirling,
high-G, gut-wrenching fight for advantage became the established
wisdom on MiG behavior and how best to counter it.

From the time of their Tonkin Gulf experience in 1964, the North
Vietnamese anticipated that all the elements of their national defense
might be called into action, and the 921st Fighter Regiment would
bear an inordinate burden. Flying hours for 921st pilots dramatically
increased over the next six months, and time on simulators, primitive
and unsophisticated though they were, ramped up as well. Chinese and
Soviet advisers focused their training regimen on integrating MiG-17
tactics into the North's expanding air defense network. Guidance was

given that "prolonged dogfights were to be avoided."[22] Pilots were conditioned by their doctrine and training to seek only intercepts and engagements where the opponent appeared isolated and encumbered with a heavy bomb load, and from which they could more easily obtain a clean escape following a slicing gun run. Hanoi's growing intelligence infrastructure was tuned to provide the best possible tactical picture for their MiG pilots. The Chinese and Soviets colluded with the VPAF to provide intelligence on carrier operations, including launch warnings and flight profiles of inbound alpha strikes.

Through most of 1965, preparation, intelligence, tactics, and aggressiveness in the face of daunting odds worked for the VPAF in claiming a semblance of parity with U.S. fighters. By the cessation of U.S. airstrikes in the North eight years later, the VPAF claimed sixteen aces with at least five aerial kills of U.S. aircraft. That contrasts with the ledger on the U.S. side of one Navy pilot and one Navy radar intercept officer ace, and one Air Force pilot and two weapons system operator aces. Allowing for inflated claims by the VPAF, the disparity is stark. Yet it fails to reveal a more critical indicator of aerial dominance achieved by the United States over time, such as a six-to-one favorable exchange rate for F-8Es.[23] The causes have been analyzed and debated but point primarily to two factors that bore most heavily on the U.S. inability to dominate completely from the air. First was battlefield geography that gave the North Vietnamese a home field advantage that they deftly exploited by coordinating the best mutually supporting effects of AAA, SAMs, and MiGs in a layered defense. When SAMs could drive attacking flights down to lower altitudes, the AAA could be used to best effect. MiGs, operating outside of prebriefed AAA and SAM envelopes and taking vectors from their ground controllers, could position for the best axis of approach to avoid detection and could pounce on ungainly bombers that had not expended their load or on stragglers coming off target runs low on fuel and making a straight line for the coast. The second factor making the task easier were U.S. rules of engagement dictated by the political leadership in Washington that played into the North's tactics: U.S. airstrikes on MiG airfields, Haiphong powerplants, Hanoi military and industrial complexes, Cam Pha port facilities, and Haiphong port operations where missile replenishment shipments were unloading on the docks were all forbidden for at least several years after the initial aerial hassle in April 1965; fortification and repositioning of defenses by Hanoi were allowed to take place during frequent bombing halts imposed by U.S. political leaders seeking some concession in negotiations; and target selection for U.S. airstrikes was meticulously controlled by Washington to avoid offending any of the communist states that were actively supporting Hanoi.

In a real sense, this was a limited war—but with the limiting constraints self-imposed by Washington. The character of the fight was of particular interest to Mac Snowden as he readied his air wing through the summer of 1965 preparing to arrive at Yankee Station in November. He followed the progress of CVW-16 in *Oriskany*, CVW-2 in *Midway*, and CVW-15 in *Coral Sea* already on station in the Tonkin Gulf through the spring and summer of 1965 and audited all available intelligence on the targets and air defenses that could be expected over the North. Mac was mindful that this limited war differed markedly from the total war described to him by his brother, Ernie. Against the Japanese twenty years before, U.S. naval aviation did not pull any punches, did not set aside enemy sanctuaries that were off limits to strikes, did not allow enemy fighters to go unmolested on their home airfields, and did not fail to commit the forces necessary to completely annihilate the enemy's naval aviation forces. Mac now prepared for the ultimate test of his flying career, and the boundaries were still being defined.

Twenty-five years before, Ernie had prepared to face a more conventional opponent, an industrial maritime nation that perceived its national interests to be best served by a blue-water navy—one that relied on aircraft carriers as an integral component of its maritime force and a corps of highly motivated aviators to operate from those carriers. The rise of Japan's naval aviation community mirrored that of the United States from its earliest days, even if it lagged by only a few years. From the first tentative steps—flying lessons for the initial student cadre under the tutelage of Glenn Curtiss at North Island—Japan's naval aviators nurtured for the next thirty years an esprit, a cultural ethos that defined their particular brand of risk-taking and aeronautical prowess prototypically embodied by Ernie's counterpart in the IJN, Takahashi Sadamu. Both had spent more than a decade of their adult lives in their naval service and, by the time the Pacific war erupted, more than half of that time in naval aviation, becoming steeped in the rituals, standards, expectations, and codes—spoken and unspoken—of a celebrated and honored warfighting union that sprouted thirty years before. Ernie and Takahashi had been peers, or at least near peers, on opposing sides, closely resembling each other by any gauge of professional competence: flying skill and experience, mastery of shipboard aviation, demonstrated record of superlative leadership in aviation squadrons, and an evident fervor for their aviation fraternity and its place in the service and for their nation.

Mac's experience was wholly different. Naturally, the tool set—ships and aircraft—had advanced technologically since Ernie's time in combat and continued to do so throughout Mac's career. But gone from the world stage were the fascist despots that had challenged the Western nations by large-scale destruction and massive death in the 1930s and 1940s, supplanted by new despots pedaling a warmed-over ideology about uniting the world's workers in a communist idyll. The world order had been rearranged such that confrontation with peer rivals devolved into brushfire wars on the edge of industrialized communities, with surrogates willing to fight and die for their communist patrons or some localized vision of workers' nirvana. The first taste of this was the Korean War, in which naval aviation adapted and acquitted itself well. Mac would soon experience it in Vietnam. But the circumstance of limited war in Vietnam meant that an opposite number for Mac such as existed for Ernie in Takahashi Sadamu would not rise in the Vietnam People's Air Force. Mac would arrive on Yankee Station in late 1965 with 15 years of unbroken ascendency in naval aviation, amassing more than 3,800 flight hours in multiple types of fighters, in all weather conditions, and with a thick portfolio of rigorous training in air combat maneuvering and air warfare simulation. His nearest competitor by age and standing in the VPAF may have been Pham Ngoc Lan, who by late 1965 was less than 2 years removed from having completed flight training and may have had 300 hours of flight time in a jet fighter with only a fraction of that time dedicated to the kind of air combat maneuvering his U.S. counterparts had seen. Indeed, if Pham Ngoc Lan was emblematic of the wise old sage in the VPAF, he would not stand equal to the typical U.S. fleet

nugget in terms of flight time and breadth of training. By that yard-
stick, the average neophyte U.S. naval aviator had accumulated at least
250 hours in basic and advanced jet training, supplemented by 100 or
so hours in the RAG learning how to fly and fight his airplane, and
added time thereafter as a new squadron member in exercises and
work-ups to hone his edge. What put the scales into equilibrium were
the onerous rules of engagement imposed on U.S. aircrews and the
VPAF's home field advantage and rules of engagement that discour-
aged prolonged dogfighting. In 1965, both sides were engaged in a
deadly dance to detect weakness, to spot deficiencies, and to develop
an advantage that could produce quick results.

8

Limited War

For the President, the Commander in Chief U.S. Pacific Fleet takes pleasure in awarding the Distinguished Flying Cross to Commander Macon Snowden, for heroism and extraordinary achievement in aerial flight while serving as Commander Attack Carrier Air Wing Five on 28 November 1965. His exceptional leadership and professional skill were in keeping with the highest traditions of the United States Naval Service.

—Adm. Roy L. Johnson, USN, Commander U.S. Pacific Fleet

Limited war—the second Asian conflict in a generation to be impaired by lack of U.S. political resolve, pursued despite painful and long-reaching sacrifice for incremental or poorly defined national goals, and waged in conformance to capricious and ill-informed rules of engagement—became Mac's all-consuming focus in August 1964. He was concluding twenty-one months as assistant and then air officer in USS *Constellation,* rotating on and off station in southeast Asian waters. Ominous portents of things to come were already starkly apparent to those in the theater in the months prior to August: an RF-8 from *Kitty Hawk,* reconnoitering the terrain in eastern Laos for communist resupply movement into South Vietnam, was lost to ground fire on June 6, and an F-8D was lost to ground fire the next day. By mid-June, *Constellation* was augmenting the reconnaissance with its own RF-8 flights.

On August 2, North Vietnamese torpedo boats approaching at high speed were met by fire from destroyer USS *Maddox* (DD 731). The encounter on this day was real enough: responding to a call for air support from *Maddox*, a formation of two F-8Es from VF-51 led by squadron skipper Cdr. Jim Stockdale and a second section from VF-53 led by executive officer Cdr. Robair Mohrhardt—both squadrons from USS *Ticonderoga*—responded with Zuni rockets and 20mm fire. One torpedo boat was rendered a smoking hulk, and two others were substantially damaged; however, the reaction from Washington was immediate. A reprisal was ordered, and sixty-seven aircraft from *Ticonderoga* and *Constellation* participated in a maximum effort to retaliate against torpedo boat bases and petroleum, oil, and lubricant storage facilities in and near the town of Vinh.[1]

As *Constellation*'s air boss, Mac was the owner of the "airfield," choreographing a highly ritualized interaction on the flight deck that aggregated weapons and aircraft, positioned aircraft in sequence, carefully calibrated the physics of mass and energy for launch, and flung fully loaded aircraft off the front end of the ship. At the center of this ballet were mostly teenage sailors who—for whatever they lacked in maturity ashore—conducted themselves with total dedication and focus. Under the air boss, they made up the V Division: moving, spotting, and fueling aircraft, operating the catapult and arresting gear, intermingling with air wing and squadron ordnance crew who groomed the aircraft for flight, and arming and uploading the weapons.

From his air boss perch above the flight deck, Mac oversaw the succession of aircraft departures off the bow on that oppressively tropical Wednesday morning, aware that a momentary lull after so big a launch would be replaced within two hours by the frenetic action of recovering those aircraft as they returned from combat. He was also aware in some inner recess of his thinking that this was not to be his opportunity to lead naval aviators into harm's way. What he could not have foreseen was that despite a successful strike that pummeled the target area, two aviators he watched depart that morning would not return. Lt. (jg) Richard Sather would perish when his A-1H Skyraider was brought down by ground fire, and Lt. (jg) Everett Alvarez would eject from his A-4C Skyhawk to be captured on the ground by the North Vietnamese. Alvarez would be the first of hundreds of naval and Air Force aviators to be taken prisoner, and he would endure eight and a half years as a prisoner of war (POW).[2]

At home, in the run-up to *Constellation*'s deployment, Mac had signed a lease on a mid-century-style bungalow in Coronado, erected among rows of tract dwellings on the last hundred acres of residential landfill property over Spanish Bight. He reasoned that a short commute to the ship, berthed quayside at North Island less than a mile away, could allow the greatest time with family in a home setting but also unbounded hours in ship's spaces attending to urgent precruise readiness issues. It was a revelation for Mac to contrast what he now witnessed on North Island and beyond the gate in Coronado with the descriptions of the area in Ernie's letters a generation before. Of course, the hundreds of aircraft parked all over the base had matured greatly in sophistication and performance. But every space on North Island not committed to runways, taxiways, aircraft parking ramps, or hangars seemed to be in use for newly organized command or administrative offices. The sprawling overhaul and repair department—then a subordinate command of the naval air station—had grown from a back-shop activity in Ernie's time to a substantial industrial complex employing thousands of machinists, aircraft electricians, welders, riveters, press operators, and jet engine mechanics, just beginning to absorb all Navy rework on the fleet of F-4 Phantoms.

Coronado was changing as well. From Ernie's time, when residents occupied in the hospitality trade supporting the Hotel Del Coronado outnumbered Navy residents, a demographic rebalance to majority Navy homes had occurred. It was said in the mid-1960s that 75 percent of the students enrolled in Coronado High were the sons and daughters of serving Navy fathers. Hollywood celebrities were still in evidence but were largely confined to the Hotel del Coronado grounds. Ernie very likely mingled with Errol Flynn, Regis Toomey, and John Payne in the North Island Officers Club when they were on location, whereas Mac only rarely would sight Charlton Heston or Robert Wagner on the Hotel Del tennis courts when taking the family for holiday brunch in the hotel. Noticeably absent from an earlier era was the frequent presence on base of Hollywood production companies and celebrity cast members playing scenes in film paeans to naval aviation. The public's appetite for aviation adventure yarns had been sated by the mid-1960s—films then celebrated the antihero and counterculture mores. And the Navy, at one time interested in the earned media public relations value of on-location shooting, was preoccupied with ramping up for a wartime commitment.

Mac detached from *Constellation* within days after the retaliatory strikes on North Vietnam—known to most in Navy circles as Operation Pierce Arrow—and was assigned to Readiness Carrier Air Wing 12 (CVW-12, or Air Wing 12), for immersion in air wing operations and refamiliarization with high-performance jet aircraft. He was now the prospective commander of Air Wing 5, the collection of squadrons that had just performed so well in the reprisals against North Vietnamese torpedo boat facilities and petroleum infrastructure. Jim Stockdale, a central figure in the Tonkin Gulf event as the commanding officer of Air Wing 5's VF-51 and the airborne leader through most of the encounter, was just a half-step behind Mac in his career progression. Having relinquished command of VF-51, Stockdale was en route to his next assignment as commander of Air Wing 16 when Mac took over CVW-5. For the remainder of 1964, Mac accumulated more than one hundred hours in the F-8E, A-1H, and TF-9J for instrument time, culminating in carrier qualifications aboard USS *Oriskany* in the A-1H. The F-8E, an updated version bearing the alphanumeric nomenclature of a new Defense Department–wide naming convention for all military aircraft, was still a type and model with which he was intimately comfortable, having flown the F8U in VF-91 but now with a new series design that added a slight bump in available afterburning thrust with the J57-P-20 and an improved fire control radar with the AN/APQ-94 by Magnavox.[3]

Not all of Mac's reimmersion in air wing routine involved flying. With the prospect of leading the air wing back to Vietnam, he and other uninitiated aircrew members were required, as potential combatants at high risk of capture, to undergo specialized training in survival, evasion, resistance, and escape (SERE). The course of instruction was broken into three phases: survival off the land; evasion, or avoidance of discovery by enemy forces lasting two days; and about four days of familiarization with life as a POW.[4] A week of survival training consisted of equal parts classroom instruction and practical fieldwork, which in Mac's class was conducted on the breakwater shoreline at the north end of Naval Air Station North Island. The survival segment taught students how to recognize and harvest edible plants, hook fish, snare small mammals, purify water, and administer basic first aid—reminding many of lessons learned in Boy Scouts but weighted with more ominous portent. Evasion picked up with personal camouflaging, concealment, discreet signaling, and orienteering over unfamiliar landscape. The final phases moved to a more remote location at Warner Springs, a stretch of northern San Diego County dominated by rolling hills and mesas capped with manzanita and sage at the base of Mount Palomar. Here, specially selected Asian-American enlisted instructors did their best to replicate conditions that might be anticipated if students were captured and detained as prisoners of war. In the fall of 1964, only a handful of Navy and Air Force pilots were held as "guests" of the North Vietnamese, and little intelligence about their experiences in captivity had yet seeped out to inform the SERE curriculum. Most of what was reinforced at this stage was limited to lessons learned from returning Korean War prisoners. Perhaps the greatest value of the training was reinforcement of the military code of conduct, and within that prescription, Article 3 may have provided the best psychological preparation: "If I am captured, I will continue to resist by all means available." As the senior officer in his class, the resistance phase proved to be personally challenging for Mac. Berated frequently in front of the assembled "POWs" by instructors acting in character, Mac endured at least one slap to the ground with a cupped fist and several hours with his six-foot four-inch frame contorted to fit the inside dimensions of a four-by-two-by-two-foot pine box specially constructed for insubordinate prisoners. As harsh and taxing as the training was, it could not begin to duplicate what American POWs were actually going through in North Vietnamese prisons: "From the very beginning of the war, North Vietnam's stated position was that American prisoners captured in North Vietnam were 'war criminals' who had committed crimes against the North Vietnamese people in the course of an illegal war of aggression and that therefore the American prisoners were not entitled to the privileges and rights granted to prisoners of war (POW) under the terms of the Geneva Convention."[5]

During that fall of 1964, engagement by naval aviation in the Tonkin Gulf was relatively limited following the Pierce Arrow strikes other than routine patrolling. What was evident from reconnaissance flights was that resupply of the insurgency in the south through Laos by the North Vietnamese continued unabated. However, in February 1965, things began to heat up when reprisals for new and more audacious attacks on U.S. and South Vietnamese facilities were unleashed under a series of Flaming Dart strikes. These actions prompted plans for a more comprehensive air campaign that focused on target priority from lists developed by the Joint Chiefs of Staff in concert with the national security staff and ultimately given the operational moniker Rolling Thunder. It was intended as a broader response to increased North Vietnamese hostilities rather than individual hostile acts that emanated from the growing tensions.[6] The political advisers and service chiefs convinced themselves that selective pressure controlled by Washington combined with diplomatic overtures would prevail and compel Hanoi to end its aggression.

Rolling Thunder's initial formulation grew out of a comprehensive target list published a year prior as the "94 target list," contained in commander in chief Pacific's operations plan 37–64. The Joint Chiefs of Staff and the civilian defense leadership, reasoning that North Vietnam's indigenous industrial capacity was practically nonexistent, devised and issued a campaign plan to take down the means of logistical resupply that might have the effect of forcing an end to North Vietnam's belligerent behavior. By focusing airstrikes on bridges, rail yards, docks, barracks, and supply dumps, U.S. airpower could reduce North Vietnamese support of communist operations in Laos and South Vietnam and limit North Vietnamese capabilities to take direct action against Laos and South Vietnam. President Lyndon B. Johnson later noted: "By keeping a lid on all the designated targets, I knew I could keep the control of the war in my own hands."[7] On March 2, the first mission of the new operation was launched against an ammunition storage area near Xom Bang, and nineteen Republic of Vietnam air force A-1 Skyraiders struck the Quang Khe naval base.[8] The sobering outcome for the U.S. Air Force and for U.S. aviators in general was that six of their aircraft were shot down during the mission. Five of the downed crewmen were rescued, but "it was a sobering portent of things to come."[9]

In mid-January 1965, Mac assumed command of Carrier Air Wing 5 (CVW-5), which was scheduled to depart on board *Ticonderoga* in the fall. He had seven months to impart his leadership style and rebuild the air wing for what would certainly be more intense and sustained combat operations in Vietnam than it experienced on its prior cruise. Performance in the air was the surest and fastest way to demonstrate his bona fides for the CVW-5 squadron aviators. Mac wasted no time in adding his name to the daily schedule in late January for several days of flying in support of Ready Strike IV, a competitive exercise under command of Fleet Air Alameda to test conventional weapons delivery tactics and accuracy. Mac flew the F-8E alternately with VF-51 and VF-53 and the A-1H with VA-52. The pace did not appreciably lessen when in February and March he joined flights with VF-51 and VF-53 supporting Exercise Silver Lance, commanded by First Fleet, as aggressor air forces in the largest peacetime Navy and Marine amphibious maneuvers conducted until that time. The entire air wing deployed to Naval Air Auxiliary Station Fallon through most of July for extensive conventional weapons training, where Mac personally coordinated and led numerous practice air wing strikes to the nearby Nellis Air Force Base, Twentynine Palms, and Fallon ranges, culminating in another weapons exercise at Marine Corps Air Station Yuma toward the end of the summer.

Dress rehearsal began in August from USS *Ticonderoga* steaming off Southern California—with mounting solemnity pervading all aspects of flight planning, in-flight mission performance, and safe recovery. *Ticonderoga's* air plan for August 29 underscored the complexity and tempo of operations as the ship and air wing prepared for imminent departure to waters off Vietnam. Issued by the ship's air operations officer, the plan set flight quarters for 0530, with the weather brief up by 0615. The ship's position at 0700 was expected to be 30 miles due south of San Clemente Island and some 75 miles west-southwest of San Diego, headed 320 degrees when the first event was to launch. Then at 1600, it would take a course of 140 degrees until 2300, when flight operations were expected to secure for the day. Routine details for flight check-in during the multiple planned events were given in numbered frequencies or preset channels to report inbound for positive control over the Chocolate Mountain aerial gunnery range and, separately, for the San Clemente impact area. References were cited for a fixed loading plan for ordnance to be carried on all strikes—every flight event would involve live fire on a target range. The Chocolate Mountain aerial gunnery range is a half-million acres of Navy-owned and -administered mountainous desert terrain just east of the Salton Sea in California, while San Clemente—also Navy-owned—is the southernmost Channel Island, covering 37,000 acres 68 miles west of San Diego.

The first event of the day that Sunday called for fighters, photographic reconnaissance, tankers, and attack aircraft to head northeast for the range in the Chocolate Mountains. F-8Es from the VF-51 Screaming Eagles and VF-53 Iron Angels would fly a practice surface-to-air missile exercise, entering and departing the target area while four A-4Cs with the VA-144 Roadrunners, four A-4Es with the VA-56 Champions, and four A-1Hs from the VA-52 Knight Riders lined up for their runs and dropped their ordnance. A lone A-3B from the VAH-4 Fourrunners was to be on hand for refueling exiting the target area, and an RF-8 from the VFP-63 detachment would provide pre- and post-strike target area photos. Then, at 1200, the sequence repeated, with four F-8Es, four A-4Cs, and four A-4Es leaving the ship for a shorter flight to the San Clemente Island target. At 1500, yet another event launched, similarly composed, bound once again for the Chocolate Mountains. The tempo continued through the last launch of the day at 2100 for another run to the Chocolate Mountains—this time in darkness. This rehearsal rhythm continued with little letup until early September when the air wing squadrons repositioned briefly at their home fields before returning for flyaboard in late September. CVW-5 and USS *Ticonderoga* started their cruise to Southeast Asian waters on September 28, 1965.[10]

Ticonderoga with CVW-5 embarked arrived and took station more than one hundred miles offshore of South Vietnam, steaming between the eighteenth and nineteenth degree parallels. This position placed *Ticonderoga* geographically within an operational area offshore from South Vietnam known as Dixie Station. Aircraft carriers arriving in Southeast Asia would normally begin operations on Dixie Station, supporting the movement of U.S. ground troops ashore, before moving north to take position on Yankee Station off the coast of North Vietnam. With a few days of preparation before combat operations began in earnest, Mac availed himself of the pause to cross-deck to USS *Bon Homme Richard* (CV 31) with his parachute bag full of flight gear. By prior arrangement with CVG-19 on *Bon Homme Richard*, Mac would fly several armed reconnaissance flights over North Vietnam with VF-194—the same Red Lightnings he had commanded a few years before, but now with a new number designation—as wingman to a combat-experienced Red Lightning skipper, both to whet his temperament for combat and to familiarize himself with the "course rules"—the communications protocols, ingress and egress procedures, and prominent terrain features. Returning to *Ticonderoga* at the end of October, he had his heavy attack squadron fly him in an air wing A-3B Skywarrior to Tan Son Nhut Air Base in South Vietnam, primarily for briefings on air rescue capabilities from the Air Force, with an interim stopover at Korat Royal Thai Air Force Base for briefings on Air Force F-105 operations in North Vietnam.

As combat intensity ramped up during this phase of the war, one archivist noted in a later retelling: "Leadership was extremely important, especially at the air wing level. Each carrier acted as an independent war-making machine, and the combat tactics employed by one air wing on-line in the Gulf of Tonkin might be far removed from another carrier air wing on-line at the same time. . . . Not all air wings were equal in the task of air combat—putting bombs on target, and survival—and the differences more often than not could be traced to leadership."[11] Mac would soon undergo his own most critical leadership test. When *Ticonderoga* and CVW-5 finally began combat flights in early November, the remainder of that month was dominated by cyclic operations against preassigned and on-call targets in South Vietnam. Mac pulled his share of assigned targets on these daily penetrations, flying twenty-eight missions in three weeks, allocating equal time between VF-51 and VF-53 sorties. November 14 was a typical day. Mac flew lead for preassigned targets—both reported to be Viet Cong resupply and troop concentrations at the base of the central highlands near the Cambodian border. The first

target was about thirty-five miles southwest of the village of Ban Me
Thuot, with a secondary target about forty miles due south of the village. The area lay at the southern terminus of a line extending northward to Pleiku that had been hotly contested by the Viet Cong, who
were making excursions from their Cambodian sanctuaries throughout October and early November. The Viet Cong gains were being
thrown back by the U.S. First Cavalry as they reinforced 5th Special
Operations Group advisers who were feeling the brunt of the offensive. Mac picked up the Nha Trang TACAN (tactical air navigation)
and calculated a direct route to the target area.

Mac's flight of four comprised VF-51 F-8s, with Lt. J. B. Allen on
his wing and Lt. Cdr. Bob Leibel leading the second section with Lt.
John Eppinger. On launch from 150 miles southeast of Saigon, each
member of Mac's Kilo flight took up a heading inside the squadron's preassigned departure sector from 310 degrees to 340 degrees
off the ship's heading, checking in and making the rendezvous with
Mac as the Kilo leader once cleaned up with landing gear and flaps
retracted and established in the climb. Once over the beach and
headed inland, Mac checked in with the tactical air control system
operating from Pleiku in II Corps area, reporting "feet dry" with
side number, mission number, flight composition, bombs, rockets,
and 20mm ordnance load, time off "Panther" (*Ticonderoga* radio call
sign), and, finally, requested identity and contact frequency of the
forward air controller (FAC) that would confirm the assigned targets. On this day, the Army's 219th Reconnaissance Aviation Company—the Headhunters—were working the target area from their
Cessna O-1 Bird Dog.[12] The Headhunters were low and slow, arcing just above the tree line at never more than 100 knots. When
it was time to mark targets for the inbound F-8s, the O-1 carried
white phosphorous rockets that left a visible trail and impact point.
Once communications were established, the FAC gave Kilo flight a
target elevation, location of friendlies still in the area, run-in direction, and expected AAA fire. Remnants of retreating Viet Cong units
remained to be marked, so Kilo flight worked over the area, reserv-
ing some of their ordnance load for the secondary target where they
picked up a second FAC to start it over again. Determined counter-
fire in form of coordinated AAA had not shown to be well disciplined

or tightly organized at this point in the central highlands of South Vietnam, if only because the battlefield was fluid, and concentrated return fire was not easy to direct while on the run under heavy tropical canopies. Opposition to close air support or interdiction airstrikes might best be characterized as benign. The principal value of Dixie Station for aviators, beyond timely on-call support to ground forces in close contact, was in acclimating new arrivals on Dixie Station to the course rules, tempo, and rhythm of daily airstrikes. That daily routine would be pressurized by a demonstrably more stressful environment over North Vietnam in due time.

When *Ticonderoga* steamed north, the character of flight operations changed markedly, now dominated by so-called alpha strikes that massed significant numbers of aircraft against highly protected infrastructure targets. At this point in the conflict, these targets were typically limited to rail and highway bridges, petroleum storage sites, and transshipment points for the movement of warmaking materials supporting insurgency in the south. That the engagement of these targets was routinely micromanaged in the planning process beforehand by a coterie of defense policy authorities in Washington was already a source of frustration and risk for naval aviators flying over North Vietnam. On November 25—Thanksgiving Day at home—prestrike planning was complete, and CVW-5 launched its first alpha strike of this cruise over North Vietnam: destruction of the Me Xa highway bridge. At least three to four MiG-17s were directed by their ground controller to intercept *Ticonderoga's* strike. It is likely that Lieutenant Pham Ngoc Lan and Phan Van Tuc, the VPAF airmen who riddled an F-8 with 37mm and 23mm fire the previous April, were piloting at least two of those MiGs. A first MiG fired without scoring any hits. A pair of MiGs followed that initial run by making a firing pass at two A-4Es from VA-56, inflicting slight damage on one with 23mm fire. The second MiG engaged in a low-altitude, twisting melee with an A-4E but broke off in less than five minutes without gaining advantage.[13] But as the first MiG lined up for its firing pass on the A-4E, the pilot radioed an urgent call to the strike group for support. Mac, hearing the transmission but minutes away on a heading opposite the A-4E's reported position, reacted immediately. Two thoughts likely raced through his mind as he processed this encounter: first, the imperative to insert himself and protect his strikers, preventing the strike from disintegrating into mayhem and ensuring everyone got safely back to the ship; and simultaneously, the overwhelming urge, even compulsion, to engage with the enemy employing everything he had trained for and learned preparing for aerial combat over the last fifteen years. Mac gave his wingman a head nod and pushed the throttle past the detent up to maximum afterburning thrust while pulling into the vertical. At the top of his climb he was inverted, rolling over to level flight to take a 180-degree change in heading. The altitude and speed gained would provide an energy advantage as he and his wingman went supersonic, headed for the A-4's last reported position. Ultimately, the MiGs had broken off and extended their separation from the area without waiting for the engagement that Mac was hoping for. All of CVW-5's aircraft returned safely on this day from the alpha strike on Me Xa, having dropped the bridge and interrupted North Vietnam's logistical resupply operation, if only briefly.

Three days later, the air wing would assemble for another alpha strike, this time on the Ha Chanh highway bridge. This would be a two-carrier strike, with CVW-5 joined by a number of aircraft from CVW-19 on *Bon Homme Richard*. Mac had the preponderance of aircraft involved in this strike, and his staff and his squadron commanders retained the central role in the prestrike planning. En route, Mac detached aircraft from CVW-19's VF-191 to strike an alternate target in nearby Thanh Hoa. The primary strike at the Ha Chanh bridge was a major success, dropping one span, damaging others, and destroying much of the surrounding infrastructure. For his overall role in planning and leading the alpha strike, Mac would be presented a Distinguished Flying Cross. The leader of the bombers in the strike, VA-144 squadron commander David B. Miller, would also be recognized with a Distinguished Flying Cross. At the alternate target near Thanh Hoa, VF-191 executive officer Cdr. Howie Rutledge would earn a Distinguished Flying Cross, but he would ultimately pay a steep price for his valor. His F-8 was downed by North Vietnamese ground fire over Thanh Hoa; he survived the ejection but would spend the next eight years as a POW in Hanoi.

Six days later—December 1—the targeting assignment was to take out a multispan bridge over the Song Thai Binh River connecting

Highway 5 to Hanoi in the west and Haiphong in the east from the city of Hai Duong, lying adjacent to the bridge. Hai Duong, due to its geography, was a major crossing point for war matériel entering the country at the port of Haiphong. Therefore, the approaches to the bridge as well as the storage areas in the city were heavily defended by an array of AAA emplacements of 37, 57, and 85mm, in addition to smaller caliber ground fire. At this point in the conflict, few of these guns were radar-controlled. Instead, "pure concentration was the name of the game—concentration and fire discipline."[14] Mac's CVW-5 staff members began their prestrike planning in earnest the day prior. If Mac had any urge to contemplate the similarities between what he was engaged in and Ernie's experiences twenty years earlier, there was scant time for it. True, the brothers' respective roles as CAGs in both wars was to plan, fly, and lead air attacks from carrier flight decks by massed numbers of aircraft—the role of CAG had not appreciably changed in the intervening twenty years. In his 1943 correspondence to Mac, Ernie noted that his air group's leaders, his squadron commanders, were all Naval Academy graduates and career officers but that most of the squadrons were populated overwhelmingly by reserve officers called up hurriedly for World War II. Ernie had clearly held both in very high regard. In Mac's 1965 air wing, the mix of academy and reserve career officers among squadron skippers was more balanced, and the same was probably true among junior officers in each of the squadrons. Ernie's squadron skippers were, on average, five to eight years younger than Mac's, with far less total flight time—the commanding officer of Ernie's torpedo squadron had earned his wings only four years prior to the group's major action in the Marianas Turkey Shoot in June 1944. If there was a difference in flying experience between the squadron commanding officers of CVG-16 in 1944 and those of CVW-5 in 1965, it was that Ernie's skippers were in almost constant action for the better part of eight months before the Turkey Shoot. The battle of the Philippine Sea was a large-scale effort, presenting enemy air, ship, and island targets unlike anything experienced later in CVW-5's strikes in Vietnam. CVG-16's squadron skippers—given their constant and intense combat flying leading up to the Turkey Shoot—proved themselves up to that challenge, with all three earning the Navy Cross for their actions on June 19–20.

The contrast in flying experience is borne out by the extensive flying backgrounds of each of Mac's squadron skippers. Most had been flying high-performance jet aircraft of different types for the better part of a dozen years. At least one had prior combat experience in Korea. Among Mac's squadron skippers and executive officers, a few were test pilot school graduates, and one had been a Blue Angel. There was an abundance of high-timers, and they provided exemplary leadership in the air. Before *Ticonderoga*'s cruise was finished, at least one skipper and his executive officer in an A-4 squadron would earn Silver Stars, and most CVW-5 squadron skippers and executive officers would earn multiple Distinguished Flying Crosses. From World War II to Vietnam, naval aviators exhibited equal amounts of aerial skill and fearlessness. If there were marked differences between 1944 and 1965, they were in the performance of the aircraft and the intensity of the opposing ground fire. Added to the ubiquitous presence and concentration of AAA was the ever-growing newer threat of SAMs to complicate Mac's problem. Finally, there was always the air threat: Ernie, leading massed aircraft attacks on Pacific island targets, could expect to encounter opposition from Japanese A6Ms that were also usually at the extent of their range tether. Naval aviators of Ernie's era learned quickly that their enemy's tight-turning performance could be offset by maintaining a speed advantage and avoiding a slow, twisting fight. Mac's aviators had already encountered the specter of ground-controlled MiG intercepts by fast movers that could fairly well match the Navy bombers in performance and had the home field advantage. Mac now had to anticipate and plan for a surprise encounter on every flight over the North Vietnamese shoreline, with MiGs taking a ground-controlled vector to the most vulnerable position of a formation. At the time of the Pierce Arrow strikes in August 1964, thirty-six MiG-15s and MiG-17s had just arrived at Phuc Yen near Hanoi. By the fall of 1965, the numbers of MiG fighters based at Phuc Yen probably exceeded fifty, with additional numbers of MiGs then based at Kep northeast of Hanoi, and more advanced MiG-21s just becoming operational from both sites.[15] The MiGs encountered by CVW-5 on Thanksgiving Day over the Me Xa highway bridge target had most likely sortied from Phuc Yen, yet preemptive or even retaliatory strikes against aircraft and facilities at

Phuc Yen were still ruled off limits by the U.S. civilian defense leadership in November and December 1965.

Another target preoccupied CVW-5 planners at the end of November. Hai Duong was a key transshipment point for war matériel situated halfway between the port city of Haiphong and the capital of Hanoi. As such, it was most assuredly well defended, ringed by well-positioned AAA gun emplacements, augmented by a well-practiced militia that on short alert could form ranks of small arms shooters ready to throw up a wall of lead to riddle low flyers. The December 1 alpha strike on Hai Duong, reconstructed from aviation histories, personal recollections, award citations, a description of a notional alpha strike in *On Yankee Station*, and notes taken during the mission by Mac, unfolded this way:[16]

0830   Strike brief: Assigned pilots mustered in the wardroom for an initial overview of the Hai Duong area and the highway bridge. CAG Mac Snowden opened the brief by describing target objectives and overall flight composition. Mac turned the briefing over to his operations officer to guide the participants through the flight order, weapons loads, communications protocol, ingress and egress routes, navigation waypoints, target layout, and division run-in order. Finally, the wing intelligence officer took over to set the threat picture by providing the latest available information on what to expect in the target area in the way of AAA concentration and disposition, SAM locations, anticipated MiG activity, and likely MiG threat approach axis. Flight composition, strike assignments, side numbers, and call signs were made clear:

Badman (Strike Lead): flak suppressors and Target CAP, Mac Snowden (#105) and wingman Fred Dale (#106)
Batterup (VF-51): flak suppressors and Target CAP, Charles McDaniel (#108) and Roy Miller (#109)
Firefighter (VF-53): MiG CAP, Bill Gureck (#224) and William Brougher (#232)

Warpaint One (VA-144) bombers: Roger Bos (#546), John McCormick (#547), Len Jenkins (#540)

Warpaint Two (VA-144) bombers: Bernie White (#545), Patrick Hale (#544), Ron Boch (#542), Bob Maier (#541)

Champ One (VA-56) bombers: Bill Nealon (#461), R. W. Sturgeon (#464), W. L. Cain (#465), D. M. Palmer (#473)

Champ Two (VA-56) bombers: Render Crayton (#468), R. Simmons (#472), J. O. Belcher (#466), E. A. Pfeiffer (#462)

0930   Ready Room briefs: The strike participants made their way to their respective squadron ready rooms to continue the strike brief in greater detail pertinent to their squadron assignments, including run-in order; approach and roll-in headings; sequence of detachment for flak suppressors; more individualized information for each member of the strike to include preferred bailout points, search and rescue safe areas and frequencies, personal identifiers for challenge and response.

1030   In the respective squadron spaces, flight gear—G-suits, torso harnesses with stitched pockets for pistol, survival knife, and personal items with oxygen mask attached, and helmet—was donned for the walk on to the flight deck for aircraft preflight.

1045   The order was broadcast from primary flight control to start engines; *Ticonderoga's* signal bridge hoisted the Foxtrot flag and accompanying corpen pennant from half-staff to fully closed, then hauled the "Fox Corpen" (flying course) signal down to signify that the ship was turning into the wind to launch aircraft with maximum wind over the deck.

1100   Launch and Rendezvous: VA-56's A-4s took an initial heading off the catapult stroke from 30 degrees to 60 degrees from the reference radial defined by the ship's heading; VA-144's A-4s went from 280 degrees to 310 degrees. VF-51's F-8s assumed their initial heading from the ship on a vector from 310 degrees to 360 degrees, with VF-53's F-8s heading from due north to 030 degrees. The strike elements climbed to assigned altitudes and started a slow orbit until the strike group was assembled. Radio silence was maintained throughout the rendezvous.

1105   Leave RZ point: CAG Mac Snowden pointed toward a prebriefed waypoint (point A) and headed off with the flight in trail, climbing to 20,000 feet altitude.

1109   Leave point A.

1128   Coast-in point: CAG Snowden called "feet dry" as the strike group crossed the beach over the North Vietnamese landmass and pilots set their arming switches in their cockpits. Mac began a gradual descent from 20,000 feet altitude to arrive at a prebriefed roll-in point on the target at 10,000 feet.

1131   Highway 18: This major east-west highway north of Hai Duong was a prominent physical landmark that served to cue the flak suppressors to begin accelerating toward the target. The flak suppressors fired their Zuni rockets and selected bursts of 20mm fire beginning at 4,500 feet and pulled off the target by 3,000 feet, shifting their scan to air threats, mindful of the potential for MiGs attempting to pounce on the A-4s. As the strike group approached the target from the north, it flew an arcing counterclockwise turn as divisions of bombers from VA-56 and VA-144 rolled in on the bridge in sequence. The attack was complete in less than six minutes as aircraft exited the area, rejoining in twos and threes headed northeast.

1137   End of ridge: Jinking their way out of the area, the strikers aimed for another physical landmark, the Ytn Tu Mountain Range that ran east-west north of Highway 18 and afforded some degree of screening cover as aircraft accelerated to maximum speed to reach the coastline and "feet wet."

**Figure 4. CVW–5 Alpha Strike on Hai Duong
Highway 5 Bridge, December 1, 1965**

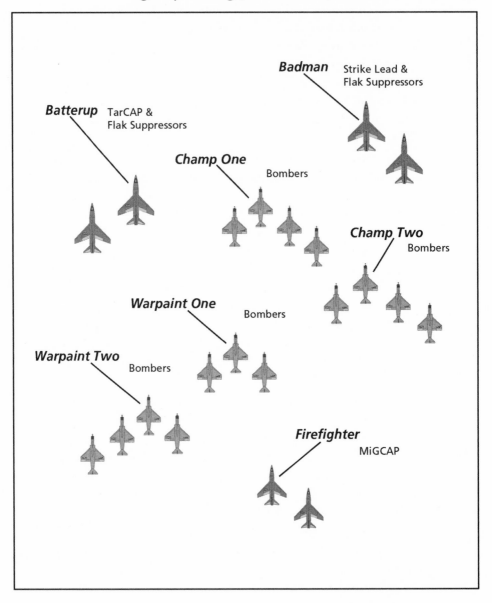

The western span of the Hai Duong Bridge was dropped after repeated bomb hits, and other spans were damaged beyond immediate use. For Mac and his CVW-5 squadron skippers and strike element leaders, this was a successful mission, tempered by the fact that one pilot did not return. Lt. (jg) John McCormick of VA-144, piloting A-4C number 547 in the second Warpaint division, was hit by suspected 57mm AAA fire on his run-in to the bridge. Other pilots pulling off the target stated in after action reports that McCormick's aircraft disintegrated in the air and the pilot was killed instantly, the wreckage impacting the ground in a rice paddy about a half-mile west of the bridge.

This was one of the earliest alpha strikes on the Hai Duong Bridge— if not the first—but it would not be the last. The North Vietnamese displayed a remarkable resilience by their ability to restore and rebuild, even when successive attacks by other air wings dropped the bridge again. It was reported later in the war that the North Vietnamese had given up rebuilding the steel and concrete spans, instead stringing cables and temporary pontoons from the remaining foundation piers at night to continue the movement of war matériel on Highway 5.

This was Mac's last flight as CAG and his last combat mission. Reluctantly, he relinquished command in early December to an incoming CAG who would take the air wing through more months of fatiguing, punishing action over North Vietnam until completing the cruise in May. The feeling engendered by his mid-cruise departure probably was similar to what older brother Ernie experienced more than twenty years prior when relinquishing command of CVG-16. After building his air group's cohesion and esprit, after the months of exacting training and preparation, after the intense initial combat experience, he had to abruptly withdraw and return to what must have seemed like less consequential work in a staff job with the hard, grueling work remaining for those left behind. In passing, he would again cross paths with Swede Vejtasa, who had been his skipper in *Constellation* three years before. Vejtasa, now as commander, Fleet Air Miramar, would note in his write-up on Mac: "He is a superb aviator having demonstrated his ability to plan and lead a combat mission evidence[d] by classified messages originated by higher authority. . . .

I have personally observed him during his air group training prior to deployment at which time he demonstrated remarkable foresight of combat requirements and oriented the training to prepare his pilots for those demanding conditions."[17]   Just as Ernie eventually made his way from CVG-16 to OPNAV to render solid work on behalf of the Navy's future carrier force structure, Mac would go directly to OPNAV to lay the foundation for the Navy's next air superiority fighter.

9

Reconstitution

Today, America can regain the sense of pride that existed before Vietnam. But it cannot be achieved by refighting a war that is finished as far as America is concerned. As I see it, the time has come to look forward to an agenda for the future, to unify, to bind up the Nation's wounds, and to restore its health and its optimistic self-confidence.

—President Gerald R. Ford

The Navy's air war over North Vietnam effectively ended in January 1973. The peace accord signed in Paris that month by U.S. secretary of state Henry Kissinger and Le Duc Tho representing Hanoi imposed a cessation on air operations north of the twentieth parallel, shielding the cities of Hanoi, Hai Duong, and Haiphong and their environs from further air attack. However the terms of the accord are assessed, the North Vietnamese were induced to take a conciliatory stance and sign it, brought to the table by the tightening vice of matériel shortages created by the mining of their major port and water tributaries eight months before. The U.S. bombings in December 1972 were thought to have spurred depletion of SAM inventories that Soviet or Chinese merchantmen could no longer replenish without risk of sinking if they entered North Vietnamese waters. In the years since Mac Snowden flew his last alpha strike against fortifications around Hai Duong commanding Air Wing 5, air combat over the North only intensified. The heightened tempo was punctuated by bombing pauses intended to extract concessions at the negotiating table, a tactic that ultimately proved illusory.

"The decade of the 1970s opened for the U.S. Navy with a resurgence of thinking about naval strategy and the role of the Navy in American defense posture. While the emphasis during the 1950s and 1960s had been on nuclear deterrence, the experience of the Vietnam War and the rising number of local crises increasingly stressed the role of conventional arms."[1] The air war was fought largely with aircraft designed and fielded in the 1950s. New technologies emerged—including radar-homing Shrike missiles, chaff and flare dispensers, electronic countermeasures gear, and laser-guided bombs—that were rushed into service. But save for the derivative EA-6B Prowler, newer aircraft introduced throughout the eight years of aerial warfare in the North were already in the development pipeline before the Tonkin Gulf incident. Navy aircraft and weapons were up to the task, but what seemed to remain static throughout the war until the mining of Haiphong was a dogged persistence for flying predictable attack profiles along the same corridors of approach and exfiltration from target areas. The North Vietnamese became very adept at reconstruction, repair, and work-arounds forced on them by repeated bomb damage, but they were also devastatingly skilled at refining their anti-air methodologies, employing ever-growing numbers of SAM sites and MiGs. For the U.S. Navy, the dismal result was 444 fixed-wing combat losses over the North during those years of aerial warfare.[2] Navy losses in isolation do not reflect what was a clear U.S. superiority in aircraft, aircrew training, and unit tactics but suggest only that overly restrictive rules of engagement imposed by senior leadership denied the strategic gains that could have been obtained years before the peace accord. In just one month—May 1972, the same month that the North's harbor areas were mined—U.S. naval aviators downed sixteen MiGs at the opening of the Linebacker campaign, underscoring the gap in air combat maneuvering advantage.[3]

With the air war over North Vietnam suspended, naval aviation retrenched to resume a more global stance that required senior leaders to address challenges in other districts on other oceans where opposing maritime players were encroaching on a free and unfettered access of U.S. naval forces. In particular, "the Soviet Navy increased its presence around the globe in a manner that the U.S. Navy saw as a challenge to American interests and American sea-control capabilities."[4] A prime example that caused great concern in senior Navy deliberations was the Soviet Exercise Okean '70 demonstration of oceanic reach involving two hundred warships exercising simultaneously in the Atlantic, Pacific, and Indian oceans and in the Mediterranean. Much depended on the leadership and vision of the leaders who would guide the Navy's reconstitution, and naval aviation's role in what emerged, through the next decade. A series of forceful and dynamic CNOs— Elmo Zumwalt, James Holloway, and Thomas Hayward—shaped the composition and posture of naval aviation in the 1970s. Even as fighting continued in Vietnam, emerging postwar trends were converging, demanding from each of these CNOs in turn a more strategic approach to the Navy's worldwide employment, modernization, and resource allocation. The nation's gross domestic product was slowing precipitously while inflation was poised to soar in the latter half of the decade; the Soviets had embarked on an unprecedented expansion of the size, capability, and global disposition of their naval forces in contravention to U.S. Navy operating norms; and a large segment of the U.S. seagoing inventory of capital ships—including World War II–vintage *Essex*- and *Midway*-class carriers—was reaching the end of useful service life and being decommissioned.

Enter Adm. Elmo Zumwalt, named CNO in 1970. Zumwalt gained favor as an aide to Assistant Secretary of Defense Paul Nitze when the two worked together on the 1963 nuclear test ban treaty with the Soviets. The relationship proved fortuitous: when Nitze was appointed Secretary of the Navy, he personally advocated with President Richard Nixon for Zumwalt's selection as CNO, and the then–vice admiral was promoted and advanced over thirty-three more senior flag officers to the post. Unlike the three naval aviators that preceded him as CNO and the two naval aviators that came after him, Zumwalt was a surface warfare officer whose most recent operational frame of reference was command of the riverine force in Vietnam. He had no instinctual feel or practical experience that could have informed his outlook regarding the flexibility and potency—or limitations—of the carrier air wing operating from large deck carriers. And so, faced with a wholly new set of challenges coming out of the Vietnam War, he and his acolytes—mainly rear admiral selectee Stansfield Turner (another surface warfare officer posted as a direct staff adviser to the CNO)—began formulating a different vision for naval aviation, one that shifted emphasis from high-end power projection emanating from large decks to equal or greater emphasis on smaller, specialized carriers hosting vertical/short takeoff and landing aircraft that could tend to lesser intensity conflicts. This specialized ship with its unique aircraft mix—named the Sea Control Ship (SCS) soon after its introduction—was a signature initiative for Zumwalt, one he envisioned as the means for protecting amphibious groups and replenishment forces that operated unaccompanied by large carriers.[5]

Admiral Zumwalt hit the deck running immediately upon his installation as CNO. With the rollout of his Project SIXTY concept paper and associated briefings, he introduced a set of proposals for how he intended to revitalize U.S. naval forces to meet the imperatives of a new naval strategy. His main point was to address the strengthening Soviet submarine threat, heralded by the deployment of *Delta*-class ballistic missile submarines with sea-launched ballistic missiles and the growing numbers of air-launched cruise missiles that could be deployed from Soviet long-range bombers. In a nod to his own community roots, he put forth a stated goal for programming actions to "elevate surface warfare programs to a level—and autonomous status—on a par with aviation programs . . . employing a powerful integrating directorate (OP-090)—supplemented by other integrating directorates—to force integration among the community 'unions'."[6] The resulting shake-up yielded three competing platform sponsors for submarine warfare, surface warfare, and aviation that survive today in more muted form.

Among the new proposals he debuted, one Project SIXTY initiative was the SCS, along with a need justification that cited a formidable Soviet threat to unprotected sea traffic and declining defense appropriations inside of which the Navy had to satisfy its modernization commitments. Ironically, given his apparent apathy for conventional large deck carrier naval aviation, he "championed the F-14 Tomcat as the Navy's replacement for the F-4 Phantom."[7] To gain the endorsement of reluctant members of Congress and defense committee professional staffers, his staff prepared a cost-benefit tradeoff analysis that was built on calculations comparing a 13-carrier force with a total of 301 F-14s to maintaining the extant 16-carrier force hosting

903 of the aging F-4s. The smaller force, he said, was "militarily more effective; $2.5 billion cheaper in procurement costs; $500 million a year cheaper in operating costs and requiring 17,000 fewer Sailors."[8] On one level, this amounted to a clever bait-and-switch ploy to quell both sides of a debate: it satisfied the proponents of the already largely developed and already flown F-14 by arguing for a production commitment, and it gave something to opponents of large deck carriers by using the cost-benefit logic to bring down their numbers while theoretically off-loading some of the capability (and ship construction dollars) to further the concept of the SCS. In the larger strategy context, it conformed perfectly to key tenets of Project SIXTY that argued for early retirement of obsolescing force structure to return savings in one area of ship construction while modernizing the fleet through addition of low-end ships to balance out the high-low force mix.

Project SIXTY was a watershed statement of strategy that had lasting influence on Navy vision and policy well beyond Zumwalt's tenure as CNO. It became an annualized template for CNO policy and planning guidance and set the stage for the 1974 "Missions of the U.S. Navy," a statement of organizing principle that related missions to tactics and provided a focal point for analyzing and debating strategic issues within the service. Critics charged that Project SIXTY placed too much emphasis on sea control as the primary thrust against the Soviets at the expense of power projection and that it promoted tactical caution by abandoning naval offensive and would have the unintended effect of degrading the fleet capability and ultimately rendering the Navy ineffective in any clash with the Soviets.[9]

Adm. James Holloway, a naval aviator with extensive aviation combat experience who followed Naval Academy classmate Admiral Zumwalt as CNO in 1974, "largely consolidated and sustained" Zumwalt's policy and organization changes.[10] Before assuming the position of CNO, Holloway served as Zumwalt's vice CNO and had much to do with implementing Zumwalt's policy and organizational changes. As CNO, he put his own twist on building the intellectual underpinnings for Navy force structure and program planning, focusing on naval warfare tasks across platforms but, significantly, highlighting the range of aircraft carrier capabilities. Perhaps Holloway's single greatest change to force construct and operational deployments came with

elimination of specialized antisubmarine warfare (ASW) carriers—
the CVS—and adoption of the CV notation in lieu of CVA to denote
the more generalized capabilities of large deck carriers. Carrier air
wings correspondingly transformed from two separate air wings tai-
lored to ASW and power projection missions to one air wing with a
range of multirole capabilities.[11] The introduction and incorporation
of the F–14, S–3, and E–2 into that generic air wing undoubtedly had
a good deal to do with generating the necessary confidence to make
that operational change. Holloway also put in motion and approved a
new fleet deployment posture that reformed the "standing operational
task force organization of carriers, surface combatants and submarines
assigned to numbered fleets . . . into battle groups consisting of one
carrier, two cruisers, four surface combatants and one or two submarines operating together in mutual support with the task of destroying
hostile submarine, surface, and air forces within the group's assigned
area of responsibility."[12]

Near the end of Holloway's tenure as CNO, his personal imprint
began to be revealed in his first major issuance, "Strategic Concepts of
the U.S. Navy," in which he laid out the rationale for, among several
enduring functions, the "implicit primacy of strike warfare and carrier platform."[13] As adherents and opponents became more or less rec-
onciled to Holloway's vision and direction and true advocacy slowly
emerged near the end of his four-year run as CNO, the amalgama-
tion of those four years of strategy refinement was issued as a defining policy document, "Sea Plan 2000," in which the argument was
forcefully for "U.S. Navy relevance to conflict with the Soviets, primarily through forward, global, offensive U.S. naval operations."[14] Of
overriding significance to naval aviation was the well-vetted need for
large deck carriers. The logic for big decks articulated in "Sea Plan
2000" was instrumental in creating the condition for congressional
action that overrode the Office of the Secretary of Defense by adding
funding for CVN-71 in the 1979 authorization bill.[15] Known for his
hands-on style, Holloway, surprisingly, was little engaged in the signoff
phase of "Sea Plan 2000." In the coordination and redraft endgame,
the policy document became more identified with Secretary of the
Navy Graham Claytor and Under Secretary Jim Woolsey, with a nod

to major contributions from commander of the Pacific Fleet and next CNO, Adm. Tom Hayward.[16] However, Holloway's shepherding of the "Strategic Concepts of the U.S. Navy" early in his CNO tour had the beneficial effect of resetting a defendable course for Navy policy by correcting some of the aberrations of Zumwalt's Project SIXTY and laying the groundwork for "Sea Plan 2000."

As much as Holloway sought to sustain Zumwalt's organization and processes initially, his own predilections were in evidence as he left office. That said, some of Zumwalt's changes were retained or only slightly modified, even by Admiral Hayward in 1978. He would issue in succession several of his own vision or posture statements, the seminal document being "The Future of U.S. Sea Power." In it, he doubled down on Holloway's course-corrective stance for large deck carriers by insisting on twelve carrier battle groups as the minimum to effect maritime supremacy. This was the centerpiece and priority of all that flowed from the document, and it would significantly influence Navy policy during Hayward's time and well beyond. It would influence global war games and spawn the stand-up of the CNO's strategic studies group in Newport, Rhode Island, as the oracle of future Navy thinking on a number of hypothetical environments.[17]

By the 1970s, Ernie Snowden had been retired from the Navy for most of the preceding decade. He had settled into a sedentary pattern of office work running a small investment banking operation, his daily regimen of desk-bound cold calls on prospective clients in the San Francisco area interrupted only by occasional business trips to Los Angeles. Practically nothing in his routine reconnected him in the slightest way to his naval aviation past, save an infrequent visit to the NAS Alameda Officers Club for dinner. In the mid-1960s, he would take the opportunity to extend his business trips about once every six months to San Diego to visit brother Mac when he was in town. These visits were bittersweet for Ernie; on one hand, he could refresh a relationship strained by years of separations, but on the other hand, he could revel only vicariously in Mac's descriptions of Navy life, of experiences at sea and in the cockpit. Whether he could consciously acknowledge the fact or not, Ernie's life had come to be defined by naval aviation, and he was having difficulty adjusting to his new post-Navy life.

Mac, on the other hand, had entered a decade of more senior responsibility where all he had learned and accomplished in naval aviation could be applied with some assurance that he could make a meaningful contribution to the trade. He was provided the rich experience of working on the staffs of two of the three CNOs that would lead the Navy during the 1970s to reconstitute and reset the Navy's direction—Zumwalt and Holloway. Three times removed from the CNO in the organizational hierarchy, Mac was placed in positions that were at once highly visible within OPNAV and outside of the Navy and highly controversial everywhere for advancing concepts or ideas not unanimously endorsed within OPNAV or certainly within Congress or the Office of the Secretary of Defense. These responsibilities would bring Mac into periodic direct contact with these CNOs, and that experience was generally positive. Under Admiral Zumwalt, Mac took more immediate direction from the deputy CNO for air, Vice Adm. Tom Connolly, through Connolly's assistant, Rear Adm. Jerry Miller. The relationship between Mac and his next two most senior bosses grew to be mutually gratifying and productive on behalf of building stability for the F-14 program. After sea duty, Mac returned to OPNAV to report to CNO Holloway's deputy for air, Vice Adm. Bill Houser, reporting daily through Houser's assistants in successive postings, Rear Adm. D. C. Davis and Rear Adm. Bill McClendon. Employing all the experience that he had amassed in twenty-five years in naval aviation at that juncture, Mac would take on the responsibilities of the director of aviation requirements but was detailed to operations analysis to craft the requirement for an air-capable ship that took life from the force structure details of Zumwalt's "Missions of the U.S. Navy" posture statement.

Outside of the CNO's immediate staff in the Pentagon where the "big picture" ideas were proposed, deliberated, and either advanced or withdrawn, the 1970s amounted to a decade of thoroughgoing change for naval aviation, even while resources were overwhelmingly absorbed in combat from Yankee Station off North Vietnam. From the beginning of the decade to the end, the number of pilots on active duty declined by fully a third, naval flight officers by 43 percent, and enlisted aviation rates by almost 9 percent. More than any other factor, the decline reflected the rapid post–1973 drawdown from the peak years of naval aviation's involvement in the Vietnam War, and the pilot training rate was plunged into modest chaos for several years. Some changes would mitigate the disruption: in 1971, CNO Admiral Zumwalt approved the consolidation of three former air training staffs into a single staff with eight training wings at major pilot training bases. A year later, the chief of naval air training would relocate to NAS Corpus Christi just as the former chief of naval air advanced training was disestablished. Concurrently, a single base training concept was created that assigned student pilots to a pipeline for more specialized training in jets, props, or rotary-wing after completion of primary training. A major step in refining the primary training equipment came in 1976 with the acceptance of the T-34C Turbo Mentor, the requirement having been drafted and signed off from Mac's director of aviation requirements tenure two years before.[18]

A new generation of aviation capability was being introduced throughout the 1970s. In the fall of 1972, VF-1 and VF-2 were established as the first two F-14 squadrons, and a year later, off Point Mugu, the F-14 fired six AIM-54 Phoenix missiles, guiding them simultaneously to six separate targets fifty miles away and obtaining four direct hits and two proximity kills. Barely four months after that success, VS-41 accepted its first S-3A ASW aircraft, and USS *John F. Kennedy*, in the same quarter, began conversion to fulfill the new CV concept accommodating a newly formed air wing with strike and ASW capability. To inject a greater degree of oversight into an acquisition process that increasingly proved insufficient to the task of maturing and fielding highly complex aviation systems, the deputy secretary of defense in 1971 rolled out a new directive on acquiring aircraft and other big-ticket hardware. The freewheeling process was reordered into three distinct phases: program initiation, full-scale development, and production and deployment, with rigorous criteria (that included a report on system efficacy and corresponding cost of the associated technology) governing successful passage from one phase to the next.

Finally, system level prototyping was mandated to permit more realistic assessment of operational suitability before a decision to enter full-rate production—the first serious adoption of "fly-before-buy."[19]

For Mac, the events of the decade prompted constant reminders of past associations, nostalgic moments of seeing aircraft and ships with which he had a close, sometimes harrowing association over his twenty-five-year career in naval aviation reach obsolescence and disappear from sight. The last A-1 Skyraider, which had populated one of his Air Wing 5 squadrons and in which he prepared for possible combat, was retired from the Navy's active list in 1971. Fifty of the Navy's remaining A-4s—the aircraft populating two of his CVW-5 attack squadrons and another one in which he had prepared for Vietnam deployment as CAG—would pass from the active inventory in 1973, transferred to Israel to replenish losses in the Yom Kippur War, and from the last active fleet A-4 squadron in 1976. The last *Essex*-class carrier, of which USS *Ticonderoga* was one and the home ship of his CVW-5, was retired in 1976. And, with heightened emotion and sentiment for Mac, the last active fleet F-8 Crusader would pass from the inventory in 1976. The operational hardware of his hardest and most rewarding flying years was fast departing, but he was in precisely the right jobs in the late 1960s and early 1970s to make a lasting contribution to the recapitalization of U.S. naval aviation.

In 1976, the Association of Naval Aviation (ANA) was founded to "stimulate and extend appreciation of Naval Aviation . . . past, present, and future." The association was open to officers and enlisted, active or retired, and civilians who contributed to or were advocates for U.S. naval aviation. ANA would figure prominently in the next episode of Mac's life after retirement from active duty.

10

Consolidation

I think the F-111B has gotten too heavy to ever be a good performing airplane. There is not enough thrust in all Christendom to put that airplane back in business really. It has gotten awfully expensive. It has gone way up in cost, and I think we ought to consider very carefully using the Navy money and the country's money in a better way.

—Vice Adm. Tom Connolly, USN

Few today have first-hand memory of the irascible Admiral Connolly and his brief rejoinder to Senator John Stennis' direct question in the Senate Armed Services Committee hearing in March 1968. His statement would prove very consequential in the unfolding history of naval aviation by setting the conditions for the ultimate demise of the Tactical Fighter Experimental (TFX) program after a tortuous seven-year acquisition path and for the emergence of the F-14 Tomcat. From 1966 until mid-1968, Mac became personally and intimately involved in the unfolding drama, in a role reminiscent of his older brother's role with OPNAV a dozen years before. The scenario, setting principled naval aviation officers against the Air Force and the Office of the Secretary of Defense in what could have been a career-ending defense of Navy acquisition discretion and its own recapitalization prerequisites, was almost identical. Principle would win out once more for naval aviation.

Mac would first encounter Vice Adm. Tom Connolly when both arrived in OPNAV in early 1966—with Mac to begin his duty as the TFX program coordinator and Connolly starting his tenure as Mac's

senior on the staff as the deputy CNO for air. That Mac was a graduate of the naval test pilot school was a plus with Connolly, who was
among the founders of the school's curriculum and the school's second director in the late 1940s and early 1950s. Although there were a
few pay grades between the two, the visibility and interservice drama
surrounding the TFX program guaranteed that they would interact
over the next two years. They formed a very collegial working relationship built upon a common language of aeronautics, spiced with
the patois of the defense acquisition process. Connolly felt strongly
enough about Mac's abilities that after his detour to deep draft command, he would pull Mac back into the job as the Experimental
Fighter Attack Aircraft (VFAX) program coordinator overseeing a
study of fighter and attack requirements that could complement the
F-111B (and eventually would evolve into the Experimental Fighter
Aircraft [VFX]) and guarantee an orderly and well-thoughtout initiation of the F-14A.

The TFX program was a fighter acquisition program that had
its genesis in two widely disparate service requirements. For the Air
Force, it was to be a long-range fighter-bomber with tree-top level
supersonic dash capabilities; for the Navy, it was the fleet air defense
mission, armed with long-range missiles.[1] Secretary of Defense Robert McNamara in February 1961 directed that the services merge their
efforts into a joint procurement program. The Navy repeatedly tried
to avoid the joint development, testifying before Congress about its
doubts that a single airplane could meet the widely divergent requirements that both services had set.[2] In the down-select process between
the two competing companies vying for the project, both services
favored a Boeing design, but they were overruled by the secretary
of defense, who wanted the General Dynamics design. McNamara
offered three rationales for imposing this decision on the services: he
believed the services' practice of "overbuying" on performance introduced extra risk (the Boeing design was superior in promised performance features); he maintained that the Air Force cost estimates were
not as reliable as his own rough judgments based on his years with
Ford Motors; and he felt that the General Dynamics design offered
the greatest commonality between Air Force and Navy variants.[3] The
General Dynamics design was proposed to be 80–90 percent common between the Air Force A and the Navy F-111B. Both variants

featured a variable sweep wing, with the Navy's variant built around the AN/AWG-9 fire control and Phoenix missile system. What was apparently not figured into the high degree of commonality at this point, but would be revealed as flight testing proceeded, was the lack of carrier suitability features that would make the initial F-111B design compatible with a flight deck environment—this despite the presence of Grumman on the General Dynamics team to ensure that carrier suitability was designed in from the start. But an overriding concern within McNamara's office was preserving the highest level of commonality.

With the Air Force appointed the lead service, the Navy's unique and necessary requirements were viewed as secondary and subject to trade-off, thus yielding a Navy derivative that was too large and heavy and under-powered for shipboard use. Flight testing, begun in late 1965, verified Navy assertions regarding TFX performance—now designated F-111B for the Navy variant. A super weight improvement program followed by a colossal weight improvement program to reshape external structural features temporarily arrested weight growth in the F-111B; however, other suitability issues were soon revealed by the flight test program, such as limited cockpit visibility, a propensity for tip-back, and inlet-induced compressor stalls.

By 1966, positions had become deeply and intractably entrenched. The Office of the Secretary of Defense was adamant that the program proceed jointly, but with the Air Force dictating design. The Air Force was satisfied that it could obtain a serviceable design as long as it could trade off Navy requirements that penalized its own, and uniformed naval aviators as a body were resolute in their rejection of the F-111B. Mac stepped into this cauldron of heated instability and rancor in 1966 to assume a central role as the TFX program coordinator in what today would be called the requirements officer in the aviation requirements directorate on the CNO staff. Mac's essential job function was to be the fleet aviator's representative in the acquisition process for the TFX—to reduce reams of aircraft design and performance data, to shine a light on areas of noncompliance with carrier suitability threshold specifications, and to interpret seemingly convoluted regulatory and statutory mandates in a manner that could be easily digested and acted upon by the Secretary of the Navy, the CNO, and the deputy chief of naval operations (air) for their interactions with Air

Force counterparts, Secretary McNamara's acolytes, and congressional members and key committee staffers. Mac's particular adeptness at this task, forged and sharpened ten years before in test pilot training and as a project test pilot, was recognized almost immediately. Five months into the job, the Secretary of the Navy personally commended Mac for his "outstanding performance in preparation of a special briefing memorandum concerning definition of F-111B aircraft performance specifications."

That commendation resulted from Mac's personal involvement preparing the CNO, Adm. David L. McDonald, for hearings with House and Senate appropriators wherein McDonald began to expose the Navy's growing dissatisfaction with weight growth—in particular, the lack of a "bring-back" margin, requiring the F-111B to jettison very expensive Phoenix missiles before being able to arrest aboard the carrier. Throughout 1966, numbers of F-111B development models were beginning to populate the ramps at Patuxent River and Grumman's nearby site in Calverton, giving the Navy's test pilots their first real hands-on experience with the aircraft. The experience was not particularly satisfying for them or for General Dynamics and Grumman. The manufacturers worked diligently on rapid design fixes but were having difficulty keeping up with carrier suitability design issues that were foregone earlier in the program in the name of commonality. In addition to the tip-back issue, the test program was revealing problems with handling qualities at approach speeds; cockpit visibility of the ship-based mirror landing system on approach; and single-engine rate of climb, a critical measure of recoverability when an engine might be lost on the catapult stroke. In truth, most of the identified carrier suitability design shortcomings were addressable. General Dynamics and Grumman were struggling but succeeding in incorporating real-time fixes such that when the F-111B actually performed its carrier trials on USS *Coral Sea* in July 1968, it passed its major thresholds. The only real drawback at the time was the development delay in maturing the AWG-9 fire control system. By then, however, momentum had already moved prevailing opinion in the naval aviation ranks away from the narrowly defined fleet air defense mission of the F-111B and toward the need for a new design that could perform effectively across multiple missions yet still host the AWG-9 and Phoenix missile system.

Roughly from Mac's arrival and throughout 1966, the Navy's preoccupation with the fleet air defense mission—the raison d'etre for TFX for the Navy—began to shift to air superiority and strike escort. Officers arrived with fresh experience over North Vietnam to fill out staff positions in OPNAV—Mac among them—and the emphasis changed to developing a dogfighting replacement for the F-4. In 1966 and continuing into 1967, Mac participated in a CNO-directed anti-air warfare study, initially undertaken by its official title VFAX, to weigh options. Even though the study endorsed the F-111B and Phoenix system as suitable for fleet air defense, the inclusion of other mission objectives and a range of air threats in the study assumptions yielded a more purely dominant fighter aircraft excursion that had great appeal and created an opening for innovative and aggressive companies to jump-start alternative concepts.

Grumman, though partnered with General Dynamics for developing the F-111B, was ready with an alternative. Its unsolicited proposal to the Navy in October 1967 adapted the F-111's variable incidence wing, Pratt and Whitney engines, and AWG-9 weapon system into a lighter, more maneuverable G-303 concept. The unsolicited proposal went not to OPNAV but to the Naval Air Systems Command for evaluation; however, Mac received regular feedback on the assessment, primarily from George Spangenberg, lead evaluator at NAVAIR. Mac became aware of Spangenberg's reputation when he returned to the Naval Air Test Center's armament test division in 1959 as a project test pilot at the same time that Spangenberg was being elevated to director of BuAer's evaluation division. Mac's initial cautious circumspection of Spangenberg, with his forthrightness and clipped tones, gave way to complete confidence and trust over the course of many meetings and closed-door reviews. By the time Mac detoured for a year of graduate school at the close of the 1960s, the bond had grown to the point that Spangenberg happily became the unofficial but acknowledged editor of Mac's thesis on aircraft design. As the VFAX evaluation got under way, Mac proceeded to Fort Worth for his own familiarization flight in the F-111. Vice Admiral Connolly had, by this point, taken his own familiarization flight in the F-111 and the Navy F-111B variant and required his own TFX coordinator to have the same hands-on experience. Mac's hour-and-a-half flight in November was conducted to divine ground truth, to discern handling and performance attributes calibrated against thousands of hours of fighter flight time. That it added new appreciation and perspective to his view of the F-111B would be reflected in a harsher critique that informed his many subsequent reports and briefings inside OPNAV up to and including the CNO and the deputy CNO (air), Vice Admiral Connolly. Mac was not a fan of the aircraft, and with the experience of four thousand hours of flight time in Navy fighters, he held grave reservations about its suitability for the fleet.

Through the winter of 1968, as Mac and his contemporaries digested NAVAIR's generally favorable assessment of Grumman's G-303 concept, there was unanimity that it offered a better option for the Navy. Joining Mac in this covey of TFX "insurrectionists" were NAVAIR civilian and principle evaluator of G-303, George Spangenberg; Mac's former fighter squadron skipper from Air Wing 5 on *Ticonderoga* and now OP-50W (operations analysis), Cdr. Robair Mohrhardt; and Rear Adm. Jerry Miller, director of aviation requirements. Their collective assessment to Vice Admiral Connolly fortified his own biases and informed his commentary with Navy Secretary Paul Ignatius (an F-111B proponent) shortly before they were called to testify to the Senate Armed Services Committee. Connolly, referring to the Grumman concept, spoke forthrightly to Ignatius:

> This proposal is a far better fighter/interceptor. I've had enough experience in these matters and I tell you that the Naval Air Systems Command isn't at all happy with the F-111B and the program. Some of our very best people are absolutely against the plane. You are just perpetuating something that's going to boomerang on you, on Mr. McNamara, the president, everyone. I'm not against a common Navy and Air Force airplane such as the F-4, but that F-111B airplane is a bad one. It's not very good for the Air Force as a low-altitude bomber, and it's a disaster for the Navy as an interceptor and fighter. I think we ought to have a competition, but this time let the Navy run

their program. They know how carrier planes must be built, not the Air Force, not a company that's never been in the act.[4]

Before the hearings, Grumman was invited once more to brief Connolly, Miller, Snowden, and the other TFX insurrectionists to update the group on progress of the G–303 concept and to make its final marketing pitch. Connolly recalled:

> Grumman came in and showed this front-back-seat version, and the selling point was that at that time the Navy hadn't put much money into the F-111B; we hadn't gone to production. Grumman showed two cost curves: one curve was the projected cost of continuing with the F-111B up through the buy, which was very large; the other showed the projected cost of dropping the F-111B and starting a new fighter/interceptor, using engines, radar, and other components that were available . . . the curve that was to apply to what is now the F-14 crossed the F-111B curve in about three years, and did not rise as fast as or as far as the F-111B.[5]

Congressional hearings in the spring of 1968 held great portent for the TFX program, as the congressional authorizers and appropriators considered a commitment of significant funding for Navy procurement of the F-111B. By now, a growing number of program detractors occupied seats in Congress and questioned the wisdom of proceeding with the F-111B. Naval aviation officers from Vice Admiral Connolly down who had more than a passing knowledge of the TFX program were frustrated that the Navy was being led unwillingly to a debacle of immense scale if the F-111B was forced on the fleet. Connolly himself, while on leave status and en route to take over the air warfare branch of OPNAV (OP-05), made a point of visiting the General Dynamics plant at Fort Worth and flying the F-111 to get a first-hand impression. At the controls, with the company test pilot in the right seat, Connolly took the airplane to 30,000 feet and attempted a supersonic run but was only able to reach high subsonic speed. Coming in to land, Connolly discovered that "the center of gravity was already aft of the aerodynamic center, which gave you an unstable coupling. . . . In the landing configuration, if it nosed up it continued up; if it nosed down it went further down. I knew damned good and well it was going to be a nightmare getting on a carrier . . . it was a terrible disappointment to me."[6] Within a year of taking the OP-05 position, Connolly arranged for a demonstration flight of the Navy variant of the F-111 at Grumman. From the left seat of the F-111B, Connolly issued an equally disappointing assessment: "I came away from Grumman disgusted and worried. . . . For another year the program went on with my constantly thinking about what could be done to fix the F-111B. . . . The Air Force was essentially unresponsive . . . and McNamara was determined that he was going to have a common airplane for the Navy and the Air Force, but this was the wrong airplane."[7] The stage was set for a defining moment in March, when Navy leadership appeared before the Senate Armed Services Committee. Senator Stennis, a TFX opponent, was becoming frustrated with the supportive "party line" testimony of the Navy Secretary and CNO. "The turning point was artfully stage-managed by a Navy officer behind the scenes (Rear Adm. Jerry Miller, present at the hearing but seated well back from the witness table)."[8] A key committee staff member whispered to Miller that Senator Stennis needed definitive language for the record upon which to act. In the staffer's office, Miller dictated a line of questioning that was to be directed to Vice Admiral Connolly, noting Connolly's irrefutable pedigree in aviation design, engineering, and testing.[9]

What followed was the death blow for the Navy's involvement in the TFX program when, on March 29, the Senate Armed Services Committee voted eleven to two against any further funding for the F-111B. That action was followed immediately on April 3 by the committee's approval of $287 million to begin development of the VFX program. Three months later, bowing to clear congressional intent, the Department of the Navy issued a stop work order on the F-111B. By the following January, Grumman was on contract under the VFX program to undertake design of the F-14 Tomcat, so named for the admiral who contravened his superiors in that Senate Armed Services Committee hearing.

Throughout a tumultuous period that saw the demise of the F-111B and the advent of the F-14, Mac and Jerry Miller worked closely together almost daily, developing a high regard for each other's professional competence and tenacity in delivering results. Miller would write of Mac, "Concurrent with the final program actions of the F-111B, and subsequent to termination, Captain Snowden assumed the additional assignment as Program Coordinator for the VFX-1. . . . He has enjoyed the complete confidence and trust of many senior officers and civilian heads of the Navy Department. . . . Highly recommended for qualifying deep draft selection. . . . I would take this man any place in any capacity. . . . Really great!"[10] Mac's contributions were immediately observed and lauded by Vice Admiral Connolly, who wrote Mac personally to "express my heartfelt appreciation for your participation in accomplishing that very difficult task" (of personally preparing the CNO for a short-notice meeting with the Senate Appropriations Defense Subcommittee to map out the development program and funding stream for VFX).[11] At Connolly's insistence and endorsement, Mac would be cited for having "established the requirements and development concept for the VFX, and in close coordination with the technical personnel of both industry and the Navy, advanced the concept through [initial planning] and into firm proposals. [Mac's] outstanding technical and operational knowledge resulted in the Specific Operational Requirements Document for the VFX-1."[12]

Deep draft command followed a screening, which placed Mac in an elite group of fewer than twenty senior aviator captains chosen every year to audition for carrier command by taking large amphibious or refueling ships to sea. Yet favor was not shining brightly on Mac as he assumed command of USS *Chilton*, a tired and neglected attack transport that had been in constant service since commissioning in the early days of World War II. Within a year, Mac earned high praise from the amphibious squadron commander for his "imagination, good judgment, and aggressive drive to contend with the manifest difficulties of maintaining and effectively operating an overage ship during a period of violent personnel turbulence." Mac's brand of tough discipline was well suited to bringing a moribund ship to life, particularly in an era of relaxed standards for grooming and behavior. But some officers, perhaps attuned to the more permissive order coming into vogue, recoiled at his no-nonsense style. The next amphibious squadron commander characterized Mac as "brusque and blunt on

occasion" in a generally less-than-stellar fitness report. The flag officer commanding the amphibious group perceived that an overly critical report had been passed into the record and wrote a special fitness
report on Mac, two-blocking the performance marks to the high side
of outstanding. But the damage already done probably extinguished
Mac's chances for promotion to flag officer.

With deep draft command behind him, he was detoured back to
OPNAV for one more turn at Pentagon staff work before learning the
outcome of his major command assignment. With his intimate familiarity with and high regard for Mac's abilities to negotiate and master
the bureaucracy from the F-111 and TFX-to-VFX experience, Vice
Admiral Connolly interceded in the personnel assignment process to
detain Mac long enough to position him as his representative to the
Air Capable Ship Study. The study was a personally directed effort by
the CNO, Admiral Zumwalt, to develop the analytical underpinnings
for a concept that was at the core of his new initiatives to "reverse
the decline of US. forces . . . to provide maintenance and depot facilities for destroyer-borne anti-submarine helicopters, to keep them airborne over a convoy."[13]

It had become evident by the late 1960s that the Soviets were
making great strides in quieting their submarines. The U.S. Navy
lacked enough convoy escorts capable of hosting a full complement
of ASW helicopters to fulfill its responsibility of keeping the sea lanes
open to the European continent in the event of hostilities with the
Soviet Union. The CVEs and CVSs adapted from World War II inventory were beginning to attrite, and mixing ASW squadrons with large
attack carrier air wings would compromise their availability for other
missions. From his perch in the OP-50W operations study group, Mac
sorted through the study precepts as the senior voice for the aviation
aspects of the study. He personally directed the panel charged with
development of roles, missions, and threat analysis and was later commended by the assistant deputy CNO for guiding the initial steps that
narrowed several aircraft concepts to a short list of preferred requirements as the basis for the Air Capable Ship's aircraft complement. His
work spawned growing interest in several types of tilt-wing medium-
sized aircraft prototypes subsequently inducted into operational

assessments, among them Canadair's CL–84 and Vought's XC–142. The early promise of new and exotic aircraft schemes exerted an inexorable tug on the basic ship design. Not long after Mac's work was done, the Sea Control Ship concept emerged as the successor to the Air Capable Ship concept. The growing fascination with medium-sized vertical/short takeoff and landing (V/STOL) aircraft in numbers that could sustain continuous ASW surveillance orbits over a transiting convoy drove the requirements process to describe an SCS that was, in effect, a more modern CVE. Four years later, mounting opposition from the naval aviation community would coalesce to kill the concept. The allure of augmenting destroyer class ships with enhanced airborne ASW for increased escort capacity—the study that had consumed Mac's energies—had metastasized after his departure into an outsized demand for a class of ships that would compete directly with large deck attack carriers for recapitalization funding.

Despite the daily to and fro, Mac, by this time, had been ordered to his major command at sea, the helicopter carrier USS *Guadalcanal*. Mac took these orders as a personal setback. He felt his career had been built on successive achievements flying fighters from attack carriers—his very persona imprinted by that aura, that elitism—and command of an attack carrier would be the capstone to a long progression of successful squadron and air wing tours. The historical record of flag promotions from major at-sea command for aviators selected from other than large attack aircraft carriers was not in the least auspicious. In the roughly ten years before and ten years after Mac would get his first look by a flag selection board, significantly more than two-thirds of skippers of attack carriers would be selected for flag, while far less than a quarter of skippers from amphibious or helicopter carriers would be selected for flag promotion. Mac's odds for attaining flag rank were greatly diminished. But, not one to bemoan his station, Mac's first priority was fulfilling an obligation to the naval service, a duty to assume command and apply his energies and wherewithal to making *Guadalcanal* ready.

In a real sense, history was repeating itself for Ernie and Mac as events from the early 1950s and nearly identical events from the early 1970s played out in similar ways. In the 1950s, Ernie performed singularly important work in OP-05 in service to the urgent need to substantiate and strengthen the Navy's new super carrier recapitalization program. For Ernie, that success was followed by a disappointing assignment to command something other than what he knew from experience: an escort carrier engaged in exercising with and appraising helicopter ASW tactics. In Mac's experience, a tour in OP-05 that proved highly visible and pivotal for the maturation of vertical lift capability at sea was followed by an equally disappointing assignment to command a helicopter carrier. The record shows that both hid their disappointment and with great determination applied themselves to making their major command tours as extraordinary and noteworthy as circumstances would allow.

Mac's command of *Guadalcanal* was eminently successful. Perhaps the penultimate gauge of his command style and its impact—and one of which Mac was proudest—was a letter from the embarked commanding officer of the 52nd Marine Amphibious Unit to Mac's superior, commander, Amphibious Squadron Eight, following a major amphibious readiness exercise. A long list of accolades was followed with: "To Captain Snowden and his crew go the sincere respect and appreciation of the entire landing force for a job well done."[14] This, in part, was a sign of the care, attention to detail, and command climate that yielded another Atlantic Fleet battle efficiency "E" award for *Guadalcanal* in Mac's final Navy command.

As the saying goes, no good deed goes unpunished. Mac drove *Guadalcanal* and her crew to attain an unprecedented record of success, only to find himself reassigned to the aviation staff in OPNAV awaiting the outcome of the next flag selection board. Returning to familiar offices in the Pentagon as the head of aircraft and weapons requirements branch (OP-506), it was clear to Mac that little had changed in his time away at sea. Many of the same fiscal and programmatic issues festered without resolution. Since its first flight during Mac's early OPNAV tenure, the F-14 had averaged about one loss a year in test failures—not an overly crash-prone program for its day given the technical sophistication of the aircraft, but one still buffeted by congressional opposition and threats to defund. Pressure was mounting from the fleet, getting its first introduction to the F-14, for an urgent modification to replace the Pratt and Whitney TF-30

engine with the General Electric F-404 engine. Marine Corps aviators were clamoring for a similar engine upgrade for their Harri-
ers and were circumventing Mac's office by petitioning Congress
directly—a contravention of the accepted process, since Navy "blue
dollars" funded Marine Corps aircraft programs. Mac found himself
at the nexus of opposition from the aviation flag officer community
and advocacy for the Sea Control Ship from CNO Zumwalt and
his acolytes. The SCS moved to the forefront of Admiral Zumwalt's
personal favorites from the moment he became CNO. He foresaw a
force of light carriers that could take up station as escorts to replenishment convoys, amphibious groups, and surface action groups that
sailed without the security of an air wing that came with a large deck
carrier. Antisubmarine helicopters, airborne early warning helicopters, and a V/STOL fixed-wing jet made up the air component of
the SCS concept, those roles initially assumed by test plan surrogates,
the SH-3G Sea King helicopter and AV-8A Harrier. To Mac and his
department heads fell the task of synthesizing the various air elements
to produce a single, coherent requirement for the SCS air capability.
As envisaged, the SCS design and its employment were similar to the
CVE "hunter-killer" operations that Ernie had pioneered from the
deck of USS *Kula Gulf* twenty years earlier. Bold concepts that seem
to offer great advantage but fall short of expectations have a tendency
of recycling a generation later cloaked in new technologies able to
rebut a new threat. The advance of rotary-wing technology and the
maturation of V/STOL technology seemed to give the SCS new life
when underwritten by the CNO. Where *Kula Gulf* experimented
with early helicopters fulfilling the role of lethal, long-range pouncers to prosecute submarine contacts, SCS seemed to hold potential as
an adjunct aviation platform for a new threat environment that was—
according to estimates from Zumwalt's analysts—one-eighth the cost
of a conventional large deck attack carrier. CNO Zumwalt perceived
SCS as the surest way to replenish the Navy's seagoing inventory
with new hulls. Naval aviators endured Admiral Zumwalt's tenure
with consternation and viewed his initiatives, especially regarding
his key naval aviation innovations, with feelings somewhere between
circumspection and disdain. Mac's feelings conformed to those of

close associate Vice Adm. Jerry Miller, who later remarked: "I do not believe a man can be a politician and a military officer simultaneously. You saw it in modern times with Zumwalt, who was politically motivated for many years before he ever got to be head of the Navy. As the head of the Navy, being politically oriented, he played politics a lot. Now that he is retired, you see it coming out constantly. He destroys some of his credibility as a military officer by exposing his lust for political power—at least in my opinion."[15]

Naval aviators found the SCS concept abhorrent and utterly bereft of warfighting or budgetary logic in a fiscally constrained era. They deemed it the first step onto a slippery slope that siphoned away precious ship construction funds intended for large deck carriers and aircraft procurement funds for frontline fighters and attack jets that populated those decks. Mac played the game as directed, marshaling the efforts of his department heads to construct an aviation program that complemented SCS, all the while detailing the arguments against SCS to seniors on the OP-05 air warfare staff. In private meetings with sympathetic professional staff members of the House Appropriations Committee (HAC), senior naval aviators shared those arguments and watched as the committee zeroed out SCS research and development funds in the fiscal year 1974 budget request. The Senate appropriators were less persuaded; however, no less a personage than Adm. Hyman Rickover, respected head of the Navy's nuclear power program, registered his opposition to the SCS at an opportune moment. The HAC held its position through the difficult conference negotiations with Senate counterparts, producing language that linked any SCS funds to a favorable outcome of a General Accounting Office study of the small carrier concept. Ultimately, Congress, starving the project of needed cash to launch, killed the SCS concept.[16]

Sea Control Ship and F-14 program issues aside, Mac worked more than a full day managing a staff of more than a half-dozen captains and twice that number of commanders, most seasoned squadron or air wing commanders. All were fully occupied with originating warfighting requirements and justifying the dollars needed to develop, field, and produce the entire portfolio of Navy aircraft, airborne sensors, and airborne weapons. In only a short time on the job, Mac signed off on a plan to re-engine the T-34B Mentor trainer, yielding its T-34C Turbo Mentor replacement; a plan to overhaul the inventory of C-2A carrier onboard delivery transports to extend their life into the late 1980s; a plan to acquire an initial cadre of five former Air Force F-5 aircraft as Navy adversaries; and a complicated arrangement to commandeer Navy A-4s for immediate transshipment to the Israeli air force to replenish losses in the Yom Kippur War—all a testament to the solid work of the OP-506 staff, to Mac's confidence in them, and to the wide latitude afforded him by his boss and director of aviation plans, Rear Adm. Donald Davis. Mac's mentor and colleague in that position from his early time in OPNAV, Jerry Miller, had moved on, but Mac and Admiral Davis were well acquainted, and the relationship was harmonious and productive, founded on their mutual esteem from years of working in close proximity. Mac was the air officer on *Constellation* when Davis brought aboard Air Wing Five in mid-1962, and Davis was the senior Navy project officer for TFX/F-111 in the Air Force Systems Command when Mac was the TFX requirements officer on the OP-506 staff. Regarding Mac's performance as OP-506, Davis wrote that his "ability in guiding the efforts of a sizable staff of highly selected and unusually talented officers is particularly noteworthy, and has generated a most impressive reputation throughout the OPNAV staff for top quality performance."[17]

It was a stressful time in OP-506 but not one without an occasional injection of levity. Capt. George Mott recalled an episode during his time on the staff:

> Mac was in charge when Lyle Bull and I were wandering back to the office and found unattended carpet lying in the fifth corridor, intended for an Air Force general's office. We looked in the general's office and no one was around. As a joke, we took the carpet into OP-506 and put it down, leaving next for lunch. When we returned, the carpet was gone. A quick look around the office revealed the carpet had been cut into many smaller pieces throughout 506 spaces with the largest piece going to 506 himself. Mac wasn't in when that happened and didn't notice the new rug. The next day the Air Force went

on the warpath, but they were clueless as to what happened to the carpet. Mac called all of us in and gave a stern lecture, asking if we had any idea what happened to the rug. After describing the missing carpet, he glanced down and realized he was standing on it. He quickly aborted the meeting, closed the door and laughed his heart out. That was the last mention of the rug. He was a great leader at a time when 506 was in everyone's gun sights.[18]

11

Legacy

The Navy has both a tradition and a future—and we look with pride and confidence in both directions.

—Adm. George Anderson, CNO

Peacetime routine was never an easy circumstance for Ernie. The animating force in his life was combat flying in the company of fellow naval aviators. Without the encouragement, challenge, and validation of that fraternity, he retreated into an abject sense of having lost his life's purpose. It may have lured him into more excessive behavior and, eventually, neglect of the toll it was taking on his health. The ships and aircraft that became so essential to his flying career and success in combat and that were the object of such great personal attachment had almost all been retired and had disappeared from view. The Dauntless and Hellcat had been struck from front line service years before he retired. USS *Lexington* sailed on as CVT 16, a training carrier reduced to short, infrequent deployments in the Gulf of Mexico to qualify student naval aviators before being decommissioned many years later. The visible reminders of Ernie's most important calling were gone, and mundane civilian pursuits could not satiate his need for a more vital existence. He founded a mortgage banking firm under his name—Snowden and Company—operating from a leased penthouse office suite on Gough Street in downtown San Francisco. He lacked any real business experience and so, as a company of one, had no real expectation of generating titanic financial growth. On his accountant's advice, he made a token effort to display all the appurtenances of entrepreneurial abundance as a

means to moderate income tax liability in retirement. He sustained
a storefront trade for nearly ten years before rising rents and business
costs forced him to file for dissolution of the business and to relocate
from his high-priced urban environment.

Ernie passed peacefully in his sleep just a mile from the approach end
of runway 34 Left at Reno-Tahoe Airport. Mac attended the funeral
alone on July 15, 1975, at the Presidio of San Francisco cemetery. It
was a modest ceremony. Ernie had withdrawn to a life marked by relative obscurity, and many of his social and service connections had
atrophied over time. Mac was one of only a handful of guests and the
only immediate family member. In a release of emotion, the gruff
style that was Mac's trademark was on display one more time: overtaken by the intense grief of the moment, he dressed down the naval
reserve honor guard at the end of the ceremony for their lack of military deportment and the disrespect for his revered brother, the fallen
warrior. Their time in uniform, their brand of aggressive flying, their
squadron, group, and ship commands mirrored each other so closely
that they might have been the same individual in some shadow universe, save the difference in their years and the vast changes in naval
aviation from the mid-1930s to the late 1970s. One constant for the
brothers—for all naval aviators, really—was the intimate association
with their aircraft that usually extended to a kind of brand loyalty to
that aircraft's manufacturer. After hundreds, then thousands, of hours
of flight time in a particular type and model, pilots became finely
attuned to the nuances of that aircraft. For Mac and Ernie, their experiences—that comfortable familiarity with cockpit layout and function, predictability of control response, finely tuned balance of throttle
position and stick motion that could extend endurance, hold tight
parade formation through obscuring weather, the ability to repeatedly
master a "three-wire" approach to a pitching deck, and the visceral feel
for stall performance and how to manage its onset in a very high-G
environment—were learned interactions that became more intuitive
with time in the aircraft. Their feel for the aircraft may have made a
difference on more than one occasion in extricating themselves from
dire circumstances in both training and combat situations. At some

level of experience, a strong personal identity with the aircraft developed. And with fellow naval aviators also experienced in that type and model of aircraft, perhaps a stronger shared sense of kinship developed—a kind of fraternity within a fraternity. For Ernie, a career of piloting widely varied types of aircraft from carriers and cruisers distilled down to two with which he felt the greatest affinity: the Douglas SBD and the Grumman F6F. The SBD represented the culmination of performance for the dive-bombing mission that arrived in the fleet just in time and became the instrument of his particular expertise. He had practiced dive-bombing in the F3F and then the SB2U, but the SBD brought together those design features most conducive to scoring bomb hits. The Douglas company name with which Ernie most associated his wartime experience for the dependability of the iconic SBD Dauntless was later taken over by the McDonnell Corporation to form McDonnell Douglas, which was ultimately subsumed in a Boeing acquisition and disappeared from the pantheon of active American aerospace companies. Only the Boeing corporate logo bears some faint resemblance to the original Douglas logo, with its globe and stylized orbiting missile contrail. Ernie lived long enough to witness the diminution of the Douglas brand with the McDonnell merger, and his disappointment was perhaps even more intensely felt as a family misfortune. Ernie's brother-in-law, Hap and Betty Arnold's second son Bruce, was married to company founder and president Donald Douglas' daughter Barbara in 1943. Thus it became a source of internal family disappointment, which Ernie shared, to see the senior Douglas' namesake company reduced in stature.

The F6F represented for Ernie an increase in performance but also a return to a pure fighter in a class that had marked the beginning of his flying career in F4B-4s. He found the heady performance gave him greatest utility, however, in making circuits of the target area in his recurring role as strike director during his time as CAG. That it also was the aircraft in which he scored one of his aerial kills probably intensified the association. Of course, with the devotion to the aircraft generally came the highest regard for the manufacturer if the aircraft had proved itself by its longevity. In the case of the F6F, the quintessential endorsement may have come from Ernie's peer and acquaintance, a World War II ace with air-to-air kills in the F4F and F6F,

Rear Adm. Edward "Whitey" Feightner. When asked by an audience
member at a 1999 Association of Naval Aviation convention address
to comment on the flightworthiness and combat performance of the
F6F, he remarked simply: "God bless Grumman." Even though Ernie
had by then passed away, this sentiment precisely encapsulated not just
Ernie's attitude but that of a generation of naval aviators that cut their
teeth in Grumman fighters. By the time of Feightner's commentary,
however, the Grumman marquee had already been transformed to a
subordinated standing through its acquisition by Northrop to form
Northrop Grumman in 1994. The goodwill and brand loyalty that
Grumman had nurtured with its naval aviator customers for its "iron
works" products were methodically excised by Northrop in the years
following the acquisition in order to create a new, unified corporate
culture.

Mac's "brand loyalty" was to Chance Vought Company, maker of
the F4U and, later, the F8U. Most of his accumulated career flight
time began with the F4U in VF-21 in the late 1940s and culminated
with the F8U in VF-91 in the late 1950s and through the mid-1960s
with Air Wing 5. Both aircraft were "world beaters" for their day in
the sense that they represented transcendent capability breakthroughs
in the design of fighter aircraft that kept the U.S. Navy in the vanguard
of fighter performance for any air force. Mac's affinity for Vought was
deep-seated and based not only on the aircraft but also on highly
rewarding interactions with Vought company representatives throughout his flying years. He never attained the flight hours that put him in
company with those Crusader high-timers who merited a most distinctive recognition. Vought placed great ceremony in presenting to
its Crusader high-timers a chrome-plated "gunfighter" .45 caliber service automatic pistol, which only a very few ultimately qualified for.
Nonetheless, Mac was highly regarded by Vought for minding fleet
Crusader needs as a collateral duty of his time as TFX requirements
officer on the OP-05 staff. With more than a twinge of regret, he witnessed the passing of Vought's marquee as it became one more disparate industrial entity in the horizontal integration that formed the
LTV conglomerate, undermined further by a Chapter 11 bankruptcy
filing, and disappearing completely during Northrop Corporation's
wave of acquisitions in the early 1990s.

Out of uniform, Mac was no less committed to applying a lifetime of experience to bettering naval aviation in particular, and the military services in general. He retired from active duty on July 1, 1974, and enthusiastically accepted orders from the Navy Department placing him in a call-up status for convoy routing duty, should that time ever come. It was not long before his OPNAV acquaintances maneuvered Mac into a new outlet for his recognized expertise and energies as a legislative assistant for military matters to Texas representative Richard White, a member of the House Armed Services Committee. Representative White was a self-avowed moderate Democrat, which likely piqued Mac's curiosity. White's history as a Marine rifleman, a veteran of the landings on Iwo Jima, and recipient of the Purple Heart for wounds received there underscored his deep-seated regard for the welfare of Navy and Marine Corps servicemen and for the Department of the Navy. White's staff director and legislative director gave Mac wide latitude to take broad pronouncements from the representative on issues of particular interest, to research the legislative history of the issue, to interview cognizant officials in Department of Defense secretariats, and to coordinate with the professional staff members on the House Armed Services Committee to draft language and shape a strategy for moving a bill forward on behalf of White. One of his initial successes out of the gate as a neophyte congressional staffer came when, as an integral part of White's office staff, he made himself a principal contributor in shaping an amendment to Title 10 of the U.S. Code, described in House bill H. R. 7682 as allowing the Armed Forces greater flexibility in calling up reserve officers and enlisted to active duty. The bill would give the defense secretary greater discretion in determining call-up time and increasing the number of reservists who could be called to active duty for other than a war or national emergency from 50,000 to 100,000 individuals. Passed by the House and by the Senate with their amendments, it was enacted into law by President Jimmy Carter in December 1980. Mac was instrumental in crafting the bill and strategy for H. R. 4448 in 1981 that would have increased the number of assistant secretaries of defense, principally by reestablishing the assistant secretary for command, control, communications, and intelligence. Representative White introduced it in committee, and it was forwarded to the full House for consideration but did not get the required support and had to be reintroduced in the following congressional session two years later. White had left Congress by then and could only draw consolation from having laid the groundwork—with the engagement and unflagging legwork of Mac and others on his staff—for the eventual passage, with some additional provisions, as part of the Defense Authorization Act of 1984 containing essentially identical language.

Finally, Mac played a key role in organizing various stakeholders and in socializing the key tenets of a resurrected Joint Chiefs of Staff reorganization act, permitting any member of the Joint Chiefs to submit dissenting military opinions to the defense secretary and then to the president and provide the secretary and the president separate military advice in his own right. It further established the position of the deputy chairman of the Joint Chiefs of Staff, prescribing that he be from a different military service than the chairman, and made the secretary responsible for the operation of the joint staff (not the chairman) so as to provide unified strategic direction of the combatant forces. The initiative was not entirely born in the 97th Congress during Mac's staff tenure—it had a history that originated in the widespread public dissatisfaction with perceived and documented interservice rivalry and inefficiency on display in the Vietnam War and still evident in the invasion of Grenada in 1983. Mac's experience gave him the standing and bona fides to again play a key role in making the salient points and doing the legwork to coordinate stakeholder buy-in such that Representative White was able to introduce the bill as H. R. 6954 in August 1982. It passed the House on a voice vote but did not sustain traction in the Senate to gain its full support. It would be another four years before sufficient momentum compelled Congress to move forward and send President Ronald Reagan for enactment what would come to be known as the Goldwater-Nichols Department of Defense Reorganization Act of 1986. The act went beyond the measures cited in the 1982 act, representing a fundamental change to the mandates of the National Security Act of 1947. By the time of the passage of Goldwater-Nichols, Mac and White had moved on to other endeavors but could still feel some satisfaction in playing an early role in propping up the movement of the legislation.[1]

Adding a fitting coda to Ernie and Mac's combined forty years in naval aviation, Mac would, as executive director of the ANA, architect and manage a gala celebration for the seventy-fifth anniversary of naval aviation in Pensacola in May 1986. Not lost on Mac was that this celebration coincided with the birthday of his older brother—the inspiration and mentor for his own lifetime of commitment to naval aviation. The ANA came about in 1974 as the brainchild of former deputy vice CNO for aviation, retired vice admiral. Bob Pirie, in league with then current deputy CNO for aviation, Vice Adm. Bill Houser. Both had been exasperated and exhausted by the struggle to save the F-14, then under unrelenting pressure from Congress and the Office of the Secretary of Defense. Nearing victory in that contest, both foresaw the need to strengthen their hand for the next fiscal and programmatic engagement by organizing the "soft" lobbying power of member advocates beyond the active duty ranks. Pirie observed that the destroyermen and battleship sailors each had their own association, and these groups often made the difference in Washington by galvanizing and mobilizing their memberships to augment the uniformed Navy's efforts. The Tailhook Association—probably the first fraternal body to organize around expressly naval aviation interests—formed in 1956 to educate the public on the appropriate role of the aircraft carrier and carrier aviation. Established as a fellowship order primarily for those achieving an arrested landing aboard an aircraft carrier, the Tailhook Association took a decidedly different path with regard to supporting the Navy's legislative agenda. Chartered along the lines of a tax-exempt social club under the federal tax code, Tailhook lacked, by design, any authority to lobby or to direct membership advocacy toward legislative initiatives inside the Washington arena and so could not lend its name or direct its membership lists to what the two senior aviators had in mind.

When Pirie and Houser gained approval from Secretary of the Navy J. William Middendorf and CNO Adm. James Holloway to implement their proposal, their announced intent was to employ the ANA in support of the deputy CNO for air's requirements and budget plans—as approved by the CNO and the defense secretary—when those requests went before Congress. A first organizational meeting was convened in Pensacola in October 1974 as an adjunct to a regularly scheduled meeting of the air board of aviation flag officers. A founding alliance of senior aviators—active and retired—was drawn together to petition for incorporation and to populate its board. To conform with the letter of the law, ANA cast itself as a tax-exempt 501c (4) organization, providing the greatest latitude for lobbying but still conforming to federal guidelines. Within only a few years, it became apparent to the board that to do its work, it had to be in closer proximity to the legislative action, necessitating a move from Pensacola to northern Virginia. Once encamped in Arlington, Virginia, ANA stalwarts Tom Moorer, Jerry Miller, Chris Cagle, and Mark Hill "performed Herculean feats in the Halls of Congress and other government offices" by educating members of Congress and their mostly neophyte staffs on the efficacy of carrier-based air power. An inadequately justified and ill-advised campaign in Congress to reduce funding and inventory of large deck carriers in the 1980s was successfully suppressed. ANA was not singularly responsible for turning the tide for large deck aircraft carriers, but its voice added greatly to a more informed and fact-based debate regarding the shortcomings of small deck carriers.

These early ANA leaders recognized that for the organization to be effective and continue to grow, a chief of staff was necessary to hold things together in the headquarters office, to oversee major events, to chart a path for growth, and to communicate frequently with the membership. All were familiar with or knew personally Mac Snowden from his tenure in OPNAV as the director of aviation plans, and specifically his work to keep the F-14 alive and thriving. Mac was the unanimous choice to be the first ANA executive director and arrived on staff as planning was getting under way for naval aviation's seventy-fifth anniversary celebration. The festivities were remarkable for entertainment value alone: show business icons and celebrities of note were present throughout the four days of performance events at the Pensacola Civic Auditorium, Pensacola Naval Air Station, and on board USS *Lexington* adjacent to the old seaplane ramps on Pensacola Bay. The involvement of *Lexington* in the celebration had particular poignancy for Mac, as hers was the flight deck from which his brother had led Air Group Five to such success in 1943–44 and was the flight deck on which his son had attained carrier qualification in 1972. Entertainers lending their reputations to this rare celebration of the history of naval aviation included Bob Hope, Elizabeth Taylor, Jonathan Winters, Brooke Shields, Sammy Davis Jr., Mac Davis, and Barbara Mandrell, who was married to a former naval aviator. There has not been a celebration before or since that showcased such star power in support of the achievements, technological progress, individual and collective valor, sacrifice, and professionalism of those who pioneered and those who continue to serve in naval aviation.

Days later, Mac would again be pulling levers behind the curtain to orchestrate a celebration surrounding the world premiere of the Hollywood motion picture *Top Gun* in Washington, D.C. After the showing of the film at a downtown theater, a lavish reception at USAir's Washington National Airport hangar was hosted by and for ANA in recognition of behind-the-scenes lobbying and support rendered by the senior Navy leadership, including the Secretary of the Navy John Lehman, for making available aircraft and flight crews to heighten the film's realism, and retired admiral Holloway, who served as a senior technical adviser on the film—and worked assiduously to make Lehman's commitments reality. Mac was briefly amused by his pleasant banter with the film's twenty-four-year-old star, Tom Cruise, but for Mac, the real value of the festivities and the public's enthusiastic embrace of the film was the universally positive impact on recruiting for naval aviation.[2]

What Mac and his peers were learning, and what Ernie, in his time, could not have foretold, was a plain truth: in the 1920s, naval aviation was new, Navy pilots were real personalities who bravely faced untold dangers mastering flight in unbelievably primitive machines and were embraced by an American public who felt a vicarious thrill and a patriotic connection to their exploits. Ernie, in his time at North Island in the 1930s, had encountered many of those celebrities and filmmakers on location who were building their own reputations by their attachment to the real heroes of the time. By the 1980s, naval aviation had matured, and its work—no less dangerous due to the exponential increases in speed, mass, and altitudes involved—was largely conducted out of view on an everyday basis. To regain the public's attention and admiration would take a dramatic celluloid representation featuring actors in flight suits from central casting. *Top Gun* succeeded beyond anyone's expectations in reconnecting the public to a very glamorized vision of naval aviation. Recruiting, by all reports, surged with new interest from an aroused pool of fresh candidates.

When the movie premiere reception ended that night in May 1986, Mac took his leave from ANA and retired from the directorship, withdrawing from any future active connection to naval aviation. Mac finally arrived at that point where he knew his service to naval aviation was at an end, where he thought his public life might be done, where he thought that he owed himself a more serene existence in less stressful surroundings. He would discover that he could not completely withdraw when there were issues that summoned his energy and experience. After leaving ANA, he decamped to Beaufort, his boyhood hometown, for a quiet retirement on the coast where he could relive some of the joy of his childhood pursuits on the water, boating and fishing. Within months, his boyhood friends, among them Graydon Paul, were exhorting him to apply his name and experience to running for the seat that would soon open for the Fourth District in the North Carolina General Assembly. He ran, and he won the 1994 contest to ride a wave that gave the North Carolina House a Republican majority and split what had been a Democrat-dominated general assembly. Mac had a particular regard for the working people in the Fourth District—farmers and fishermen. He ran on a platform that promised his full support to those groups to fend off encroachments by overzealous environmentalists. But at the top of his legislative priorities were issues that could make life a bit easier and reduce onerous tax and business burdens for the enlisted and junior officer Marines that lived in his district and commuted to Marine Corps Air Station Cherry Point. The strength of his name and his reputation in naval aviation carried an overwhelming majority of the vote from this demographic group.

Sadly, Mac's term in office lasted only four months before a virulent form of lung cancer ended his life. Diagnosed late in the progression of the cancer, he was told by Navy doctors that very little in the arsenal of known and accepted treatments could be applied to arrest or reverse the effects. He volunteered for a radical protocol involving experimental chemotherapy, understanding that his physical response might be used to advance the state of knowledge. His first treatment was so toxic that he lived only twenty-four hours beyond its application. He was buried with military honors at Arlington Cemetery on May 10, 1995. North Carolina governor James Hunt took the floor of the state house of delegates to acknowledge the loss of one of their own recently installed members who, in just three months in office, had already drawn unanimous attention from the legislative members and had made an impact on the state's business.

When surveying the overlapping careers of Mac and Ernie, one sees, through the rare fraternal connection that influenced them both, more than fifty years of naval aviation from the perspective of two who had enormous impact on the evolution of carrier fighters and their employment—from leather flying caps and goggles peering out from open-cockpit wood-and-rag biplanes to anti-G suits and torso harnesses in supersonic combat. The constants throughout were their close affinity and mutual respect, and their esteem for carrier aviation and frequent exchange of professional counsel and advice from twin perspectives that bracketed so much of naval aviation history. Many hundreds of clearly superlative officers served naval aviation over that time. Many have become more illustrious for singular milestone achievements or were more advanced in rank than Ernie or Mac. Neither brother rose to flag rank in a real sense—Ernie was awarded that promotion as an inducement to exit the rolls of active officers and clear the way for rising new talent, but without filling a flag billet; Mac was told in confidence by a highly placed and well-known flag officer that he had made the promotion list for admiral but at the last minute was removed to make room for a returning Vietnam POW. Ernie took his proxy promotion and flag title in stride; Mac would harbor a measure of pique and indignation for years but suppressed any ill feeling to apply himself to the next job before him. There was no shortage of motivated, competent, and aspiring naval aviators surrounding both Ernie and Mac. What set these two journeymen practitioners apart is a nearly identical—perhaps, in part, genetic—predisposition for a conspicuous display of combat leadership; an aptness for flying; the highest regard for naval traditions and ceremony; the good fortune to be positioned at the forefront of foundational change from 1937 to

1986; and the fortitude and will to exert themselves totally to influence change positively for naval aviation.

In assessing the record, Mac was one of a very small number of squadron aviators to be in a position to innovate delivery schemes for tactical atomic weapons from fighters. He was, perhaps more than any other mid-grade peer at that time, the leading expert for the Atlantic Fleet in the arming and delivery profiles required for the BOAR store from the F2H Banshee. He was skilled at air-to-air gunnery—possessing an instinctual feel for the interplay and physical dynamics of aircraft and projectile movement through space—garnering Atlantic Fleet honors for his scores on the towed banner. That knack would be retained and redirected again when as commanding officer of VF-91, his mentorship resulted in the squadron posting the highest Pacific Fleet scores for aerial gunnery. In every assignment, from department head in VF-41, to executive officer of VF-91, to commanding officer of VF-91, to commanding officer of USS *Chilton*, to commanding officer of USS *Guadalcanal*—every unit in which Mac served won the fleet battle efficiency "E" during his tenure. Those successes resulted from the contributions of many, but Mac's presence and ample display of leadership had an overwhelming influence on the outcome. A career-long compilation of carrier-based fighter experience provided Mac the wherewithal to make himself a pivotal influence for the suspension of the F-111B program and the birth of the VFX. He was the indispensable staff officer at that moment who embodied the necessary knowledge and skill to formulate and draft the arguments that successfully shot down the F-111B and gave carrier aviation its iconic showpiece, the F-14 Tomcat.

Mac would fly from or serve on aircraft carriers that were successfully commissioned in part due to the experience, perseverance, and skill of his older brother, Ernie, who held essentially the same position in OPNAV as the program coordinator for carrier modernization and recapitalization that Mac would later occupy for the advanced fleet air defense requirement that produced the F-14. In *Ranger* as commanding officer of VF-91, in *Constellation* as air officer, and finally in *Ticonderoga* as commander of Air Wing Five, Mac benefitted from improvements, upgrades, and "new steel" that older brother Ernie shepherded through the labyrinth of Pentagon acquisition. As the commanding officer of

USS *Kula Gulf* (CVE- 108), Ernie was among a very few who pioneered the employment of helicopter-based ASW hunter-killer operations. Earlier, as operations officer for air for the Eighth Fleet, Ernie refined and applied lessons learned in the Marianas Turkey Shoot for positioning of fleet air cover that would, in its time, underscore the viability of the aircraft carrier in the face of intense Air Force efforts to reveal the carrier's vulnerability. In the fateful battle of the Philippine Sea, Ernie was at least initially the sole voice for arming VF-16's Hellcats with armor-piercing bombs for the long search on June 20 for the remnants of the Japanese fleet. He reasoned that Hellcats, by their speed and maneuverability, would possess the best chance of surviving the withering antiaircraft fire from enemy vessels, but also had the ability to fend off and neutralize any aerial opposition on the way in and out. This concept was unconventional and not widely embraced at the time, but Ernie presented the scheme to Vice Admiral Mitscher, who approved. Save limited application in Vietnam by bombing from F-8s and F-4s, the concept would lose its appeal until resurfacing with the F-14 "Bomb-cat" in the air-to-ground delivery role in Bosnia fifty years later.

And at the beginning of this story of two overlapping careers in naval aviation, older brother Ernie, with fellow aviators from those early squadrons in carriers such as *Ranger* (CV 4), *Lexington* (CV 2), and *Saratoga* (CV 3), set down the early precepts for tactics and maneuver in Fleet Problems XIX and XX—rigorously exercised models for squadron and air group operations that would carry them through the early stages of the war in the Pacific. Both brothers were presented a rare opportunity to spearhead the application and validation of carrier air tactics, under fire, in the earliest stages of an air war as commanders of aviation units—Ernie as skipper of VS-72, leading squadron attacks against experienced and highly resolved and capable air, land, and sea targets, and Mac as commander of Air Wing Five. In retirement, Mac recalled in an interview:

> During pre-deployment to Vietnam operations, I had set up Operation Singing Sword. Air Wing Five was probably the first carrier air wing to attempt extensive wing training exercises in preparation for a tour at Yankee Station. We flew a number of

mass A-4 flights from NAS Lemoore, joined by F-8s from NAS Miramar, to various target areas on the West Coast and east of the mountains. Coordinated attacks were the routine. Opposition to the flights was provided by VF-126 TF-9Js out of Miramar. Later in the training cycle, we deployed the entire air wing plus detachments to NAS Fallon for strike training, emphasizing all aspects of live ordnance. We also provided cross-training, in that VF pilots taught fighter tactics to VA pilots in the classroom and in the air. Conversely, the attack folks taught the VF guys tactics of bombing. Remember, at this time the F-8s were largely pure VF and some had acquired rocket tubes, but there had not been much in the way of bombing.[3]

Mac's work, and that of contemporary commanders that summer of 1965, presaged what would become standard air wing training at Fallon in future years.

Both Mac and Ernie, against intense air and ground opposition in their time, tested the limits of interwar training doctrine, absorbed the lessons of leading naval aviators into unanticipated enemy countertactics and the brunt of losing those under their command. Finally, in subsequent assignments, they used that experience to advance the mechanics, maneuvers, stratagems, and procedures, even perhaps the artistry, of naval aviation through a fifty-year continuum. Thus, two brothers, with no predilection for flight save a physical gift for that all-important hand-eye coordination, by dint of leadership—inherent, learned, and applied, and equal parts tactical and administrative acumen—helped shape the course and growth of naval aviation from the earliest inelegant biplane gambols on narrow wooden flight decks to the crushing mass and power of supersonic operations from steel decks.

Notes

Introduction

1. Wolfe, *The Right Stuff*, 16.

Chapter 1. Beginnings

Epigraph. McCain, "Remarks by Senator John McCain at the Tailhook Symposium Honoring the Centennial of Naval Aviation."

1. Grossnick and Evans, *United States Naval Aviation, 1910–2010*, vol. 2: *Statistics*, 208.
2. Currituck County Archives, "Currituck County War of 1812 Veterans."
3. Evans and Grossnick, *United States Naval Aviation, 1910–2010*, vol. 1: *Chronology*, 5.
4. Grossnick and Evans, *United States Naval Aviation, 1910–2010*, 2:5.
5. Groom, *The Aviators*, 12.
6. Ibid., 15.
7. Rankin, "The Navy's Schneider Cup Racers," 802.
8. Ibid.
9. Reynolds, *Famous American Admirals*, 240–41.
10. Rankin, "The Navy's Schneider Cup Racers," 803.

Chapter 2. Foundations

Epigraph. Trimble, *Admiral William A. Moffett*, 110.

1. Evans and Grossnick, *United States Naval Aviation, 1910–2010*, 1:65.
2. Nofi, *To Train the Fleet for War*, 105.
3. Ibid., 67.
4. Evans and Grossnick, *United States Naval Aviation, 1910–2010*, 1:488.

5. Hill Goodspeed, "Foundation for Victory: U.S. Navy Aircraft Development, 1922–1945," in Smith, *One Hundred Years of U.S. Navy Air Power.*

6. Evans and Grossnick, *United States Naval Aviation, 1910–2010,* 1:488.

7. Downs, "Calvin Coolidge, Dwight Morrow, and the Air Commerce Act of 1926."

8. Nofi, *To Train the Fleet for War,* 64.

9. Wagemann, "The Admiral."

10. Trimble, *Admiral William A. Moffett,* 4.

11. Ibid., 11.

12. Evans and Grossnick, *United States Naval Aviation, 1910–2010,* 1:101.

13. Cutler and Burgess, "Lest We Forget."

14. "Swede Vejtasa: In Memoriam."

15. Ibid.; Vejtasa, "Fitness Report on Macon Snowden."

16. Spangenberg oral history.

Chapter 3. Preparation

Epigraph. *Lucky Bag,* 1932.

1. Keillor and Keillor, *Images of Aviation— Naval Air Station Pensacola,* 9.

2. Siegfried, "Naval Air History Part 3."

3. Ibid.

4. Grossnick, *Dictionary of American Naval Aviation Squadrons,* 1:11.

5. Yenne, *The Story of the Boeing Company,* 18.

6. Nofi, *To Train the Fleet for War,* 303.

7. Friedman, *U.S. Aircraft Carriers,* 11.

8. Ibid.

9. Felker, *Testing American Sea Power,* 141.

10. Ibid., 58–59.

11. Chant, *The World's Greatest Aircraft,* 45.

12. Francillon, *Grumman Aircraft Since 1929,* 89.

13. Nofi, *To Train the Fleet for War,* 231–32.

14. Wildenberg, *Destined for Glory,* 174.

15. Linder, "Field Guide to Coronado History: Glenn Curtiss' Coronado Home."

16. Larkins, *Battleship and Cruiser Aircraft of the United States Navy, 1910–1949*, 11.
17. Ibid., 18.
18. Ginter, *Curtiss SOC Seagull*, 1–3.
19. Larkins, *Battleship and Cruiser Aircraft of the United States Navy*, 43–45.
20. Huston, *American Airpower Comes of Age*, 11.
21. Ibid; Coffey, *Hap*, 180.

Chapter 4. Peer Rivalry

Epigraph. Peattie, *Sunburst,* 61.

1. Coffey, *Hap*, 180.
2. Evans and Peattie, *Kaigun*.
3. Peattie, *Sunburst*, 55.
4. Ibid., 11; Bergerud, *Fire in the Sky*, 326.
5. Bergerud, *Fire in the Sky*, 323–26.
6. Tagaya, *Aichi 99 Kanbaku "Val" Units: 1937–42*.
7. Nofi, *To Train the Fleet for War*, 231.
8. Ibid., 235.
9. Smith, *Fist from the Sky*, 152–54.

Chapter 5. Total War

1. Guyton, *Whistling Death*, 88–89.
2. Naval History and Heritage Command, "Wasp VIII (CV-7)," *Dictionary of American Naval Fighting Ships*.
3. Guttman, "Interview with World War II SB2U-3 Pilot Sumner H. Whitten."
4. Lundstrom, *The First Team and the Guadalcanal Campaign*, 19.
5. Chant, *The World's Greatest Aircraft*, 182.
6. Hammel, *Carrier Clash*, 35–36.
7. Morison, *History of United States Naval Operations in World War II*, 5:ix.
8. Lundstrom, *The First Team and the Guadalcanal Campaign*, 27.
9. Ibid., 33.
10. Ibid., 34.
11. Ibid., 38.
12. Coggins, *The Campaign for Guadalcanal*, 31.

13. Christ, *Battalion of the Damned*, 108–10.

14. Lundstrom, *The First Team and the Guadalcanal Campaign*, 28.

15. Morison, *History of United States Naval Operations in World War II*, 5:58.

16. Ibid.

17. Lundstrom, *The First Team and the Guadalcanal Campaign*, 158–59.

18. Ibid., 222.

19. Morison, *History of United States Naval Operations in World War II*, 5:132–33.

20. Lundstrom, *The First Team and the Guadalcanal Campaign*, 228–29.

21. Huston, *American Airpower Comes of Age*, 51.

22. Gendell, "Annapolis's Last Army-Navy Game."

23. Arnold, *War Department Correspondence*.

24. *Providence Journal*, "Four Navy Fliers Get Decorations," 8.

25. Snowden, "Wake Mission Summary."

26. Ibid.

27. *Raleigh News and Observer*, "Snowden Tells of Navy Raid."

28. Potter, *Admiral Arleigh Burke*, 120.

29. Hornfischer, *The Fleet at Flood Tide*, 23.

30. Cagle, "Arleigh Burke–Naval Aviator," 3.

31. Ibid., 5.

32. "The West of Tokyo Missionary Society," http://www.rb-29.net/HTML/81lexingtonstys/07.01wotms.htm.

33. Hornfischer, *The Fleet at Flood Tide*, 35.

34. Sears, *Pacific Air*, 299.

35. Ship Staff, *Tarawa to Tokyo 1943–1946*.

36. Naval History and Heritage Command, "Action Reports: Task Force 58, 11–21 June 1944," in *Papers of Admiral Arleigh A. Burke*.

37. Ibid.

38. Kennedy, "Back from the Biggest Air Battle of the War."

39. Ibid.

40. Ibid.

41. Naval History and Heritage Command, "Action Reports: Task Force 58, 11–21 June 1944."

42. Potter, *Admiral Arleigh Burke*, 164.

43. Tillman, *Clash of the Carriers*, 205.

44. Bryan and Reed, *Mission Beyond Darkness*, 15.

45. Ibid., 17.

46. Sears, *Pacific Air*, 17.

47. Sinton, "Plans for Night Rendezvous—Request for."

48. *Pilot's Flight Operating Instructions for Navy Model SBD-6 Airplanes.*

49. Tillman, *Clash of the Carriers*, 226.

50. Bryan and Reed, *Mission Beyond Darkness*, 108.

51. Van Voorhis, "March of Time."

52. Ship Staff, *Tarawa to Tokyo 1943–1946.*

53. Snowden, "Air Group Sixteen End of Tour Report."

54. Commander, Task Force 58, Naval Dispatch 092117.

55. Commander in Chief, Pacific, Naval Dispatch 160440.

56. Bohl, "Annapolis Architecture."

57. 1946 *Lucky Bag,* 57.

Chapter 6. Transition

Epigraph. 1946 *Lucky Bag*, 57.

1. Naval History and Heritage Command, "Ticonderoga IV (CV-14)," *Dictionary of American Naval Fighting Ships.*

2. 1946 *Lucky Bag.*

3. Potter, *Admiral Arleigh Burke*, 272.

4. Ibid.

5. Wooldridge, *Into the Jet Age*, xix.

6. Ibid.

7. Rosenberg, "Air Warfare Division (OP-55) Study on Future Development of Carrier Aviation with Respect to Both Aircraft and Aircraft Carriers," 262.

8. Coffey, *Hap*, 382.

9. Newport Fleet Officers Wives, *Guidelines: Naval Social Customs.*

10. Rubel, "The U.S. Navy's Transition to Jets," 50.

11. Dunn, "Six Amazing Years; RAGs, NATOPS, and More," 98.

12. Ibid.

13. Tillman, *Vought F4U Corsair*, 73–74.

14. Swihnart, "The Vought F4U Corsair."

15. Harris, "Fitness Report on Lieutenant M. S. Snowden."

16. Buttler, *Early U.S. Jet Fighters*, 27.

17. Ibid.

18. Ginter, *McDonnell F2H-3/4 Big Banjo*, 34–35.

19. Marolda, *The U.S. Navy in the Korean War*, 33.

20. Rubel, "The U.S. Navy's Transition to Jets," 55.

21. Friedman, *U.S. Aircraft Carriers,* 24–25.

22. Ibid.

23. Fechteler, "Remarks on Navy Department Appropriations for 1954."

24. Ofstie, "Remarks on Navy Department Appropriations for 1954."

25. Rubel, "The U.S. Navy's Transition to Jets," 53–54.

26. Chambers, *Images of Aviation: Naval Air Station Patuxent River,* 34, 57, 58.

27. Gillcrist, *Sea Legs,* 131.

28. Ibid.

29. Satterfield, "Fitness Report on Lieutenant M. S. Snowden."

30. Buttler, *Early U.S. Jet Fighters,* 183.

31. Ibid.

32. Tillman, *MiG Master.*

33. Mersky, *F-8 Crusader vs. MiG-17,* 12.

34. Rubel, "The U.S. Navy's Transition to Jets," 51.

35. Ibid.

36. Evans and Grossnick, *United States Naval Aviation, 1910–2010,* 1:302.

37. Rudowsky, "Review of the Carrier Approach Criteria for Carrier-Based Aircraft," 8–9.

38. Ibid.

39. Dorr, "From Props to Jets and Angled Decks: Centennial of Naval Aviation."

Chapter 7. Dvinas and Silver Swallows

Epigraph. Tuoi Tre News, "General Vo Nguyen Giap's Immortal Sayings."

1. Karnow, *Vietnam,* 380.

2. Johnson, "Address on Gulf of Tonkin Incident."

3. Toperczer, *MiG-17 and MiG-19 Units of the Vietnam War,* 27–28.

4. Boniface, *MiGs Over North Vietnam,* 4–6.

5. Mersky, *F-8 Crusader Units of the Vietnam War,* 7.

6. Nichols and Tillman, *On Yankee Station,* 54.

7. Schuster, "The Rise of North Vietnam's Air Defenses."
8. Ibid.
9. Nichols and Tillman, *On Yankee Station*, 164.
10. National Museum of the U.S. Air Force, "SA-2 Surface-to-Air Missile."
11. Freed, "The Missile Men of North Vietnam."
12. Nichols and Tillman, *On Yankee Station*, 58.
13. Ibid., 56.
14. Hobson, *Vietnam Air Losses*, 270–71.
15. Nichols and Tillman, *On Yankee Station*, 168.
16. Mersky, *F-8 Crusader vs. MiG-17*, 26.
17. Ibid.
18. Ibid., 47.
19. Ibid.
20. Woodford, "Have Drill/Have Ferry Tactical Evaluation."
21. Barnes, "The MiGs of Area 51."
22. Morocco, *Thunder from Above*, 40.
23. Mersky, *F-8 Crusader Units of the Vietnam War*, 43, 56.

Chapter 8. Limited War
1. Mersky, *F-8 Crusader Units of the Vietnam War*, 19.
2. Ibid.
3. "Products: F-8E," *Vought Heritage*, http://www.vought.org/products/html/f8u-2ne.html.
4. Nichols and Tillman, *On Yankee Station*, 127.
5. Pribbenow, "Treatment of American POWs in North Vietnam."
6. Morocco, *Thunder from Above*, 40.
7. Goodwin, *Lyndon Johnson and the American Dream*, 264–65.
8. Van Staaveren, *Gradual Failure*, 86.
9. Morocco, *Thunder from Above*, 54.
10. Cross, "USS *Ticonderoga* (CVA-14) Air Plan."
11. Levinson, *Alpha Strike Vietnam*, 58.
12. "Army 3rd Brigade 1st Cavalry Division Operation Silver Bayonet 1965 #5A59," Vietnam Center and Archives.
13. Van Staaveren, *Gradual Failure*, 193.
14. Nichols and Tillman, *On Yankee Station*, 51.

15. Ibid., 68.
16. Ibid., 103–9.
17. Vejtasa, "Officer Fitness Report on Macon Snowden."

Chapter 9. Reconstitution
Epigraph. Ford, "Remarks of the President to the Tulane University Student Body."
1. Hattendorf, *U.S. Naval Strategy in the 1970s.*
2. Nichols and Tillman, *On Yankee Station*, 164.
3. Evans and Grossnick, *United States Naval Aviation, 1910–2010*, 1:393.
4. Hattendorf, *U.S. Naval Strategy in the 1970s,* xi.
5. Swartz, *U.S. Navy Capstone Strategies*, 19.
6. Swartz, *Organizing OPNAV (1970–2009)*, 22.
7. Naval History and Heritage Command, "Admiral Elmo R. Zumwalt Jr."
8. Ibid.
9. Ibid.
10. Swartz, *Organizing OPNAV (1970–2009)*, 15.
11. Swartz, *U.S. Navy Capstone Strategies*, 79.
12. Holloway, *Aircraft Carriers at War*, 388–89.
13. Swartz, *U.S. Navy Capstone Strategies*, 95.
14. Ibid., 112.
15. Ibid., 127.
16. Ibid., 177.
17. Evans and Grossnick, *United States Naval Aviation, 1910–2010*, 1:389–98.
18. Davis, "Report on the Fitness of Captain M. S. Snowden."
19. Evans and Grossnick, *United States Naval Aviation, 1910–2010*, 1:389.

Chapter 10. Consolidation
Epigraph. Tailhook Daily Briefing, "TFX and Turkeys—Part II."
1. Curtis, "The Sad Story of the TFX."
2. Art, *The TFX Decision*, 125.
3. Wooldridge, *Into the Jet Age*, 80.
4. Ibid., 81.

5. Ibid., 77.

6. Ibid., 79.

7. Ibid.

8. Thomason, *Grumman Navy F-111B Swing Wing*, 53.

9. Miller, "The Crash of TFX," 34–35.

10. Miller, "Supplement to Regular Fitness Report on Captain M. S. Snowden."

11. Connolly, "Letter of Appreciation."

12. Cone, "Recommendation for the Legion of Merit to Be Awarded Captain Macon Snowden."

13. Friedman, *U.S. Aircraft Carriers*, 352.

14. Harter, "Letter of Appreciation."

15. Woolridge, *Into the Jet Age: Conflict and Change in Naval Aviation*, 168.

16. Friedman, *U.S. Aircraft Carriers*, 354.

17. Davis, "Report on the Fitness of Captain M. S. Snowden."

18. Mott interview.

Chapter 11. Legacy

Epigraph. Anderson, "Remarks on the Retirement of Arleigh Burke."

1. Hall, "Top Gun."

2. Lawson, "Recollections from Air Wing Commanders," 33.

3. Ibid.

Bibliography

"Army 3rd Brigade 1st Cavalry Division Operation Silver Bayonet 1965 #5A59." December 24, 1965, folder 01, box 00, Bud Harton Collection, Vietnam Center and Archive, Texas Tech University. https://www.vietnam.ttu.edu/virtualarchive/items.php?item=168300010049.

Anderson, George. "Remarks at the Retirement of Arleigh Burke, 1 August 1961." https://www.history.navy.mil/browse-by-topic/heritage/famous-navy-quotations.html.

Arnold, H. H. *War Department Correspondence.* Washington, D.C.: Headquarters of the Army Air Forces, November 20, 1942.

Art, Robert J. *The TFX Decision: McNamara and the Military*. Boston: Little, Brown and Company, 1968.

Barnes, Thornton D. "The MiGs of Area 51." http://area51special projects.com/migs.html.

Bergerud, Eric M. *Fire in the Sky*. Boulder, Colo.: Westview Press, 2000.

Bohl Architects. "Annapolis Architecture." http://www.bohlarchi tects.com.

Boniface, Roger. *MiGs Over North Vietnam: The People's Air Force in Combat, 1965–1975*. New York: Stackpole Books, 2010.

Bryan III, Joseph and Philip G. Reed. *Mission Beyond Darkness*. New York: Duell, Sloan and Pearce, 1945.

Buttler, Tony. *Early U.S. Jet Fighters: Proposals, Projects, and Prototypes*. Manchester, U.K.: Hikoki Publications, 2013.

Cagle, M. W. "Arleigh Burke—Naval Aviator." *Foundations* 2, no. 2 (September 1981).

Chambers, Mark A. *Images of Aviation: Naval Air Station Patuxent River*. Charleston, S.C.: Arcadia Publishing, 2014.

Chant, Christopher. *The World's Greatest Aircraft*. New York: Chartwell Books, 2014.

Chief of Naval Operations Staff, Air Warfare Division (OP-55). *Study on Future Development of Carrier Aviation with Respect to Both Aircraft and Aircraft Carriers,* August 22, 1949, AHU Files.

Christ, James F. *Battalion of the Damned: The 1st Marine Paratroopers at Gavutu and Bloody Ridge.* Annapolis, Md.: Naval Institute Press, 1942.

Coffey, Thomas M. *Hap.* New York: Viking Press, 1982.

Coggins, Jack. *The Campaign for Guadalcanal.* New York: Doubleday and Company, 1972.

Commander in Chief, Pacific. Naval Dispatch 160440, July 16, 1944.

Commander, Task Force 58. Naval Dispatch 092117, July 10, 1944.

Cone, Davis. "Recommendation for the Legion of Merit to Be Awarded Captain Macon Snowden." Office of the CNO, Letter OP-506/bam, serial #6291P50, September 6, 1968.

Connolly, Thomas. Letter of Appreciation, OP-05A/MTST, serial #17P05, June 11, 1968.

Cross, W. E. "USS *Ticonderoga* (CVA-14) Air Plan," August 29, 1965. Daily publication by USS *Ticonderoga*'s admin office while deployed, now in author's personal collection.

Currituck County Archives. "Currituck County War of 1812 Veterans." http://cc.ciniva.net/veterans.cfm.

Curtis, Carl. "The Sad Story of the TFX." Remarks on the Failure the TFX Program on the Senate Floor by the Senator from Nebraska, Section 29310-29315. *Congressional Record, Proceedings and Debates of the 90th Congress, 2nd Session,* January 15, 1968 to October 14, 1968. Washington D.C., U.S. Government Printing Office.

Cutler, Thomas J. and Rick Burgess. "Lest We Forget: Swede Vejtasa, VF-51." U.S. Naval Institute *Proceedings* 132/11/1,245 (November 2006).

Davis, D. C. "Report on the Fitness of Captain M. S. Snowden." NAVPERS 1611, February 13, 1973.

Dorr, Robert F. "From Props to Jets and Angled Decks: Centennial of Naval Aviation." Defense Media Network, May 27, 2010. http://www.defensemedianetwork.com/stories/naval-aviation-centennial-from-props-to-jets-and-angled-decks.

Downs II, Charles F. "Calvin Coolidge, Dwight Morrow, and the Air Commerce Act of 1926." Calvin Coolidge Presidential Foundation, https://coolidgefoundation.org/resources/essays-papers-addresses-13/.

Drew, Dennis. *Rolling Thunder 1965: Anatomy of a Failure*: Air University Technical Report No. AU-ARI-CP-86–3. Maxwell Air Force Base, Ala.: Air University Press, October 1986.

Dunn, Robert F. "Six Amazing Years; RAGs, NATOPS, and More." *Naval War College Review* 64, no. 3 (Summer 2011).

Evans, David and Mark Peattie. *Kaigun: Strategy, Tactics, and Technology in the Imperial Japanese Navy, 1887–1941*. Annapolis, Md.: Naval Institute Press, 1997.

Evans, Mark L. and Roy A. Grossnick. *United States Naval Aviation, 1910–2010*, vol. 1., *Chronology*. Washington, D.C.: Naval History and Heritage Command, 2015.

Faltum, Andrew. *The Essex Aircraft Carriers*. Baltimore, Md.: The Nautical and Aviation Publishing Company of America, 1996.

Fechteler, William N. "Remarks on Navy Department Appropriations for 1954." U.S. House of Representatives Defense Appropriations Subcommittee Hearing, HRG-1953-HAP-0029, May 27, 1953.

Felker, Craig C. *Testing American Sea Power: U.S. Navy Strategic Exercises, 1923–1940*. College Station: Texas A&M University Press, 2007.

Ford, Gerald R. "Remarks of the President to the Tulane University Student Body," April 23, 1975. https://digitallibrary.tulane.edu/islandora/object/tulane%3A75293.

Francillon, Rene J. *Grumman Aircraft Since 1929*. Annapolis, Md.: Naval Institute Press, 1989.

Freed, David. "The Missile Men of North Vietnam." *Air & Space Magazine* (December 2014).

Friedman, Norman. *U.S. Aircraft Carriers*. Annapolis, Md.: Naval Institute Press, 1983.

Gendell, David, "Annapolis's Last Army-Navy Game," *SpinSheet Magazine*, October 1, 2013. http://www.spinsheet.com/annapoliss-last-army-navy-game.

Gillcrist, Paul T. *Sea Legs*. Lincoln, Neb.: Universe, Inc., 2000.

Ginter, Steve. *Curtiss SOC Seagull*. Simi Valley, Calif.: Ginter Publications, 2011.

———. *McDonnell F2H-3/4 Big Banjo*. Simi Valley, Calif.: Ginter Publications, 2011.

Goodwin, Doris Kearns. *Lyndon Johnson and the American Dream*. New York: Harper and Row Publishers, 1976.

GovTrack. "Rep. Richard White: Former Representative from Texas' 16th District." https://www.govtrack.us/congress/members/richard_white.

Groom, Winston. *The Aviators*. Washington, D.C.: National Geographic Society, 2013.

Grossnick, Roy A. *Dictionary of American Naval Aviation Squadrons*, vol. 1: *The History of VA, VAH, VAK, VAL, VAP, and VFA Squadrons*. Washington, D.C.: Naval Historical Center, 1995.

——— and Mark L. Evans. *United States Naval Aviation, 1910–2010*, vol. 2: *Statistics*. Washington, D.C.: Naval History and Heritage Command, 2015.

Guttman, Jon. "Interview with World War II SB2U-3 Pilot Sumner H. Whitten." *World War II* (July 2002). http://www.historynet.com/interview-with-world-war-ii-sb2u-3-pilot-sumner-h-whitten.htm.

Guyton, Boone. *Whistling Death*. Atglen, Pa.: Schiffer Publishing, 1994.

Hall, Carla. "Top Gun: Where the Flyboys Are." *Washington Post*, May 19, 1986.

Hammel, Eric. *Carrier Clash: The Invasion of Guadalcanal and the Battle of the Eastern Solomons*. Pacifica, Calif.: Pacifica Press, 2010.

Harris, L. E. "Fitness Report on Lieutenant M. S. Snowden." NAVPERS 310A, October 26, 1951.

Harter, R. K. "Letter of Appreciation." 52d Marine Amphibious Unit, RKH:eb, 1541/1, September 14, 1971.

Hattendorf, John B., ed. *U.S. Naval Strategy in the 1970s—Selected Documents*. Newport, R.I.: Naval War College Press, September 2007.

Hobson, Chris. *Vietnam Air Losses: United States Air Force, Navy and Marine Corps Fixed-Wing Aircraft Losses in Southeast Asia 1961–1973*. Hinckley, U.K.: Midland Publishing, 2001.

Holloway, James L. *Aircraft Carriers at War: A Personal Retrospective of Korea, Vietnam, and the Soviet Confrontation*. Annapolis, Md.: Naval Institute Press, 2007.

Hornfischer, James D. *The Fleet at Flood Tide*. New York: Bantam Books, 2016.

Huston, John W., ed. *American Airpower Comes of Age: General Henry H. "Hap" Arnold's World War II Diaries*. Maxwell Air Force Base, Ala.: Air University Press, 2002.

Johnson, Lyndon B. "Address on Gulf of Tonkin Incident." August 4, 1964. https://usa.usembassy.de/etexts/speeches/rhetoric/lbjgulf.htm.

Karnow, Stanley. *Vietnam: A History*. New York: Penguin Books, 1984.

Keillor, Maureen Smith and Richard P. Keillor. *Images of Aviation— Naval Air Station Pensacola*. Charleston, S.C.: Arcadia Publishing, 2014.

Kennedy, George. "Back from the Biggest Air Battle of the War." *Sunday Star*, September 3, 1944.

Larkins, William T. *Battleship and Cruiser Aircraft of the United States Navy, 1910–1949*. Atglen, Pa.: Schiffer Publishing, 1996.

Lawson, Robert L., "Recollections from Air Wing Commanders," *The Hook Magazine* (San Diego, The Tailhook Association) 45, no. 2 (Summer 2017): 33.

Levinson, Jeffrey L. *Alpha Strike Vietnam*. Novato, Calif.: Presidio Press, 1989.

Life Magazine. "The West of Tokyo Missionary Society." June 3, 1944. http://www.rb-29.net/HTML/81lexingtonstys/07.01wotms.htm.

Linder, Bruce. "Field Guide to Coronado History: Glenn Curtiss' Coronado Home." *Coronado Patch*, June 10, 2013. https://patch.com/california/coronado/field-guide-to-coronado-history-glenn-curtiss-coronado-home.

Lucky Bag: Yearbook of the Regiment of Midshipmen. Annapolis, Md.: U.S. Naval Academy, 1932, 1946.

Lundstrom, John. *The First Team and the Guadalcanal Campaign: Naval Fighter Combat from August to November 1942*. Annapolis, Md.: Naval Institute Press, 2013.

Marolda, Edward J., ed. *The U.S. Navy in the Korean War*. Annapolis, Md.: Naval Institute Press, 2007.

McCain, John. "Remarks by Senator John McCain at the Tailhook Symposium Honoring the Centennial of Naval Aviation," September 12, 2011. https://www.mccain.senate.gov/public/index.cfm/speeches?ID=5d91c166-9cf0-8139-9fe1-32a39173548c.

Mersky, Peter. *F-8 Crusader Units of the Vietnam War*. Oxford, U.K.: Osprey Publishing, Ltd., 1998.

———. *F-8 Crusader vs. MiG-17*. Oxford, U.K.: Osprey Publishing, Ltd., 1998.

Miller, G. E. "The Crash of TFX." *Foundations* (Fall 1988).

———. Officer Fitness Report on Commander M. S. Snowden. Washington, D.C.: Chief of Naval Operations staff, May 12, 1968.

———. Officer Fitness Report on Commander M. S. Snowden. Washington, D.C.: Chief of Naval Operations staff, September 10, 1968.

———. "Supplement to Regular Fitness Report on Captain M. S. Snowden," Memorandum OP-50/jjj dated November 24, 1967.

Morison, Samuel Eliot. *History of United States Naval Operations in World War II*, vol. 5: *The Struggle for Guadalcanal, August 1942–February 1943*. Boston: Little, Brown and Company, 1958.

———. *History of United States Naval Operations in World War II*, vol. 8, *New Guinea and the Marianas, March 1944–August 1944*. Annapolis, Md.: Naval Institute Press, 2011 (1953).

Morocco, John. *Thunder from Above: Air War, 1941–1968*. Boston: Boston Publishing Company, 1984.

Mott, George. Interview, September 4, 2015.

National Museum of the U.S. Air Force. "SA-2 Surface-to-Air Missile." http://www.nationalmuseum.af.mil/Visit/Museum-Exhibits/Fact-Sheets/Display/Article/196037/sa-2-surface-to-air-missile/.

Naval History and Heritage Command. "Admiral Elmo R. Zumwalt Jr., Nineteenth Chief of Naval Operations." https://www.history.navy.mil/browse-by-topic/people/chiefs-of-naval-operations/admiral-elmo-r-zumwalt-jr-.html.

———. *Dictionary of American Naval Fighting Ships*. 2014. https://www.history.navy.mil/research/histories/ship-histories/danfs.html.

———. *Papers of Admiral Arleigh A. Burke*. "Action Reports: Task Force 58, 11–21 June 1944."

Newport Fleet Officers Wives. *Guidelines: Naval Social Customs*. https://www.history.navy.mil/research/library/online-reading-room/title-list-alphabetically/g/naval-social-customs.html.

Nichols, John B. and Barrett Tillman. *On Yankee Station*. Annapolis, Md.: Naval Institute Press, 1987.

Nofi, Albert A. *To Train the Fleet for War*. Newport, R.I.: Naval War College Press, 2010.

Nelson, Derek and Dave Parsons. *Official and Unofficial U.S. Navy Air Patches, 1920s to Today*. Osceola, Wis.: Motorbooks International, 1990.

Ofstie, Ralph A. "Remarks on Navy Department Appropriations for 1954." U.S. House of Representatives Subcommittee Hearing on Defense Appropriations, HRG-1953-HAP-0029, May 27, 1953.

Peattie, Mark. *Sunburst: The Rise of Japanese Naval Air Power, 1909–1941*. Annapolis, Md.: Naval Institute Press, 2001.

Pilot's Flight Operating Instructions for Navy Model SBD-6 Airplanes. NavAer 01–405C-1, September 1944.

Potter, E. B. *Admiral Arleigh Burke*. New York: Random House, 1990.

———, ed. *Sea Power: A Naval History*. Annapolis, Md.: Naval Institute Press, 1981.

Pribbenow, Merle. "Treatment of American POWs in North Vietnam." Wilson Center Cold War International History Project, February 14, 2012. https://www.wilsoncenter.org/publication/treatment-american-pows-north-vietnam#sthash.AdYQAXD1.dpuf.

Providence Journal. "Four Navy Fliers Get Decorations," April 4, 1943.

Raleigh News and Observer. "Snowden Tells of Navy Raid," December 11, 1943.

Rankin, Robert H. "The Navy's Schneider Cup Racers." U.S. Naval Institute *Proceedings* 81/7/629 (July 1955).

Reynolds, Clark G. *Famous American Admirals*. Annapolis, Md.: Naval Institute Press, 1978.

Rosenberg, David. "Air Warfare Division (OP-55 Study on Future Development of Carrier Aviation with Respect to Both Aircraft and Aircraft Carriers." In *American Postwar Air Doctrine and Organization: The Navy Experience*. Washington, D.C.: Proceedings of the 8th Military History Symposium, Office of Air Force History, Headquarters USAF, 1979.

Rubel, Robert C. "The U.S. Navy's Transition to Jets." *Naval War College Review* 63, no. 2 (Spring 2010).

Rudowsky, Thomas. "Review of the Carrier Approach Criteria for Carrier-Based Aircraft." Naval Air Warfare Center Aircraft Division Technical Report #NAWCADPAX/TR-2002/71, 2002.

Satterfield, L. M. "Fitness Report on Lieutenant M. S. Snowden." NAVPERS 310, September 13, 1956.

Schlight, John. *A War Too Long: The USAF in Southeast Asia, 1961–1975.* Washington, D.C.: Air Force History and Museums Program, 1996.

Schuster, Carl O. "The Rise of North Vietnam's Air Defenses." *HistoryNet .com.* June 2016. http://www.historynet.com/13703647.htm.

Sears, David. *Pacific Air: How Fearless Flyboys, Peerless Aircraft, and Fast Flattops Conquered the Skies in the War with Japan.* Boston: Da Capo Press, 2012.

Siegfried, Doug. "Naval Air History Part 3." Working draft for *Hook* magazine, 2015.

Ship Staff, USS *Lexington. Tarawa to Tokyo 1943–1946.* https://www .navysite.de/cruisebooks/cv16-46/index.html.

Sinton, William. "Plans for Night Rendezvous—Request for." AIR-PAC memorandum, January 22, 1944.

Smith, Douglas V., ed. *One Hundred Years of U.S. Navy Air Power.* Annapolis, Md.: Naval Institute Press, 2013.

Smith, Peter C. *Fist from the Sky: Japan's Dive-Bomber Ace of World War II.* Mechanicsburg, Pa.: Stackpole Books, 2005.

Snowden, E. M. "Air Group Sixteen End of Tour Report," June 1944.

———. "Wake Mission Summary." AG16/A16–3 Serial 194, November 3, 1943.

Snowden, M. S. "Strike Mission Notes," December 1, 1965.

Spangenberg, George A. Oral history, August 31, 1997. www.secret-projects.co.uk/gasoralhistory.pdf.

Steichen, Edward. *The Blue Ghost: A Photographic Log and Personal Narrative of the Aircraft Carrier USS* Lexington *in Combat Operations.* New York: Harcourt Brace and Company, 1947.

Swartz, Peter. *Organizing OPNAV (1970–2009).* Alexandria, Va.: Center for Naval Analyses. CAB D0020997.A5/2Rev, January 2010.

———. *U.S. Navy Capstone Strategies.* Alexandria, Va.: Center for Naval Analyses. MISC D0026414.A1/Final, December 2011.

"Swede Vejtasa: In Memoriam." *Naval Aviation News,* May 9, 2013. navalaviationnews.navylive.dodlive.mil/2013/05/09/.

Swihnart, Earl. "The Vought F4U Corsair." Aviation History Online Museum, 2014. http://aviation-history.com/vought/f4u.html.

Tagaya, Osamu. *Aichi 99 Kanbaku "Val" Units: 1937–42*. New York: Bloomsbury Publishing, 2013.

Tailhook Daily Briefing. "TFX and Turkeys—Part II." February 22, 2008. http://wwww.tailhookdaily.typepad.com/tailhook_daily_briefing/2008.

Thomason, Tommy. *Grumman Navy F-111B Swing Wing*. Simi Valley, Calif.: Ginter Publications, 1998.

———. *U.S. Naval Air Superiority: Development of Shipborne Fighters 1943–1962*. North Branch, Minn.: Specialty, 2007.

Tillman, Barrett. *Clash of the Carriers: The True Story of the Marianas Turkey Shoot of World War II*. New York: Penguin Group, 2005.

———. *The Dauntless Dive Bomber of World War II*. Annapolis, Md.: Naval Institute Press, 1989.

———. *MiG Master: Story of the F-8 Crusader*. Annapolis, Md.: Naval Institute Press, 1990.

———. *Vought F4U Corsair*. North Branch, Minn.: Specialty Press, 2001.

Toperczer, Istvan. *MiG-17 and MiG-19 Units of the Vietnam War*. Oxford, U.K.: Osprey Publishing, Ltd., 2001.

Trimble, William F. *Admiral William A. Moffett: Architect of Naval Aviation*. Annapolis, Md.: Naval Institute Press, 1994.

Tuoi Tre News. "General Vo Nguyen Giap's Immortal Sayings." October 9, 2013, https://tuoitrenews.vn/society/13947/general-vo-nguyen-giaps-immortal-sayings.

Van Voorhis, Westbrook. "March of Time," documentary, CBS Radio, August 17, 1944.

Van Staaveren, Jacob. *Gradual Failure: The Air War Over North Vietnam 1965–1966*. Washington, D.C.: Air Force History and Museums Program, 2002.

Vejtasa, S. W. "Fitness Report on Macon Snowden (NAVPERS 310)," February 23, 1966.

Vraciu, Alex. *Fighter Pilot*. Indianapolis: Indiana Historical Society Press, 2010.

Wagemann, Kurt. "The Admiral." Forrest Sherman Foundation, Inc. http://www.ussforrestsherman.org/the_admiral.htm.

Wildenberg, Thomas. *Destined for Glory*. Annapolis, Md.: Naval Institute Press, 1998.

Wolfe, Tom. *The Right Stuff*. New York: Picador, 2008.

Woodford, Thomas R. "Have Drill/Have Ferry Tactical Evaluation." National Air and Space Intelligence Center Report.
https://nsarchive2.gwu.edu/NSAEBB/NSAEBB443/docs/
area51_51.PDF.

Wooldridge, E. T., ed. *Into the Jet Age: Conflict and Change in Naval
Aviation, 1945–1975*. Annapolis, Md.: Naval Institute Press, 1995.

Yenne, Bill. *The Story of the Boeing Company*. San Francisco: American Graphic Systems, Inc., 2005.

Index

About the Author

Ernest Snowden is the son of Macon Snowden and nephew of Ernest Snowden. The author is a 1970 graduate of the U.S. Naval Academy and a former naval aviator. After active duty, he continued in the Naval Reserve as an aeronautical engineering duty officer until his retirement in 2000. As a Navy civilian, he served as the business manager for the Maintenance Policy Division of the Naval Air Systems Command, followed by a tour as staff assistant to the deputy director for research and engineering in the Office of the Secretary of Defense.